WITTGENSTEIN ON THE HUMAN SPIRIT

a volume in
Philosophy, Literature, and Politics
PLP
Leonidas Donskis and J.D. Mininger, Editors

WITTGENSTEIN ON THE HUMAN SPIRIT

Yuval Lurie

Amsterdam - New York, NY 2012

Cover photo: “Haus Wittgenstein”, Flickr, Martin Pulaski

Cover Design: Studio Pollmann

The paper on which this book is printed meets the requirements of “ISO 9706:1994, Information and documentation - Paper for documents - Requirements for permanence”.

ISBN: 978-90-420-3517-1
E-Book ISBN: 978-94-012-0792-8

Printed in the Netherlands

Printed by Printforce, the Netherlands

Philosophy, Literature, and Politics (PLP)

Leonidas Donskis

and

J. D. Mininger

Editors

Previous PLP Volumes

Leonidas Donskis, Editor, *Niccolò Machiavelli: History, Power, and Virtue.* 2011. VIBS 226

Leonidas Donskis and J. D. Mininger, Editors, *Politics Otherwise: Shakespeare as Social and Political Critique*, 2012. VIBS 242

CONTENTS

EDITORIAL FOREWORD

The Rodopi VIBS sub-series *Philosophy, Literature, and Politics*, in which *Wittgenstein on the Human Spirit* appears, locates itself in the overlapping thematic and methodological pools, where these traditional disciplinary waters spill through their porous borders, collect and swirl together, refracting the light of knowledge in new and original patterns and configurations. *Wittgenstein on the Human Spirit* sails bravely and successfully through these interdisciplinary waters, leaving a unique intellectual wake for readers to mark to its course. But perhaps some may have concerns that this project is, rather, lost at sea.

Therefore, let us briefly take account of its bearings. Wittgenstein's work is thoroughly philosophical—he is considered by many to be the most important philosopher of the twentieth century. He was not a literary critic and not an author of literature (though I have found great insight and pleasure in reading the *Tractatus* as a kind of modernist poem). Still, his lessons on philosophy of language bear mightily on concerns both literary and aesthetic. With that said, where and how does one locate the Wittgensteinian ship with a political compass?

The political points on the Wittgenstein map are not always readily apparent, and it is surely one of the greatest merits of Yuval Lurie's book to navigate along some of these lines.

Wittgenstein on the Human Spirit steers through the political-cultural waters by the stars—in this case, by locating a constellation of three points: Wittgenstein on Jews and Judaism; Wittgenstein on the philosophy of culture and civilization; and Wittgenstein's musings on the stakes of clarifying the problem of the spiritual nature of human beings. At each point in the constellation, Lurie offers at least three different, yet often overlapping and exchangeable, masks of Wittgenstein: as conceptual persona; as spiritualist; and as historical character. The fact that each of the book's three major sections are capable of standing on their own, yet inextricably interrelated—offering continuity and insight in varying and multiple combinations—reflects Wittgenstein's own methodological preferences.

The constellatory organization of Lurie's volume is an exemplary instance of a Wittgensteinian approach to thought. Part of the extraordinary significance of Wittgenstein's work lies in its challenge and appeal to various and often acrimoniously divorced branches of philosophy, such as the Continental and Analytic traditions, whether because of or in spite of its cross-pollination of logical, linguistic, and cultural concerns.

The very force of Wittgenstein's polymathic approach constitutes an important political intervention unto itself. Lurie's treatise redoubles this political angle: not only does this volume locate politicized cultural sites of tension and controversy in Wittgenstein's writings and submit those aspects to lively reflection and commentary, but also, its thematic constellations and transdisciplinary methods equally access the political in Wittgenstein.

Lurie's work may be accurately described as a Wittgensteinian book on Wittgenstein: rigorously argued, sensitively considered, and utterly readable. With Yuval Lurie at the helm of *Wittgenstein on the Human Spirit*, you will surely find strong winds and happy sailing in these interdisciplinary waters.

J.D. Mininger
Philosophy, Literature, and Politics, Co-Editor
Vytautas Magnus University
Kaunas, Lithuania

PREFACE

Wittgenstein on the Human Spirit embraces three philosophical studies of mine, concerning Ludwig Wittgenstein's remarks on the spirit of human beings in culture. Given the focus of Wittgenstein's remarks, they constitute three studies in the Philosophy of Culture, aiming to bring philosophical insight to the expressive meaning of human cultural practices, innovations, and deeds. The studies are set out in the form of philosophical investigations that describe, explain, examine, explore, and evaluate Wittgenstein's remarks on this subject within three philosophical frameworks of discussion: the *Spirit of Jews*, the *Spirits of Culture and Civilization*, and the *Common Spirit of Human Beings*.

Philosophical studies that focus on a philosopher's remarks on expressive cultural matters tend to converge on their author. Therefore, these studies also provide three philosophical portraits of Wittgenstein drawn against the background of philosophical problems, puzzling questions, cultural worries, spiritual concerns, self-reflection, artistic sensibilities, aesthetic attitudes, conceptual clarifications, and philosophical insights that had deep personal meaning for Wittgenstein.

Two concepts are at the center of these studies: culture and spirit. I also discuss such concepts as high culture, civilization, creativity, observance, tradition, genius, talent, cultured taste, appreciation, great works of art, artistic ideals, Jews, stereotypes, national character, anti-Semitism, ideology, modernity, myth, magic, religion, ritual, symbols, humanity, and more. I also discuss various conceptions and views that have been put forward to enrich and explain these concepts, disclosing how Wittgenstein confronts them through the use of conceptual clarifications.

This volume transcends the common distinction between Analytic and Continental philosophy. It affords a philosophical discourse on the conceptual underpinnings of views and discussions emerging out of philosophy, aesthetics, anthropology, and cultural studies. Although the three studies comprising this book are related to one another, each is devoted to a different philosophical perspective taken by Wittgenstein on the expressive nature of the human spirit in culture. As such, each one stands on its own and can be read without reference to the others.

The first two studies derive from earlier articles of mine: "Jews as a metaphysical species," *Philosophy: The Journal of the Royal Institute of Philosophy*, 64 (1989); and "Wittgenstein on Culture and Civilization," *Inquiry*, 32 (1989) www.tandfonline.com. Some of the topics discussed in them appeared earlier in my "Jews as a Parable," *Iyyun,* 37 (April 1988), pp. 95–127 (in Hebrew). I thank these journals for permission to use material that appeared in their publications. Peter Hacker, Ruth Mansur, Haim Marantz, and Ithai Smoliar offered helpful suggestions. Nimrod Maman helped with the typescript. Ruvik Danieli and Amiel Schotz suggested helpful stylistic corrections. I thank all of them. Lars Hertzberg commented in detail on the third study, and I am thankful to him in particular for his great help. Finally, I am thankful to the Israel Science Foundation, which generously provided research support for these studies.

First Study

THE SPIRIT OF JEWS

There are certain remarks in *Culture and Value*, in which Ludwig Wittgenstein writes about Jews and what he calls their "Jewish mind."[1] In these remarks, he appears to draw a distinction between two different spiritual forces, both of which operate in Western culture and give rise to two different types of cultured human beings and, along with them, two different types of artists and works of art. On one side of the divide are Jews and artists imbued with Jewish spirit. On the other side are others who have a non-Jewish spirit. In what follows, I discuss these statements and their place within Wittgenstein's philosophical thinking, self-reflection, and European discourse about culture and Jews.

One

REMARKS ON THE SPIRIT OF JEWS

1. A Surprising Encounter with Jews

In a manuscript published after his death as *Culture and Value*, Ludwig Wittgenstein included several remarks that he wrote about Jews. In them, he offers the following thoughts about the nature, mentality, character, and artistic achievements of Jews. For example: "You get tragedy where the tree, instead of bending, breaks. Tragedy is something unJewish."[1] Following Ernest Renan who, in a celebrated lecture, claimed, "a nation is a soul, a spiritual principle," he writes:

> What Renan calls the *bon sens précoce* of the Semitic races (an idea that I already entertained a long time ago) is their *unpoetic* mentality, which heads straight for what is concrete. Which is characteristic of my philosophy.[2]

He explains this claim by noting that Jews are attracted by "pure intellectualism." "I think today there could be a form of theatre played in masks. The characters would be just stylized human beings." (In his opinion, this feature is suited to the plays written by the prominent Viennese cultural critic, Karl Kraus and to their abstract nature, which manifests his Jewish origins.) "And masked theatre, as I believe, is in any case the expression of an intellectual character. Perhaps (too) for this reason only Jews will be attracted to this theatre."[3]

Wittgenstein views intellect as a spiritually barren region that typifies the Jews' intellectual attitude toward cultural affairs and life: "The Jew is a desert region under whose thin layer of rock lies the molten lava of spirit."[4] Since the Jews' "molten lava of spirit" remains hidden beneath their "thin" intellectual "layer of rock," no original cultural creation emerges from it. Therefore, Jews lack genius:

> The saint is the only Jewish "genius." Even the greatest Jewish thinker is no more than talented. (Myself for instance.) . . .
>
> It might be said (rightly or wrongly) that the Jewish mind is not in a position to produce even so much as a tiny blade of grass or flower, but that its way is to make a drawing of the blade of grass or the flower that has grown in the mind of another & then use it to sketch a comprehensive picture. This is not to allege a vice & everything is all right as long as what is being done is quite clear. Danger arises only when someone confuses

> the nature of a Jewish work with that of a non-Jewish work & especially when the author of the former does so himself, as he so easily may. ("Doesn't he look as proud as though he were being milked himself.")
>
> It is typical of the Jewish mind to understand someone else's work better than he understands it himself.[5]

In Wittgenstein's view, the absence of creative power in the Jews' approach to cultural life manifests the fact that of themselves Jews are nothing:

> The Jew must in a real sense "make nothing his business." But for him especially this is particularly hard because he, as it were, has nothing. It is much harder to be poor voluntarily if you *can't help* being poor, than when you might also be rich.[6]

This absence of creative power can also be discerned in the Jews' typical attitude toward property and cultural assets. In his opinion, Jews strive to augment their (lack of creative) power by various means. Therefore, they treat property as a means of increasing their power:

> Power and possession are not the *same* thing. Even though possession also gives us power. If Jews are said not to have any sense for possession that is presumably compatible with their liking to be rich; for money is for them a particular sort of power not possession.[7]

Jews also tend, in his opinion, to hide their true nature beneath a cloak of cunning and secrecy:

> It has sometimes been said that the Jews' secretive & cunning nature is a result of their long persecution. That is certainly untrue; on the other hand it is certain that, despite this persecution, they continue to exist only because they have the inclination towards this secretiveness. As we may say that such & such an animal has escaped extinction only because it has the possibility or capability of concealing itself. Of course I do not mean that one should commend this ability for such a reason, not by any means.[8]

Wittgenstein also remarks that while the unique contribution of Jews to Western civilization is often noted, it is not often noted how different the Jews' contribution to Western civilization is from that of non-Jews:

> In Western Civilization the Jew is always being measured according to calibrations which do not fit him. That the Greek thinkers were neither philosophers in the Western sense, nor scientists in the Western sense, that those who took part in the Olympic Games were not sportsmen &

> fit into <no> Western occupation, is clear to many people. But it is the same with the Jews too.
> And insofar as the words of our <language> seem to us the only possible standards of measurement we are always doing him injustice. And he is first overestimated then underestimated . . . .[9]

At the same time, Wittgenstein suggests that the obsessive European preoccupation with Jews does not stem from their direct influence on European affairs, but from experiencing them as a sort of human anomaly and disease—from which a negative attitude toward Jews emerges. This is particularly the case in connection with the emerging national self-consciousness of European nations and the Jews' attempt to affiliate themselves with the cultural and social life of these nations in the modern period:

> "Look on this wart as a regular limb of your body!" Can one do that, to order?
> Do I have the power to decide at will to have, or not to have, a certain ideal conception of my body?
> Within the history of the peoples of Europe the history of the Jews is not treated so circumstantially as their intervention in European affairs would actually merit, because within this history they are experienced as a sort of disease, anomaly, & nobody wants to put a disease on the same level as normal life.
> We may say: this bump can be regarded as a limb of one's body only if our whole feeling for the body changes (if the whole national feeling for the body changes). Otherwise the best we can do is *put up with* it.
> You may expect an individual to display this sort of tolerance or even to disregard such things; but you cannot expect this of a nation since it is only a nation by virtue of not disregarding such things. I.e., there is a contradiction in expecting someone to retain the original aesthetic feeling for his body & also to make the swelling welcome.[10]

In addition to such general remarks about (the spiritual nature of) Jews, there are also specific remarks about (the artistic character of) certain creative personalities in relation to their Jewishness. Thus, for instance, Wittgenstein appears to follow Richard Wagner's diatribe in his *Das Judenthum in der Musik* by defining Mendelssohn as a Jewish composer. Therefore, he notes, Mendelssohn's work is devoid of tragedy; it is a plateau. When at its best, it consists of "musical arabesques."[11] Also: "If one wanted to characterize the essence of Mendelssohn's music one could do it by saying that there is perhaps no music by Mendelssohn that is hard to understand."[12] Wittgenstein also describes Mendelssohn as someone who adapts himself to his social environment, which then determines his character:

> Mendelssohn is like a man who is cheerful only when everything is cheerful anyway, or good only when everyone around him is good, & not self-sufficient like a tree that stands firmly in its place, whatever may be going on around it. I too am like that & tend to be so.[13]

Therefore, "Mendelssohn is perhaps the most untragic of composers."[14] And more: "What is lacking in Mendelssohn's music? A 'courageous' melody?"[15]

Sometimes Jewish character does not coincide with being Jewish. It turns out, "There is something Jewish in Rousseau's character."[16] Likewise, Wittgenstein's creative achievements exhibit a Jewish mentality. Everything previously said about the nature of a Jewish mind permeates his own work as well.[17] He is devoid of genius. He is talented but unoriginal. In his artistic work he shows himself to possess "good manners," and nothing else.[18]

2. First Reaction

In many of us, these remarks of Wittgenstein about Jews create a growing sense of unease as we stumble over them. The ideas expressed in them—namely that Jews possess a different spirit than that which is embodied in other human beings, that they lack originality and cultural depth, that they have adhered to a culture that is not theirs and penetrated it by virtue of their cleverness and cunning, altering it to fit their own sophisticated but shallow spiritual disposition—are reminiscent of familiar anti-Semitic diatribes and ideologies. For those of us who have been accustomed to the *Tractatus Logico-Philosophicus* and *Philosophical Investigations*, these remarks are also a source of great astonishment, such as one might experience at suddenly discovering a skeleton in the closet of a close acquaintance. For behind all the talk about "mentality," "spirit," "nature," and "character," there seem to reverberate familiar anti-Semitic strains.

Perceived as such, Wittgenstein's remarks on Jews are apt to be dismissed as unfortunate relics of inherited stereotypical cultural images of Jews, manifesting ingrained anti-Semitic prejudices that are irrelevant to the main body of his philosophical discourse. Knowing that Wittgenstein's family was of Jewish origins, we might find biographical interest in them, as revealing Wittgenstein's psychological difficulties with his self-identity, but lacking genuine philosophical interest.[19] We might also note in this connection that these statements begin upon his return to both philosophy and Cambridge, England, in 1929, and wonder what caused them at this juncture in his life. I shall return to this question and answer it later. However, to prepare the ground for this answer, it is useful to recall first some crucial junctions in his philosophical journey.

Wittgenstein first came to Cambridge in 1911, to study with Bertrand Russell. This was after he already received an engineering degree in Berlin and was doing aeronautical research in Manchester, where he became interested in logic and its relationship to the problems of philosophy. He left Cambridge for a secluded place in Norway in 1913, to pursue philosophical work on his own. Throughout the First World War, from 1914 to 1918, he served in the Austrian army. During this time, he wrote a manuscript that was later published and translated into English as *Tracataus Logico-Philosophicus*. The book had a powerful effect on what became known as Analytic Philosophy. At the time of its publication, Wittgenstein was working as a lower school teacher in rural Austria, having declared his belief in the book that he "found, on all essential points, the final solution of the problems."[20] Later, he gave up teaching and was occupied with the design and construction of his sister's house in Vienna. When it was finished, he again became interested in the problems of philosophy and soon returned to Cambridge. At this time, he began to write down his new philosophical thoughts. At first, he was still working out some old ideas, but soon began to change his approach to philosophical problems, the culmination of which is expressed in books that were published after his death in 1951, most notably in his *Philosophical Investigations*.

Whatever instigated Wittgenstein's remarks on Jews upon his return to both philosophy and England, the above first reaction to these remarks, which would dismiss them as irrelevant to his philosophical project, is too hasty. For they encode a more complicated story, enclosing a personal, cultural, and philosophical tangle whose crucial effect on both his life and philosophy is not always perceived through Analytic eyes. In what follows, I tell this story and shed interpretive philosophical light on it. My aim is to reveal (rather than unravel) the tangle that lies at its core and the way it extends and reaches deep into Wittgenstein's philosophy, cultural viewpoint, and self-reflection.[21]

Two

PHILOSOPHICAL CLARIFICATIONS

Before discussing the ideas expressed in Ludwig Wittgenstein's remarks on Jews and their significance for his self-reflection, spiritual concerns, and philosophical project, I want in this chapter to describe the philosophical framework in which they are formulated.

1. Essence and Clarification

The first thing I wish to suggest is that, in these remarks, Wittgenstein is describing the way the essence of Jews is embodied in the nature, character, mind, and spirit of Jews. The point of this comment is that we often use the concepts of nature, character, mentality, and spirit when we typify people in some intrinsic manner, thereby explaining what constitutes their inner human core and disposes them to behave the way they do. On the basis of these concepts, we might describe someone as being of a trusting or suspicious nature, having a friendly or reserved character, possessing an inquisitive or dull mind, engaging life in a high or low spirit, and so forth. As I read Wittgenstein in this connection, he is reflecting on the nature, character, mentality, and spirit of Jews as a way of noting how their Jewish essence is manifested through these human features. That is because, as he remarks much later, "the *essence* is not something that can be shown; only its features can be described."[1] The features of the essence of Jews that he describes in these remarks are the Jews' nature, mentality, character, and spirit. As emerges, he describes these essence-embodying features as being inherently different from those of other human beings. They are Jewish features, disclosing a Jewish essence.

To speak of the essence of things is to speak of that which makes them into the kind of things they are. A central way of doing so in modern philosophy is to relate the essence of things to how we conceptualize them. In the philosophical view that underlies these remarks, the concept of a Jew, which is employed to identify certain people as "Jews," both embodies and manifests the essence of a Jew. In this connection, we might compare the way the concept of a dog or a bird is likewise held to both embody and manifest the essence of dogs or birds. As such, the essence of different creatures—dogs, birds, and Jews—is both embodied and manifested through the concepts used to refer to them. In the case of Jews, it is revealed in their human features that provide them with a Jewish nature, Jewish character, Jewish mentality, and Jewish spirit: human features that both embody and manifest the essence of their Jewishness.

Another way of stating the point I am elucidating here is to say that, in Wittgenstein's remarks on Jews, he refers to Jews as a different kind of human being from all other human beings put together. This is due to their possession of a completely different kind of spiritual nature (or character) and mentality. In the conceptual distinction he is drawing, Jews differ in their spiritual nature from the spiritual nature of all other cultured human beings. In the way in which cats and dogs are different natural kinds, Jews and all other cultured human beings are different spiritual kinds. Thus, the distinction he is drawing between Jews and other human beings is a conceptual dichotomy concerning the human spirit. On one side of the divide are human beings imbued with Jewish spirit. On the other side are all other human beings possessing a non-Jewish spirit.

The second thing I wish to suggest is that in his remarks on Jews, Wittgenstein is seeking to "clarify," as he calls it, the essence of Jews in three ways: as it is incarnated in the very concept of a Jew, as it is manifested in the cultured behavior and attitude toward life of Jews, and as it is experienced—by others and by himself. His remarks in this connection are not empirical generalizations based on an historical, sociological, or psychological study of Jews and their artistic creations in comparison to others. They are clarifications of the concept of a Jew in various cultural contexts of confronting, experiencing, and reflecting on their spiritual nature.

In the philosophical approach underlying Wittgenstein's discourse throughout his writings, concepts are linked to the meanings of words, which are manifested through the use of language in the stream of human life. Therefore, his conceptual remarks are usually focused on the use of words, aiming to bring philosophical insight to our understanding of them. In seeking to clarify the concept of a Jew, Wittgenstein places his remarks on Jews within his overall philosophical project of clarifying our understanding of the meaning of words by describing their use and what we experience in their connection. It is a philosophical project that he characterizes as "my work of clarification."[2] As he explains, the task in this project, in contrast to his past logically oriented philosophical venture:

> the task of philosophy is not to create a new, ideal language, but to clarify the use of our language, the existing language. Its aim is to remove particular misunderstandings; not to produce a real understanding for the first time.[3]

In this particular case, such misunderstanding may be that the word "Jew" is used like other words designating national or ethnic identities, such as "German" or "African," whereas it is used to refer to a human beings possessed of an altogether different kind of spirit than that which embodies all other national or ethnic identities: a different human spiritual category, as it were.

Put in terms of "linguistic meanings," the concept of a Jew that Wittgenstein seeks to clarify is expressed by use of the word that is synonymous with the word "Jew" in the language of his culture.[4] To state this point in English, it can be said that he seeks to clarify the meaning of the word "Jew" used in the stream of social and cultural life in which he partakes. He does so by describing the nature, character, mentality, and spirit of Jews, both as they are manifested in the meaning of the word "Jew" and as they are grasped when interacting with people identified as "Jews." This is where the "real understanding" of the meaning of the word "Jew" is acquired "for the first time." It may be worthwhile to recall now some of the ways in which Wittgenstein goes about his "project of clarification," which may have bearing on his clarification of the concept of a Jew.[5]

2. Clarification of the Grammar of Words

At first, upon his return to both philosophy and England, Wittgenstein was still pursuing his project of clarification by reflecting about the nature of language and the meaning of words according to what he claimed in his *Tractatus Logico-Philosophicus*. There, language was described as a system of propositional signs for representing (or picturing) states of affairs through propositions. The elements of a propositional sign constituted names, which were held to correspond to "the objects of the thought."[6] A name, he declared in this connection, means a certain object of thought.[7] On the basis of this logical view of language, he claimed that the problems of philosophy are posed because our language is misunderstood.[8] To overcome these problems and the disputed metaphysical answers given to them in philosophy, we need to say things in a logically clear way that precludes raising metaphysical problems and devising disputed metaphysical answers to them. The way to do so is to "make use of a sign-language that excludes them by not using the same sign for different symbols," meaning for different concepts.[9] Such a sign language was supposed to constitute a conceptual system based on what he called "*logical* grammar." It provides a transcendental framework underlying all languages for entertaining propositions that picture states of affairs. He noted that Gottlob Frege and Bertrand Russell were the first to formulate it.

In the approach of both Frege and Russell, an analysis of language was supposed to make linguistic meaning clear by displaying the logical form or structure of propositions. This structure, or form, was deemed to explain the basic relationship between subject and predicate. In Aristotle's *Metaphysics*, the relationship between subject and predicate constituted the basic structure or form of reality. Frege was the first to develop the logical means for analyzing propositions into such logical forms. When Wittgenstein first encountered Frege's and Russell's logical methods of analysis, he expressed his understanding of their aims by noting, "every proposition that says something indefinable about one thing is a subject-predicate proposition . . . ."[10] He also remarked that this is not always discerned from the linguistic expression of a proposition. It requires a logical analysis to clarify it. On the basis of this view of language and meaning, he described the task of philosophy as the clarification of propositions. This was supposed to be achieved through their logical analysis into basic constituents that provide "logical clarification of thoughts."[11] Hence, "whenever someone . . . wanted to say something metaphysical, to demonstrate to him that he had failed to give meaning to certain signs in his propositions."[12] With this goal in mind, he noted in the preface to *Tractatus Logico-Philosophicus* that "the whole sense of the book might be summed up in the following words: what can be said at all can be said clearly, and what we cannot talk about we must pass over in silence."[13]

In accordance with the above view about the logical nature of the world, language, and thought, Wittgenstein declares in the opening remark to *Philosophical Remarks*—the first manuscript he wrote upon his return to philosophy and England: "A proposition is completely logically analyzed if its grammar is made clear . . . ."[14] By "grammar," he still means "logical grammar." As he had been previously criticized for merely setting out the formal requirements for a logical clarification of concepts but not exemplifying it, he now commenced to provide such clarification for certain concepts by describing the relationship between them and possible experiences. He notes in this connection, "an octahedron with the pure colors at the corner-point, e.g., provides a *rough* representation of colour-space, and this is a grammatical representation, not a psychological one."[15] It provides, he says, "a *bird's-eye view* of the grammatical rules" for concepts depicting colors. However, he also notes, "the chief trouble with our grammar is that we don't have a *bird's-eye view* of it."[16] In this conception of linguistic meanings, the task of philosophy is to offer such a *bird's-eye view* of the grammar of words, which constitutes their universal and transcendental basis. (As after a while it must have dawned on him, this makes the philosophical analysis of the linguistic meaning of words, which describes all the possible instantiations of the concept of color in all possible languages according to its purported logical grammar, a dubious undertaking.)

Some time after writing the above remark, Wittgenstein began to transform some of his previous assumptions about the nature of language and its grammar, as well as the nature and purpose of philosophical clarifications.[17] He now began to regard linguistic meanings as manifested in linguistic practices that govern the use of words, rather than through some mental representation of basic signs transfixed in the logical forms of propositions. Unlike mental representations and logical forms that underlie names and propositional signs, linguistic practices are activities. As such, they have all sorts of uses, some of which he later lists:

> Giving orders, and obeying them—
> Describing the appearance of an object, or giving its measurements—

Constructing an object from a description (a drawing) —
Reporting an event—
Speculating about an event—
Forming and testing a hypothesis—
Presenting the results of an experiment in tables and diagrams—
Making up a story; and reading it—
Play-acting—
Singing catches—
Guessing riddles—
Making a joke; telling it—
Solving a problem in practical arithmetic—
Translating from one language into another—
Asking, thanking, cursing, greeting, praying.[18]

They are also both cultural and normative. They manifest shared ways of doing things with words in a culture, which are governed by the application of common judgments concerning right and wrong, correct and incorrect actions. As such, they reveal normative uses of words in a culture, which he now refers to as the "grammar of words."

At this stage in his thinking on language, Wittgenstein often refers to linguistic practices as "language games." Since there are many different shared linguistic practices, there are also many different language games and many different grammars that are manifested through them. To note the varied uses of language through the metaphor of language game is to draw attention to the linguistic fact that these practices may have nothing in common. This insight is in contrast to his former view, in which language was described as the use of propositions to represent states of affairs. As such, linguistic practices may develop in time and they may differ from one culture to another, which Wittgenstein sometimes describes as constituting different imagined "tribes." They not only use different words in their communication; they also use the same words in similar practices, but nonetheless, to some extent differently. Thus, their words for number and color, for example, may be incorporated in somewhat different practices. As such, they will manifest a somewhat different grammar for the meaning of "number" and "color," manifesting a somewhat different concept of number and color from ours.

Importantly, when the discussion is restricted to only our own "tribe," we still do not possess a *bird's-eye view* of all the (future) possible uses of a word and its grammar. In *Philosophical Investigations* he notes in connection with the philosophical desire to attain such a view the following: "A main source of our failure to understand is that we do not command a clear view of the use of our words. Our grammar is lacking in this sort of perspicuity."[19] The understanding that we fail to achieve thereby is philosophical understanding, not ordinary understanding of language in human communication. It is the sort of understanding that we desire when we wonder "what is a proposition, the meaning of a word, or how we are able to understand language." To achieve such philosophical understanding requires what he now calls "A perspicuous representation" that "produces . . . understanding which consists in 'seeing connections'"—presumably between different uses of the same word in different contexts.[20] However, this way of representing the use of a word is limited to a particular edifying example. It does not provide a complete description of the use of a word in all possible cases. Thus, both the goal and method of philosophical clarifications now change. Previously, these were to attain a bird's-eye view of the logical grammar of words, which provides an analysis of their meaning and determines all the logically possible applications of a word. Now, it is to bring philosophical insight to only a certain aspect of the meaning of a word, by describing the connection between different uses of it within certain cases. This sort of clarification is supposed to help us overcome what is philosophically puzzling to us, or misleading us in its connection. "The concept of a perspicuous representation is of fundamental significance for us," he asserts. "It earmarks the form of account we give, the way we look at things . . . ."[21]

Curiously, the above remark itself is bereft of any insightful example to demonstrate how this is done. A statement of Wittgenstein that might provide such an example is the following: "You can't hear God speak to someone else, you can hear him only if you are being addressed.—That is a grammatical remark."[22] Read in one context, this remark might be an instance of clarifying self-reflection on the problematic state of his quest for religious faith. Read in another, it turns this private instance of self-reflection into an insightful "grammatical" remark that clarifies the conceptual nature of religious discourse in which the words "to hear God speak" are used. In either context, it reminds us that while religious discourse is similar (in its surface grammar) to everyday discourse, it also differs from it in its deep grammar. In doing so, it provides a "perspicuous representation" of the "grammar" of the words "hearing X speak" when used in these two different circumstances. It thus enables us to see philosophically edifying connections and differences between the concepts of God and person, and thereby between everyday discourse and religious discourse.

Of course, "perspicuous representations" of the grammar of words are not a so-called analysis of the meanings of words. Analysis of meaning is purported to be exhaustive. It aims to reduce the meaning of words to their essential and basic constitutive elements. Perspicuous representations focus on certain aspects of meaning only, seeking to bring limited but edifying insights to them: not what Wittgenstein had previously called "a complete description."[23] Hence, to say "you can't hear God speak to someone else, you can hear him only if you are being addressed" is not to analyze the meaning of the word "God" or to describe its entire grammar. The remark provides only a restricted, if nonetheless insightful perspective into its meaning by describing the use of the word "God" in a given religious practice of worshiping God. This focus on the practice rather than on the meaning of the word is not unlike the way he also clarifies the concept of pain. He does that by noting that in the practice of using it we both express our pain and recognize that others are feeling pain.

Therefore, perspicuous representations of the grammar of words are also not explanations of the meaning of words. Explanations of the meaning of words, like instructions on how to reach a certain destination by an unfamiliar route, are geared for someone who is both ignorant of them and in practical need of them. They aim to convey new information that is useful for those lacking it. Perspicuous representations of the grammar of words are insightful clarifications of the uses of words with which we are already familiar. As such, they may be confusing or useless for someone unfamiliar with the use of the words they undertake to clarify.

Someone unfamiliar with religious discourse and the concepts underlying it will not gather philosophical insight from Wittgenstein's remark about hearing God speak only if you are addressed. Such a person may conclude from it that God is a person who addresses people only through their e-mail. He or she will also not get the point of the humorous remark according to which in the modern period, a religious person is someone who prays to God. A person to whom God speaks is mad. On the other hand, someone familiar with religious discourse should find Wittgenstein's remark to be a religious banality. To gather philosophical insight from it one needs to be both familiar with religious discourse and philosophically puzzled by how it differs from ordinary discourse. As may be seen from the last example, philosophical clarifications bring edifying understanding to something we already know.

3. Clarifications through Insightful Metaphors, Reminders, and Examples

Another way in which Wittgenstein pursues his work of clarification is by inventing philosophically insightful metaphors for our varied normative uses of language, such as language game. In that particular case, it "is meant," he explains, "to bring into prominence the fact that the speaking of language is part of an activity, or of a form of life," rather than a way of representing things through propositions.[24] A similar example is his calling the normative shared use of language in a culture "the grammar of words."

Still another way in which Wittgenstein clarifies uses of language is by placing philosophically puzzling concepts under proper categories. In this connection, for example, he notes that "intention is neither an emotion, a mood, nor yet a sensation or image. It is not a state of consciousness. It does not have genuine duration."[25] The remark that intention is not a process or mental state, because it lacks genuine duration may be a particularly insightful reminder in the context of philosophical discourse that strives to explain the mind as comprised of mental processes and states. It reminds us of the relationship between the concepts of duration and state, suggesting that there is more to the concept of mind than just mental states and processes. Such clarifications are not of the same category as scientific explanations. They aim to bring conceptual insight into a philosophically puzzling phenomenon, which scientists in their quest to explain how it works may not find conceptually puzzling.

Philosophical clarifications are often procured by Wittgenstein through edifying examples or striking expressions that bring new insight into the conceptual nature of what puzzles him and that he is seeking to clarify. In doing so, he is making use of an artistic discourse to provide insight through a striking example or a form of expression. In this venture, philosophically insightful remarks are not unlike edifying metaphors and jokes. Typically, such insights are difficult to paraphrase. They embody their insightful point of view. Like powerful pictures that impose a unique perspective on us, they force us to see things in a particularly significant manner. They provide expressive ways of seeing things that are conjoined to their embodied ways of expression. To try to separate the insightful points of view they create from their forms of expression is like trying to explain the humorous point of a joke. In the transaction, the humorous insight derived through it is lost. To attempt to express and preserve this insight in the explanation is not unlike attempting to bounce a ball after it has been deflated.

To appreciate the significance of an artistic discourse that acquaints us with insightful points of view about life, it is useful to imagine people who lack a sense of humor or who fail to enjoy a striking metaphor and to reflect on how we might try to convey to them the metaphoric or humorous insights we gather from it.

4. Experiencing the Meaning of a Word

One important task pursued by Wittgenstein in his project of clarification is to bring philosophical insight to the relationship between experience and understanding. In the case of understanding certain music, this may involve clarifying the experience of hearing it in a musically meaningful manner. In the case of understanding mathematics, it may involve noting that understanding how to follow a rule of addition is not a particular experience. He also strives to clarify the relationship between our understanding the meaning of words and what we experience in their connection. In one such case, he seeks to clarify the way in which we experience the meaning of names of people that are personally significant to us. For example, "I feel as if the name 'Schubert' fitted Schubert's works and Schubert's face."[26] "The name S is surrounded in that manner, at least if we are talking about the composer. But these surroundings seem to be fused with the name itself, with this word."[27] That is in contrast to the way a "convict has a number for a name . . . ,"[28] which reduces a person's significant individuality to a meaningless number.

One would like to dismiss this idea as a curious psychological phenomenon that has little to do with the linguistic role of names, which determines the meaning of names. The linguistic role of names is to individuate, not to produce experiences that may vary for different users of a name in referring to the same individual. One would like to say that our ability to mean a given person through the use of a name does not depend on what we experience when we use a name. However, Wittgenstein is seeking to bring out the way in which the significance of certain names is manifested for us in what we experience when we use them to refer to a given person. In this case, a name may be experienced as expressing the significance of the person to which it refers. He notes that this phenomenon is typical of our use of names that refer to significant (or meaningful) persons for us:

> —But remember how the names of famous poets and composers seem to have taken up a peculiar meaning into themselves. So that one can say: the names "Beethoven" and "Mozart" don't merely sound different; no, they are also accompanied by a different character. But if you had to describe this character more closely—would you point to their portraits, or to their music?[29]

The point of the last question does not emerge from an answer given to it by someone. Rather, it is to note that our use of names significant to us may be accompanied by certain significant experiences. He imagines in this regard someone who is not inclined to experience anything of the sort in connection with the use of names, referring to such a person as a "meaning-blind" person:

> And now the meaning-blind man again: He would not feel that the names, when heard or seen, were distinguished by an imponderable Something. And what would he have lost by this?—And yet, when he hears a name, first one bearer of it, and then another, may occur to him.[30]

In this example Beethoven's and Mozart's names are experienced by cultured human beings in the West as fitting their works:

> It is as if the name together with these works formed a solid whole. If we see the name, the works come to mind, and if we think of the works, so does the name. We utter the name with reverence.
>
> The name turns into a gesture; into an architectonic form.[31]
>
> If anyone didn't understand this, we should want to designate him as, say, "prosaic." And is that what the "meaning-bind" would be?[32]

Earlier, Wittgenstein expressed this thought thusly: "sometimes we project the character into the name & treat that as given. Thus, we get the impression that the great masters we know so well have just the names that suit their work."[33]

Of course, sometimes the "surroundings" of a name may be indeterminate, particularly in the case of a person we learn about from stories, such as Moses in the Bible. In this case, he claims, we use various descriptions to "define" Moses when referring to him. For example, as "the man who led the Israelites through the wilderness"; "the man who lived at that time and place and was then called 'Moses'"; "the man who as a child was taken out of the Nile by Pharaoh's daughter" and so on.[34] Thus, it is possible that different people experience the meaning of the name "Moses," when used to refer to the person in the Bible and who fits these definitions, in different ways under different circumstances. We might also consider the use of the name "Moses" to refer to different people: say a friend named "Moses" and the prophet Moses in the Bible, and being able to mean at a given time one of them only. We might also have different experiences when referring to these different people. Although we want to say that the use of the same name to refer to different people is not determined by the "experience of meaning" that accompanies it, the experience may manifest significant aspects of its meaning to the user.

In some of his clarifications, Wittgenstein also explores the relationship between the meaning of words that are not proper names and experiences that may accompany them. In one place, he considers pointing to the color and pointing to the shape of an object. He claims that there are "characteristic experiences" accompanying these different cases of pointing and meaning shape or color, although "not always."[35] In another place, he considers words that have two different meanings, such as "bank":

> As I heard "bank" the meaning money-bank came to mind. It is as if a germ of meaning were experienced and then got interpreted. Now is that an experience?
>
> One might precisely say: "I had an experience which was the germ for this use." That might be a form of expression that was natural to us.[36]

At the same time, Wittgenstein is wary of philosophical claims about experiences determining the meaning of words. He considers a claim, "every familiar word, in a book for example, actually carries an atmosphere with it in our minds, a 'corona' of lightly indicated uses. . . ." In response, he notes that this assumption is not adequate to explain intention, as "we communicate with other people without knowing if they have this experience too." The same holds for someone who says, "that with *him* knowing how to play chess was an inner process—We should say that when we want to know if he can play chess we aren't interested in anything that goes on inside him." If the person replies that this experience is what constitutes knowing how to play chess, "then we shall have to draw his attention to the criteria that would demonstrate his capacity, and on the other hand to the criteria for the 'inner states.'"[37]

Note that the same could also be said about the previous example, concerning the name "Schubert" or the meaning of the word "bank." So the point is not that some words are accompanied by particular experiences and some are not. Rather, the point is that, in the stream of life, when we communicate with people, we are not usually concerned about what they experience in connection with the words they use. Thus, in Wittgenstein's famed example of "a language meant to serve for communication between a builder A and an assistant B," what is important for the builder is the ability of the assistant to react correctly, not what he or she experiences.[38] Understanding the meaning of words used in human communication is ability. Abilities and capacities are not experiences, even if certain experiences sometimes accompany them:

> Even if someone had a particular capacity only when, and only as long as, he had a particular feeling, the feeling would not be the capacity.
>
> The meaning of a word is not the experience one has in hearing or saying it, and the sense of a sentence is not a complex of such experiences . . .
>
> Are you sure that there is a single if-feeling, and not perhaps several? Have you tried saying the word in a great variety of contexts?[39]

In my reading of the above remarks, experiences do not in general determine the meaning of words or our ability to understand their meaning. Their use according to "the grammar of the language" does that. Nonetheless, users of a language may have various experiences in connection with their use of words, particularly when this is a significant name for them or when a given word has different meanings or when it is used in the stream of life within different contexts. One way of noting this fact is by removing a word from the contextual stream of life in which it is used, such as by repeating it over and over again, without actually using it in some linguistic practice. It may then be experienced as a strange or foreign word, lacking any meaning.[40]

5. Aspect-Blindness

At this point, it might still seem that the ability to experience the meaning of a word is a curious psychological phenomenon that has little to do with the meaning of words used in the stream of life according to shared practices. However, Wittgenstein connects the ability to experience the meaning of words with the ability to see aspects of things. To bring out this point, he first notes that there are two uses of the word "see," manifesting what he calls "the difference of category between the two 'objects' of sight."[41] The example he uses to clarify this distinction is the picture of a face. In one case, we simply see it as such. In another, we see *in* it a likeness to someone: "I contemplate a face, and then suddenly notice its likeness to another. I see that it has not changed; and yet I see it differently. I call this experience 'noticing an aspect.'"[42] He goes on to provide several examples of seeing aspects of things. In one, he describes it in connection with our ability to acquire the concept of a triangle and to recognize triangles according to it, while failing to see various non-theoretical aspects of a triangle:

> Take as an example the aspects of a triangle. This triangle:
>
> 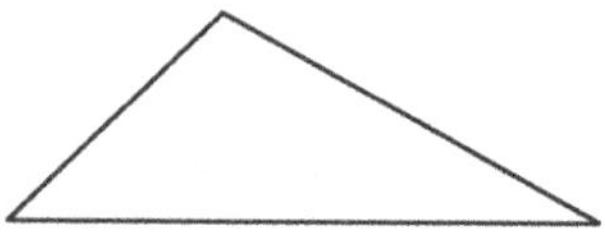
>
> can be seen as a triangular hole, as a solid, as a geometrical drawing; as standing on its base, as hanging from its apex; as a mountain, as a wedge, as an arrow or pointer, as an overturned object which is meant to stand on the shorter side of the right angle, as a half parallelogram, and as various other things...
>
> But how is it possible to see an object according to an interpretation?—The question represents it as a queer fact; as if something were being forced into a form it did not really fit. But no squeezing, no forcing took place here.[43]

Seeing a triangle in this way is to see more than the drawing of a closed geometrical figure made up of three straight lines. It is to see it *as* possessing certain features that are not described in the geometrical definition of the concept of a triangle. Nonetheless, they may be an intrinsic part of our experience of seeing it. They are not "squeezed" or "forced" by intellectual interpretations. In my reading of this phenomenological insight, it is intended to undermine the metaphysical distinction between concepts and judgments. In it, Wittgenstein demonstrates that often when we perceive an object as exemplifying a certain concept, such as that of a triangle, we also see *in* it certain features that are not part of the concept used to describe it. Nonetheless, they characterize our way of seeing this particular triangle. The fact that it is seen as standing on its base is one of the distinguishing features of both this particular triangle and our particular way of seeing it. Accordingly, we may suppose that some people may not see this triangle as standing on its base or as a mountain, although they share with us the concepts of a triangle, base, and mountain. In a similar way, some people may not be able to see an arrow as pointing in a certain direction, although they may recognize it to be an arrow. The inability to see such features is a form of what he calls both "aspect-blindness" and meaning-blindness:[44]

> Anyone who cannot understand and learn to use the words "to see the sign as an arrow"—that's whom I call "meaning-blind."
>
> It will make no sense to tell him "You must try to see it as an arrow" and one won't be able to help him in that *way*.[45]

It is not clear from the example discussed whether Wittgenstein envisions someone who is incapable of seeing an arrow as pointing in a certain direction, or someone who is incapable of seeing anything as this or that—someone who lacks both the concept and the ability to see something as having a certain significant feature that is not part of the concept used to distinguish it. I take it that what is at stake in these examples is not the success of seeing in a given drawing of a triangle that it is standing on its base or a given sign as pointing in a certain direction, because we may fail to do that in certain cases but succeed in others. Wittgenstein is envisioning an inability to do so in more than just a particular case: "Anyone who cannot understand and learn to use the words 'to see the sign as an arrow'—that's whom I call 'meaning-blind.'"[46] He notes that it makes no sense to tell such a person to try to see it as an arrow. Apparently this is akin to telling a color-blind person to try to see colors. In Wittgenstein's use of the locution "meaning-blind" such a person is blind to the meaning of words that name colors.

In a similar manner, Wittgenstein sees an inherent connection between the ability to see various aspects of things and the ability to experience the meaning of certain words. When these non-theoretical aesthetic abilities are missing, he speaks of aspect-blindness and also of meaning-blindness. In both, the experience of the meaning of a word or an object is missing:

> The importance of the concept aspect-blindness lies in the kinship of seeing an aspect and experiencing the meaning of a word. For we want to ask: "What are you missing if you do not experience the meaning of a word?"—If you cannot utter the word 'bank' by itself, now with one meaning, then with the other, or if you do not find that when you utter a word ten times in a row it loses its meaning, as it were, and becomes a mere sound.[47]

In contrast to the above experience, in which the words of our language are rendered strange to us, we may also have an experience of familiarity with certain words used in the stream of life:

> It's as if the word that I understand had a definite slight aroma that corresponds to my understanding of it. As if two familiar words were distinguished for me not merely by their sound or their appearance, but by an atmosphere as well, even when I don't imagine anything in connection with them.[48]

We may note in connection with an experience of meaning that to understand the meaning of words requires an understanding of the linguistic practices in which they are used. To experience their meaning requires being sensitive to their particular significance for us in the context of their use. Therefore, Wittgenstein notes, "Aspect-blindness will be akin to the lack of a 'musical ear.'"[49]

6. Preliminary Conclusions

I have described several ways in which Wittgenstein goes about his project of clarification so as to focus on the philosophical framework in which his statements on Jews are also written. Thus, just as his "grammatical remarks" on the meaning of other words "earmark the way we look at things," his grammatical remarks on Jews also purport to earmark the way we look at things, namely, upon Jews. The "we" in this case are members of the culture in which he is affiliated and in which the concept of Jew is employed.

These remarks clarify the concept of a Jew used therein by means of similes and metaphors that aim to afford articulated conceptual insights into the Jews' unique spiritual nature, as it is experienced and grasped from within the concept of a Jew. They may now be seen to do so by either offering a *bird's-eye view* of the grammatical rules for representing the concept of a Jew or perspicuous representations of the spiritual nature of Jews, expressed as grammatical remarks on the concept of a Jew.

In either case, they describe how Jews are grasped and experienced in several cultural contexts of reflection on Jews and on their abilities, propensities, and achievements: social, psychological, economical, historical, and artistic. They clarify the concept of a Jew by describing the spiritual essence of Jews as it is manifested in different contexts of life. Moreover, as they are clarifications of a concept that serves him to reflect both on the spiritual nature of Jews in comparison to that of other people and on his own spiritual nature, they also provide Wittgenstein with self-clarifications about these matters.[50] In doing so, he distinguishes Jews from other people, as forming a different spiritual category of humanity, describes how he and others both grasp and experience the spiritual nature, character and mentality of Jews, and expresses his critical attitude toward Jews and their effect on Western culture.

Three

CLARIFYING THE CONCEPT OF A JEW

As may be seen from Wittgenstein's remarks on Jews, he describes Jews as possessing a shared spiritual nature, namely a Jewish one. Although this spiritual nature may afflict some people who are not Jewish, such as Rousseau, people identified as "Jews" are typified by it. As may also be seen, he appears to identify Jews as people who are of a common Jewish ethnic origin, not a common Jewish religious or cultural affiliation. Given this overview of Jews, he seeks to clarify the concept of a Jew by considering the spiritual nature of Jews in several cultural contexts of reflection. It is edifying to examine some of them more closely now.

1. Jews in Society

One context in which Wittgenstein reflects on the spiritual nature of Jews is social, pertaining particularly to the Jews' attempt in the modern period to integrate into society and assimilate. He reflects on the success of this venture by describing and thereby clarifying how non-Jews relate to such Jews as to an alien human element seeking to affiliate itself with a cherished national and cultural enterprise, experiencing them as a diseased growth on the healthy national body. That is because, as he explains it, within the history of the Jews' existence in Europe "they are experienced as a sort of disease, anomaly, & nobody wants to put a disease on the same level as normal life." Jews are experienced in this way because they are perceived to embody a deviant spiritual nature, different from that which is embodied in all other human beings throughout all cultural and national affiliations. As such, the attempt of Jews to assimilate fails, for their Jewish essence still informs their spirit, generating hostile anti-Semitic sentiments towards them for infringing on the wholesome and organic national body. Thus, there is something deviant and unalterable about the very spiritual nature of Jews. Even when Jews assimilate, it still manifests itself in a way that is easily detected by others. It makes ordinary, non-Jewish Europeans experience assimilated Jews as both retaining and concealing their alien, deviant, secretive, harmful Jewish essence and spiritual nature, motivating them to turn against assimilated Jews.

Wittgenstein's approach to this big ideologically charged and complicated subject is the same as his approach to many other subjects that arise in intellectual and cultural discourse. It is a philosophical approach that seeks to "clarify" a given concept or the essence of a given cultural innovation, artistic expression, ritual or natural phenomenon, by noting how we operate with it, how it manifests our sensibilities and attitudes, and how it affects us. In this case, he turns to clarify the concept of a Jew by describing how non-Jews both experience and relate to assimilated Jews from within the social surroundings of their emerging self-identity as a people who share a common social identity that historically excluded Jews.

It may be useful to recall at this point that throughout their history, Jews living in Europe were usually distinguished from the rest of the population. They had a different legal standing from others. They required an authorized grant by the regime to dwell where they were born and they lived under their own cultural laws. Accordingly, others often regarded them as aliens living within their midst, familiar with their surroundings and culture, but not belonging to either of them. Through the impact of religious ideology, they were often also regarded as the spiritually impoverished successors of a people who both bequeathed the Bible to the world and rejected Christ, relying instead on their sophisticated and contrived Talmudic religious discourse. Exiled from their ancient homeland, they were seen to subsist in what for them is "Diaspora." To persevere within the economic and civil restrictions laid on them, they were often forced into mercantile practices, arousing negative reactions to them. They were then held to rely on their practical intellectual abilities to wheel and deal and to conceal their true cunning nature. Wittgenstein expresses this received perception of the Jews by noting that Jews "continue to exist only because they have the inclination towards . . . secretiveness." He then compares Jews to an animal that "has escaped extinction only because it has the possibility or capability of concealing itself." From this perspective on Jews, they appear to lack some of the basic cultural forms of life that people living within their own homelands tend to create and cultivate, such as agriculture, industry, government, military organization, and arts.

In Wittgenstein's clarification of the above perception of Jews and their contrived, secretive, and anomalous way of subsisting within the geographical, social, and cultural realms of other nations, they are experienced by others as a people dispossessed of their own organic bodies, living by their intellectual wits only. When, in the modern period, they try to assimilate, they are grasped by others as seeking to fit in by attaching themselves to a country, culture, and nationality to which they do not really belong, and to be doing so by means of pretence. He clarifies this perception of assimilated Jews and the negative attitude toward them that it evokes by a basic experience, relating to what we grasp as a part of our body and what we grasp as an unhealthy growth on it. Thus, he uses the popular anti-Semitic metaphor, equating assimilated Jews with an unhealthy growth upon the healthy national body to "clarify" the concept of an assimilated Jew. In doing so, he describes how non-Jews grasp Jews. He thus articulates the basic experience underlying both national and anti-Semitic sentiments, providing for their powerful influence on those who succumb to them. As such, the phenomenological description of Jews and their parasitic spirit as others experience them, expresses the basic attitudes toward Jews and towards national self-identity on which anti-

Semitic ideologies are constructed and propagated. It clarifies the way Europeans respond to assimilated Jews living among them in an antagonistic manner, by experiencing them as a parasitic growth on their cherished culture and nationality. (To note that historically Jews were first forbidden to follow many professions, to farm the land, or produce and then were excoriated precisely because they did not do so is both to provide an historical explanation for experiencing them as a parasitic growth and to note the irony of it.)

What does not immediately emerge is how similar this way of grasping the spiritual nature of Jews is to ways of grasping both the nature and meaning of things that he considers elsewhere. If you grasp the spiritual nature of Jews in such a meaningful fashion is it akin to understanding that "you can't hear God speak to someone else." Or is it akin to seeing a particular aspect of something, such as seeing the figure of a triangle as "a triangular hole, as a solid, as a geometrical drawing; as standing on its base, as hanging from its apex; as a mountain" and so forth. Or, is it akin to using a name according to a certain definition: for example, the name Moses as "the man who led the Israelites through the wilderness," or "the man who lived at that time and place and was then called 'Moses,'" or "the man who as a child was taken out of the Nile by Pharaoh's daughter"? Or is it akin to experiencing the meaning of the word (used in his culture that is synonymous with) "Jew" in a particular way, such as one might experience the meaning of the word 'bank' differently when referring to the bank of the river or the institution for conducting money transactions.

Either way, anti-Semitic attitudes toward Jews emerge from immediate ways of grasping the Jews' deviant human spiritual nature. They are ways of experiencing the spiritual feature of Jews in immediate fashion without any interpretation. On this clarification, anti-Semitic ideologies only draw from and build on these experiences and ways of grasping the spiritual nature of Jews; they do not induce them. Those who fail to perceive these features of Jews are not sufficiently spiritually discriminating. They are like someone lacking a musical ear or like someone who is unable to see a triangle as standing on its base.

The difficulty with this interpretation is that it suggests that the spiritual features of Jews can be perceived, just as a melody can be heard and a triangle can be seen standing on its base. Although some anti-Semites claim that they can recognize Jews in a crowd, this claim pertains mostly to Jewish physical features. However, the phenomenological features of the Jews' spiritual nature that may be experienced in a social context, wherein they are perceived as "a sort of disease," are not sufficiently filled in. (Is it that Jews are more "pushy" than other people, as the locution "pushy Jews" suggests?) Moreover, it is not clear from this analogy whether identifying people as Jews promotes this way of grasping their Jewish spiritual nature, or the other way around.

Another possibility is that the very meaning of the word (used in his culture that is synonymous with the word) "Jew" promotes such an experience when interacting with people that are identified as Jews. In this interpretation, the concept of a Jew is that of a spiritually diseased human being, just as the concept of cancer is of a diseased growth on the organic body or the concept God entails that you can only hear God speak if you are addressed. In interactions with people identified as Jews, it casts its dark shadow on how they are grasped, regardless of how we may think of them personally. (This allows for the possibility that some of your best friends are Jews, even if you recognize Jews as belonging to a "diseased" human spiritual category.) In either case, anti-Semitic ideologies are founded on such immediate ways of reacting to people identified as Jews. Those who do not share these perceptions and experiences use the concept of a Jew as they would any other national characteristic. They are not aware of the "deep grammar" that underlies the use of the word "Jew," which determines its meaning and the attitudes toward Jews that it produces. It renders the claim that Jews possess an anomalous and diseased spirit into a grammatical remark that expresses a conceptual truth.

Whether the diseased parasitic spiritual nature of Jews is an inherent part of the concept of a Jew expressed in the language of Wittgenstein's culture or whether it is an experience that accompanies its use, it manifests an attitude toward Jews that he seeks to clarify. In the context of his previous examples of meaning-blindness, it might be said that those who do not experience the meaning of the word "Jew" as referring to someone with a diseased parasitic spirit are meaning blind to it. They are like someone who may recognize a drawn figure as triangle but not be able to see that it is standing on its base. They use the word "Jew" only in its "prosaic" meaning, referring through it to human beings of a given nationality: like French, English, or the like. They are like foreigners who have mastered the technical or prosaic use of the language of a culture but not its shared spirit. They are like people who only know that Beethoven was a great composer and Goethe a great writer, but have no appreciation of their works. Or they may even remember the different definite descriptions identifying each of them. But having no appreciation for their works of art, they do not experience anything especially meaningful about their names in connection with them.

What disturbs many of us upon reading these remarks of Wittgenstein on Jews is the impression that they do not just describe the way in which anti-Semitic attitudes emerge against the background of both national sentiments and the attempt of Jews to assimilate. Nor do they only offer a "perspicuous representation" of the concept of a Jew by "clarifying" the phenomenological ways in which Jews are experienced through the negative attitudes they promote because of emerging national sentiments. They also appear to *justify* them, expressing along the way the author's *own* negative attitude toward Jews, because of what he perceives as the Jews' alien, secretive, diseased and parasitic spiritual nature.

2. Jews in History, Economy, and Art

The impression that Wittgenstein is not merely clarifying the concept of a Jew used in his culture, but is also clarifying his own attitudes toward Jews, is strengthened by another context of reflection on Jews. This is the Jews' psychological nature, as manifested in the ability of Jews to persevere despite their turbulent and calamitous history. According to Wittgenstein, Jews tend to hide their true psychological nature, which is both "secretive and cunning." He rejects the view that this psychological trait in Jews is a result of the Jews' long history of persecution. Rather, it is because of this trait that Jews have survived their long history of persecution, perhaps because, unlike a tree that cannot bend before a strong wind, Jews can. Since their spiritual nature allows them to bend in the face of social upheavals. Therefore, the fate of Jews in history is not tragedy. Tragedy befalls a people who are unable to bend before historical calamities. Jews, however, can, as they are intellectually practical, spiritually flexible, and psychologically secretive and cunning. Therefore, they manage to persevere even when calamities overtake them, making them inherently different from non-Jews, whose lives can be tragic.

Wittgenstein does not disclose how he reaches this description of the spiritual nature of Jews. Nor does he say how he reaches the conclusion that this spiritual disposition explains the ability of Jews to survive, rather than it being a development due to their persecution. To the extent that he is not engaged in an actual historical discourse but in his project of clarification, these remarks are clarifications of the spiritual nature of Jews as it emerges out of received historical discourse about them. To say that Jews have become what they are because of their persecution is to offer a causal explanation for their deviant spiritual nature. To say that they survived their persecution because of what they are is to clarify their spiritual nature as it is manifested through their history. It is similar to suggesting that dogs befriend human beings because they are tame, rather than that they have became tame because they befriended human beings. (In a similar manner, Wittgenstein claims elsewhere that we are not inclined to follow a rule because of what it means: it means what it does because we are inclined to follow it.) In this methodological procedure, philosophical clarification of the spiritual nature of Jews is not a scientific, causal, hypothetical explanation of how Jews came to be what they are. It is a descriptive effort that brings philosophical insight to the meaning of their cultural dispositions within a specified context of reflection on them.

Further to Wittgenstein's previous insight, the flexible spiritual disposition and cunning psychological trait manifest themselves also in the Jews' approach to economic and financial matters. Typically, Jews are perceived as making their living by selling and financing what other people produce. Wittgenstein explains this propensity on the part of Jews as manifesting the fact that they are noncreative human beings. Lacking an inherent powerful creative spirit that may sustain them by motivating them to create what they lack, they are spiritually poor. This makes existence difficult for them, since of themselves they have "nothing" of value. Therefore, they both esteem money and have a great ability to make money, seeking to augment their lack of creative spiritual power by their typical attitude toward property and assets, such as "their liking to be rich; for money is for them a particular sort of power not possession."

In my reading of these remarks, they are aimed at clarifying the concept of a Jew by describing the attitude of Jews toward economical and financial matters. As such, the remark that Jews love money is a grammatical remark, expressing a conceptual remark within an economic context of description. Moreover, as emerges from these clarifications, Jews do not simply love money more than other human beings love money. They love it in a different way. It provides them (in a sublimated form) something they lack: namely, spiritual power.[1] Thus, for Jews financial matters are a substitute for spiritual matters.

Still another context in which Wittgenstein writes about Jews, and which embraces most of his remarks about them, concerns the Jews' involvement in culture as an artistic enterprise or *Kultur*. In this context of reflection, he does not seek to clarify how others relate to them, but how he himself experiences their creative endeavors and influence on the cultural affairs of art in Europe. His remarks about the spiritual nature of Jews in this context of reflection are prompted by describing how he relates to works of art that are produced by artists of Jewish origins, including his own. As emerges, he experiences them as intellectually clever, but not demonstrating any genuine creative power, and therefore as spiritually both sterile and parasitic, making use of the artistic creations of non-Jews in a clever fashion. Since Jews are incapable of creating cultural works of art on their own, there are no Jewish geniuses in the arts. At most, Jews are talented artists, not true geniuses.

As Wittgenstein now makes clear, he perceives Jews to embody in their approach to cultural affairs in the arts an intellectual force that is alien to the powerful creative spiritual forces that lie at the basis of Western culture, or, for that matter, the creative spiritual forces at the basis of *any* human culture. The metaphor he uses to clarify the Jews' lack of creative power is "a desert region." Nothing belonging to the arts is capable of growing in this region. He claims that below this "thin layer of rock lies the molten lava of spirit."[2] However, this spirit seems to be only a very powerful intellectual force. It is incapable of creating original and powerful works of art on its own. Even when it is transplanted into a lush cultural region, it will not yield anything of artistic value that is original. At most, it is an intellectual force that can only refine and elaborate on what others have created. Therefore, it attaches itself to cultures that others have created in a spiritually authentic fashion. It reprocesses their original artistic creations, using the cultural contributions that others have made to reproduce and refine them in a clever manner. In so doing, Jews change the spirit formerly embodied in the culture in which they have integrated themselves, rendering it a more sophisticated but also spiritually less powerful culture.

As may now be seen, in all contexts of reflection on Jews, Wittgenstein describes the Jews' involvement in cultural affairs as a parasitic intellectual intrusion by a people lacking a genuine spiritual nature of their own, and therefore lacking powerful creative cultural abilities. As now also becomes clear, these remarks do not just *clarify* how others experience the attempt on the part of Jews to assimilate into non-Jewish society. Nor do they merely *describe* the way in which artists of Jewish origins create and how the Jews' intrusion on the cultural enterprise affects artistic achievements in the modern period. They also *express* the way in which *he* experiences certain works of art produced by Jews as an expression of a Jewish spirit, and his critical assessment of the Jews' spiritual intrusion on and contribution to European cultural affairs.

In clarifying the nature of Jewish expressions in art, Wittgenstein contrasts an intellectual and practical attitude toward life and its expression in art with a poetic and tragic attitude toward life and its expression in art. Jews are people possessing an intellectual character, endowing them with an "*unpoetic* mentality, which heads straight for what is concrete." He distinguishes such an approach to life and art with one that is manifested in what he states Schiller called a "poetic mood": "I think I know what he means," he comments. "I think I am familiar with it myself. It is the mood of receptivity to nature & one in which one's thoughts seem as vivid as nature itself . . . ."[3] In contrast with a poetic character that promotes a poetic mood, Jews are intellectual and practical. They are not receptive to nature and their artistic expressions are not "vivid as nature itself." As I interpret this, he means that Jews do not express themselves out of the depths of their human spirit, because their Jewish sprit lacks natural human depth. It is all intellect. Therefore their self-expressions are not vibrant powerful similes and metaphors, which have an artistic life of their own. At the most they are contrived and artificial expressions that are the product of thinking.

Jews are also typified by not being tragic, so that "tragedy is something un-Jewish." It is not clear from his remarks whether these two characterizing features of the Jews' spirit, their unpoetic mentality and their lack of a tragic attitude toward life, are interrelated, and if so, how. One way of seeing the connection between them is to note that both a poetic and tragic nature are an expression of an ability to be true to one's basic character, as it is manifested in an authentic attitude toward life and what it encloses. Reflecting on the concept of tragedy, Wittgenstein first notes, "a tragedy might really always start with the words: 'Nothing at all would have happened, had it not been that . . . .' (Had he not been caught in the machine by a corner of his clothing?)." However, he also comments critically on this comment: "But isn't it a one-sided view of tragedy to think of it merely as showing, that an encounter can decide one's whole life."[4] Indeed, several years later he offers examples of tragedy that relate it to a hero's courageous confrontation with death: "In a bullfight, the bull is the hero of a tragedy. First driven mad by suffering, he dies a slow & terrible death.[5] He notes in this connection, "a hero looks death in the face, real death, not just a picture of death."[6]

In my reading of the above remarks, they aim to clarify the concept of tragedy as it is manifested in both art and life. In the first, tragedy is the product of an untimely accidental death. In the second, it derives from a hero's courageous attitude towards death. It is the second conception of tragedy that is relevant to Wittgenstein's discussion of Jewish spirit. In this conception, a tragic attitude toward life emerges from a nature that is both unable and unwilling to adjust, but remains true to itself in the face of death. But Jews have a cerebral, practical attitude toward life, adjusting themselves to the circumstances that confront them. Such an attitude toward life manifests itself in the Jews' intellectual character. They adjust to life's changes, rather than remaining true to themselves when looking at "death *itself* in the eye."[7] Therefore, the ethical attitude toward life and death on the part of Jews is never tragic. He notes critically in this connection, "fear in face of death is the best sign of a false, i.e. a bad, life."[8] It typifies the ethical attitude toward life of Jews. Earlier he pronounced that "ethics and aesthetics are one and the same."[9] Thus, the remark on the ethical attitude of Jews to life and death also brings a further dimension to Wittgenstein's critical comments on the spirit of Jews in the arts.

3. Self-Reflection in the Context of Jewish and non-Jewish Spirits

Since Wittgenstein regards himself as endowed with a Jewish spiritual nature, his clarifications of the concept of a Jew and of the Jews' unique spiritual nature often turn into self-clarifications. Wittgenstein refers to Felix Mendelssohn in this connection, both because he typifies an assimilated Jew, who creates in the arts and, perhaps also, because he could see a similarity between Mendelssohn's cultural predicament and his own. Like Mendelssohn, Wittgenstein's family origins were Jewish. Although he was raised as a Catholic, his grandparents on his father's side were former Jews who converted to Protestantism. His grandfather on his mothers' side was also a Jew who had converted to Catholicism. Only his grandmother on his mother's side lacked Jewish ancestry.

Wittgenstein uses Mendelssohn and his music to clarify his understanding of three things: (1) how a Jew's spiritual attitude toward life and art persists even when working within the cultural tradition of German music; (2) what he dislikes in the Jews' attitude toward life and art, which is expressed even when operating within an authentic cultural tradition; (3) to reflect on his own spiritual nature, which he takes to be mirrored in Mendelssohn's spiritual attitude toward life and art as expressed in his music: "Mendelssohn is like a man who is . . . good only when everyone around him is good. . . . I too am like that." This is in contrast to someone possessing a strong spiritual character. Such a person is like a tree that does not bend before the wind, expressing a tragic attitude toward life and death. But he, like Mendelssohn, is different:

> Tragically holding on, defiantly holding on to a tragic situation in love always seems to me quite alien to my ideal. Does that mean my ideal is feeble? I cannot & *should not judge*. If it is feeble then it is bad. I believe that fundamentally I have a gentle & calm ideal. But may God protect my ideal from feebleness & mawkishness![10]

Thus, his comments on Mendelssohn's spiritual character are also an expression of self-clarification.

Wittgenstein's reflections on Mendelssohn's and his own spiritual character connect an aesthetic ideal to an existential attitude toward life itself. In both cases, it is seen to derive from an intellectual character. In his own case he thinks it manifests a lack of powerful creative ability in philosophy as well:

> I think there is some truth in my idea that I am really only reproductive in my thinking. I think I have never *invented* a line of thinking but that it was always provided for me by someone else & I have done no more than passionately take it up for my work of clarification. That is how Boltzmann, Hertz, Schopenhauer, Frege, Russell, Kraus, Loos, Weininger, Spengler, and Sraffa have influenced me. Can one take Breuer & Freud as an example of Jewish reproductive thinking?—What I invent are new *comparisons*.[11]

Note that he is not criticizing here the philosophical project of clarification itself, only the way in which he goes about it by passionately working out ideas that originate with others. This comes out more clearly in his self-clarification of his artistic efforts:

> At the time I modeled the head for Drobil too, the stimulus was essentially a work of Drobil's & my work was again really one of clarification. I believe that what is essential is for the activity of clarification to be carried out with COURAGE; without this it becomes a mere clever game.[12]

In artistic and philosophical endeavors, courage is a virtue that Wittgenstein contrasts with being merely clever. To clarify further the difference between these two different creative abilities and attitudes, and to caution against confusing between them, he relates a kind of aesthetic delusion to which he was sometimes prone concerning his own creative powers:

> When I have had a picture suitably framed or have hung it in the right surroundings I have often *caught* myself being as proud as though I had

> painted the picture. Actually that's not right: not "as proud as though I had painted it" but as proud as though I had helped to paint it, as though I had so to speak painted a little bit of it. It is as if an exceptional arranger of grasses were at last to think that he too had produced at least a quite tiny blade of grass himself. Whereas it ought to be clear to him that his work lies in a different region altogether. The process through which even the tiniest & meanest blade of grass comes into being is quite foreign and unknown to him.[13]

In this example, Wittgenstein's contribution to art is meant to strike an analogy with the contributions to culture of artists endowed with Jewish spirit. Like them, Wittgenstein works with an already existing cultural product. Like them, he operates upon what culture bequeaths him, in such a way as to improve the cultural product. It can even be said that he contributes to the making of a prettier picture. However, he is not the one to paint the picture. He does not even take part in its painting. His contribution lies merely in advancing the artistic achievement it embodies by integrating it in a sophisticated and intelligent manner in a given cultural undertaking.

As before, with regard to Wittgenstein's clarification of national sentiments that give rise to ant-Semitic sentiments, the impression is that he is not merely describing the creative effort that provides for art, nor just explaining how Jews might delude themselves into thinking that they are original creators of works of art, when their contribution to art is merely to advance the artistic creation of someone else. He is criticizing Jewish artists, like himself, for failing to note how they rely on the creative work of others, because they are incapable of creating something original on their own. This is an aesthetic criticism that encompasses ethical disapproval as well. For "danger arises only when someone confuses the nature of a Jewish work with that of a non-Jewish work & especially when the author of the former does so himself, as he so easily may." So the effort in which Wittgenstein is engaged is not only an edifying self-reflection about his own achievements or aesthetic and conceptual clarifications about the artistic achievements of Jewish artists in general, but an effort to curtail artistic and conceptual "confusion." This turns into an ethical effort, as it warns of a "danger" that arises for an author, like himself, when the Jewish spiritual origins of his work are not properly noted and distinguished. Such an author may then delude himself into thinking that he has actually created something on his own, and feel unjustly proud of himself. "Doesn't he look as proud as though he were being milked himself," when he, in fact, has only milked other creators of their original artistic contributions.[14]

Although Wittgenstein notes his Jewish "unpoetic mentality" and his Jewish inclination to elaborate on what others have created, rather than creating something original himself, he refers to Jews in third person: as either "they" or as "the Jew." Jews, it might be said, are not, for Wittgenstein, "us guys." They are "those people." It is as though his Jewishness is a spiritual disease with which he is afflicted, making him, against his wish, a party to all those who are afflicted by it as well. However, he aspires to overcome this affliction, and he has no feelings of loyalty to those who are afflicted with this disease with him.

4. Creativity in Philosophy

The importance of the subject of creativity for Wittgenstein emerges from what Bertrand Russell has told of his first encounters with him. In Russell's account, Wittgenstein asked Russell to tell him what he judged to be his abilities in philosophy. He added that unless they were exceptional, he would become an aeronautical engineer. In the ensuing weeks, Russell conferred on him the mantle of genius, suggesting to Wittgenstein's astonished sister that he expected the next big step in philosophy to be taken by her brother. However, as these comments now disclose, Wittgenstein saw himself possessed of a Jewish spirit, inclining him to be influenced by others and to be merely a "reproductive" thinker: not what is expected of genius.

The problem for Wittgenstein was that while he aspired to purge himself of his Jewish spirit and to create—in an original, poetic, courageous, "non-Jewish manner"—on his view of philosophy, it is not a culturally creative enterprise, which has a meaningful, powerful, authentic spiritual voice of its own. When explaining things completely on its own, philosophy becomes a senseless metaphysical enterprise, building "houses in the air." In contrast to such metaphysical efforts, philosophy, pursued by means of conceptual clarifications of various uses of language or artistic works, subsists in the homeland that others have created. It is a descriptive effort that manifests a clever Jewish spirit, lacking the ability to create something genuine on its own. At most, it is akin to a cultural effort aimed at having "a picture suitably framed" or "hung . . . in the right surroundings."

The way in which Wittgenstein seeks to overcome this problem is, first, by relinquishing any attempt to procure intellectual, metaphysical, scientific-like explanations in philosophy, consigning his project to procuring insightful clarifications of what both puzzles and inspires him. Second, he notes that to provide deep insight, philosophical clarifications need to be pursued with what he terms "courage." Presumably, creative courage enables even a philosopher, who strives for self-clarification rather than for metaphysical explanations and who tends to evoke "comparisons" between different phenomena, to express his basic human nature when bringing conceptual insights to bear on the way things are rendered meaningful to him. It demands being true to oneself, expressive, straightforward, and not contrived or merely clever, even when engaging in insightful philosophical clarifications. It thus demands overcoming what he regards as his Jewish "*unpoetic* mentality, which heads straight for what is concrete. Which is characteristic of my philosophy." Nonetheless, he wants to integrate his philosophy with artistic poetic expression:

"One should write philosophy only as one writes a poem."[15] By basing his clarifications of the meaning of words—which underlie our use of language and ways of engaging life—on edifying examples, enlightening similes and insightful metaphors, it is possible to achieve this goal. For it is to use an artistic, poetic mode of expression to procure deep philosophical insights, and to do so in a powerful and original way.

Four

THE PHILOSOPHICAL BACKGROUND

It is tempting to stigmatize Ludwig Wittgenstein's remarks on Jews as an unfortunate relic of anti-Semitic stereotyped conceptions about Jews prevalent in his time and contributing to his difficulties with his self-identity. While this claim may be correct, it does not sufficiently elucidate Wittgenstein's philosophical attempt to clarify the concept of a Jew in the way he does, placing the concepts of disease, imitation, talent and cleverness at its spiritual core. Nor does it explain why he considers the clarification of the stereotypical concept of a Jew propagated in his culture a proper philosophical topic at all, revealing important aspects of both the spiritual forces operating in a culture, the Jews' particular spiritual nature and their damaging affect on the arts in the modern period. As though in response to such implied criticism, he snipes back: "One age misunderstands another; and a petty age misunderstands all the others in its own ugly way."[1] To understand these matters better, it may help to look into the philosophical background of these comments, at which Wittgenstein mostly only hints. For they stem from his interweaving of two similar, but different, ideas about the spiritual forces underlying modern culture. These ideas are derived primarily from two different philosophical sources, which he both acknowledges and employs to reflect on the spiritual nature of Jews and their impact on modern culture and society. It is edifying to trace their impression on his thinking.

1. Spengler's Spiritual Dichotomy

The first idea about the spiritual forces embodied in modern culture that underlies Wittgenstein's remarks is that there are two fundamentally different attitudes toward life from within which human beings live and engender. First, a more basic attitude, the spiritual life force of which is manifested in will, emotion, action, and response, and second, a more artificial attitude, the spiritual life force of which is manifested in intellect and abstract reasoning. What emerges is a metaphysical distinction concerning two different fundamental ways in which human beings operate, pursue their existence, and express what is valuable to them. It provides a central and dominant metaphysical theme in both Romantic philosophy and conservative ideology. It is a theme that in existential philosophy was transformed into an ontological distinction between authentic and inauthentic modes of existence-in-the-world.[2] Wittgenstein derives this approach mostly from Oswald Spengler, who wrote on the spiritual underpinnings of human cultures as manifested in prominent historical communities and whose pessimistic volume on the spiritual decline of the West as a culture appeared at the end of the First World War.[3]

According to Spengler, that to which we refer as "a culture" is the spiritual orientation of an historic group of people who have achieved a unitary conception of their world, which is oriented on a distinctive conception of the physical space in which they live and act. This spiritual orientation informs all their activities: in art, religion, philosophy, politics, economics, and ways of waging war. Transcending the distinction between culture and civilization, which equated culture (*Kultur*) with the arts and civilization with practical innovations, Spengler distinguished between four separate periods in the history of all great human communities, the first three of which he called (following Nietzsche) periods of culture and the last, a period of "civilization." Culture, he explained, is an historical period in which original and authentic human activity takes place. Civilization is an historical period in which refined, theoretical, technical, and sophisticated elaboration on what has previously been created takes place. In civilization, explained Spengler, the highest creative works are those of administration and the application of science to industry. It is a period in which the spiritual forces that in the past had provided for an historical community's culture are in decline, heralding its demise. (Culture, explained Spengler by way of one illustration among several, is classical Greece; civilization is Rome.)

Although the culture and civilization of an historical society are linked by being a continuing historical effort to live, create, and act out of the same conception of the world and human life, the spiritual disposition behind periods of culture is different from that of civilization. The spiritual disposition that gives rise to culture stems from an effort that is more primitive, basic, and instinctive to human beings—one that is closer in nature to action. The spiritual disposition that finds expression in civilization stems from a more artificial and complex effort, one that belongs to the realm of thought. Culture, Spengler claimed, is soul. Civilization is intellect—a period when a culture has lost its soul. Culture resembles the spiritual world of a child, civilization that of an adult. The two spiritual dispositions behind culture and civilization find expression in the history of all mature human communities, through two separate social classes: peasants and nobles, on the one hand, priests and bourgeoisie, on the other. The former are dynamic and spontaneous, the latter search for eternal truths. Spengler compared the former to a plant that sprouts directly from the earth, the latter to an animal roving the land for its sustenance. These two classes' control of society in various periods coincides, in his view, with the existence of either culture or civilization in each period.

Wittgenstein, it seems, takes the Spenglerian distinction between two different spiritual dispositions underlying culture and civilization and applies it to Western culture in the modern age, regardless of historical periodicity. In this way, according to him, it is possible in modern Western culture to detect and distinguish between artists operating within a spiritual disposition that underlies a period of culture and artists operating within a spiritual disposition that underlies a period of civilization. Finally, and here lies his major effort, Wittgenstein reshapes the metaphors and similes used by Spengler in order to arrive at a clearer, more powerful, and insightful description of these two different spiritual dispositions. Within this framework, he identifies artists of a spiritual disposition that underlies civilization as Jews, while artists of a spiritual disposition that gives rise to culture are non-Jews (thereby transforming Spengler's priests and bourgeoisie into Jews and his peasants and nobles into non-Jews). This results in the Jewish mind becoming synonymous with a cultural attitude whose formative spirit is intellect.[4]

2. Weininger's Spiritual Dichotomy

The last move, namely identifying Jews with the spirit that underlies modern civilization, stems from the second idea that Wittgenstein is propagating in these remark. It is that the Jews' involvement in Western culture, as discussed earlier, displays a spirit different from that on which Western culture, or for that matter, any culture, is based. This second idea is one at which Wittgenstein arrives mainly through the writings of Otto Weininger. Weininger, born in 1880 as a Jew, lived in Vienna, converted to Christianity, and, upon completing his doctoral degree in philosophy at the University of Vienna, committed suicide in 1903, in the house were Beethoven had died. Shortly before that, he had published a book that subsequently sparked considerable discussion in European intellectual circles. The title of Weininger's book, *Sex and Character*, is apt to mislead nowadays.[5] The book is about two different spiritual dispositions and attitudes, which mould people's lives and shape culture. (Perhaps today the book would have been called *Gender and Character*.) Weininger describes them through what he terms "the ideal human male type and the ideal human female type." The former manifests pure masculinity and is passionate, rational, firm, and creative. The latter manifests pure femininity and is sexually driven, chaotic, fickle, and spiritually sterile. Weininger claims that no human being manifests either pure masculinity or pure femininity; rather, each individual is a combination of both. However, in general, pure femininity is manifested to a greater extent in women, just as pure masculinity is in men.

Weininger views the feminine type as an extremely negative cultural type. Adopting a philosophical conception of culture as a mode of human existence that embodies self-creation, he renders cultural existence into a spiritual mode of existence. In contrast to this creative cultural endeavor, women are by nature reproductive creatures and this is also their nature as a cultural type—a cultural type that is not a true producer of new cultural creations. It only enhances and reproduces cultural innovations that others have created. It is also a cultural type that is mostly immersed in everyday details of life, not in abstract ideas, defining itself through attachments to other people, not through spiritual ideals and metaphysical principles. In keeping with this view, Weininger expresses repugnance at the feminine cultural type as demonstrated in the behavior of women and calls for sexual abstinence.

I have mentioned Weininger's view regarding women because it also serves as a launching pad for his remarks about Jews. For Weininger, femininity and Jewishness are inextricably linked. Fittingly, he devotes a special chapter in his book to Jews. He views Jews and their attitudes toward life as the manifestation of a feminine culture. As when discussing femininity, so too he claims here that in speaking of "the Jew," his reference is only to the "Platonic" idea of Jews and not to actual Jews: to the abstracted metaphysical idea of a Jew underlying the Jews' ways of engaging life. In his pronouncements, the Jew, like the Aryan or the Christian, is supposed to denote a metaphysical cultural type. Therefore, he takes himself to be expounding on the spiritual nature of metaphysical Jews—as well as on the spiritual nature of metaphysical men and women.

In the case of the Jew, this is a metaphysical cultural type whose underlying spirit is devoid of any divine inspiration, sublime metaphysical aspiration, moral quality, or self-awareness. The Jew, writes Weininger, attempts to frame as shallow and banal a worldview as is possible and refuses to see the arcane and spiritual significance of things. To the extent that there is no extreme good or bad in either Jews or women, so too they can never exhibit either great genius or stupidity. Weininger emphasizes that, in his comments on Jews and women, he is concerned not with biological traits, but spiritual ones. The intellectual capability of spiritual Jews and women makes itself evident in vigilance and egoism. Human beings whose spirit is of this cultural type can pursue any matter to the same degree, lacking any independent standard of their own. Metaphysical Jews, like metaphysical women, are nothing in and of themselves. This spiritual disposition and attitude toward life is expressed in the Jews' great talent for journalism. Jews, writes Weininger, adapt themselves to every situation and every race, becoming parasitic. They believe in nothing, neither inside nor outside themselves. In our day, Weininger claims, Jewishness is the spirit of the age. The modern era is the most Jewish and the most feminine. Finally, he calls for a clear choice to be made between these two cultural types.

Weininger's train of thought is assimilated by Wittgenstein into his own philosophical way of thinking, by first reforming its blatant and derogatory metaphysical claims, turning them into what he regards as "clarifications" of the concept of the Jew. In Wittgenstein's philosophy, at the time he came under the influence of these ideas, concepts that enable us to refer to things are presumed to be embodied in mental imagery that provides for a representational prototype of what they denote. Wittgenstein, in his *Notebooks 1914-1916*, initially introduced the idea of such a prototype and subsequently integrated it into his *Tractatus Logico-Philosophicus*. It was used therein to explain how a linguistic sign could be undetermined and still have meaning, for example, in the case of a "generality-sign" having universal scope. In this view, a prototype is a representational entity through which conceptual distinctions are both made possible and grasped. It is a mental aid used to represent conceptual distinctions made in a language, enabling us to apprehend certain phenomena as falling under a common concept and, therefore, as constituting instances of the same kind of phenomenon. When, for example, we see various shades of color as instances of the color red, we are making use of some mental prototype of the color red to distinguish and grasp them as such. The concept of red is embodied for us in such a prototype, which serves as its mental representation.

Thus, while Weininger takes himself to be describing the spiritual nature of *metaphysical* Jews, manifesting the Platonic idea of a Jew, Wittgenstein takes himself to be describing the spiritual nature of Jews as they are represented by *the mental prototype* of the concept of the Jew. And, like Weininger's metaphysical pronouncements about Jews, his conceptual remarks about prototypical Jews are derived from the stereotypical concept of the Jew that was circulating at the time in his culture. As is the case with conceptual clarification in general, Wittgenstein appears to assume that in clarifying the concept of the Jew, he is not talking about actual Jews, only about the prototype of the Jew that represents the concept of a Jew in our minds. In Weininger's metaphysical pronouncements, this was not always clear. Wittgenstein's criticism of such metaphysics is that it obliterates the distinction between factual and conceptual investigations:

> The essential thing about metaphysics: that the difference between factual and conceptual investigations is not clear to it. A metaphysical question is always in appearance a factual one, although the problem is a conceptual one.[6]

Thus, unlike Weininger's metaphysical assertions about Jews, which conflated conceptual distinctions with factual ones, his remarks about Jews are supposedly merely conceptual clarifications, pertaining only to the prototype of the concept of a Jew.

Once this philosophical transition from confused metaphysical pronouncements to conceptual clarifications that focus on prototypical mental representations is accomplished, Weininger's pronouncements about the spiritual nature of Jews are then taken over by Wittgenstein with what appear to be two provisos. He distinguishes (in a more universal way) between Jews and non-Jews, rather than Jews and Aryans or Christians and he does not call for a choice to be made between these two cultural types. He then reduces Weininger's various metaphysical pronouncements concerning Jews to the slogan that Jews lack (spiritual) character. Instead of character, their spirit is infused with what Spengler ascribed to human beings who are immersed in civilization—pure intellect.

Wittgenstein now turns to distinguishing between human beings and works of culture that express a Jewish spirit and human beings and works of culture that express a non-Jewish spirit. The idea is that the intellectual and characterless spirit manifested in Jews does not organically belong to any culture in which they operate. The cultural survival of this spirit is dependent on the spirit that underlies the cultures of other nations. It lacks the ability to create a culture of its own. Jews, being people who operate from a spiritual disposition of pure intellect, are forced to attach themselves to the cultures of others to reflect genuine (spiritual) character. However, in so doing, they transform these cultures into civilizations. That is what is happening to Western culture in the Modern Age. When the new, characterless, and intellectual spiritual force that manifests itself in the Jewish affiliates of a culture conjoins with the original and authentic, non-Jewish spiritual force of Western culture, this culture begins to change and become transformed into civilization. Nonetheless, if we look closely, we can still distinguish between works of culture that stem from a Jewish spirit and works of culture that stem from a non-Jewish spirit. It is as if "Jewish artists," even when operating *in accordance* with the spirit of Western culture, nevertheless fail to operate *from within* the spirit underlying that culture.

3. Merging the Two Ideas

As may now be seen, in Wittgenstein's remarks on Jews, the Spenglerian idea about a spiritual difference between culture and civilization and the Weiningerian idea about a spiritual difference between Jews and Aryans are merged into one. That is because the concepts of Jewish spirit and mentality serve Wittgenstein both as a concrete means for illustrating a conceptual distinction between two different ways in which the human spirit manifests itself and as a means of describing the Jews' spiritual nature and spiritual effect on Western culture. Indeed, as can now also be seen, the spiritual divide drawn by Weininger between Jews and Aryans and by Spengler between culture and civilization is used by Wittgenstein to distinguish and describe two spiritual prototypes operating in Western culture in modern times. These prototypes are drawn through the stereotyped images of Jews and non-Jews that emanate from this culture. Thus, Wittgenstein spends much of his effort in these remarks describing and clarifying the stereotypical conceptions that underlie these two spiritual prototypes.

The first spiritual prototype, the Jew, embodies the rootless entrepreneur, the stylish urban intellectual, the talented but somewhat shallow artist who has nothing deeply meaningful to give of his or her self. The second spiritual prototype, "the non-Jew," embodies the deeply rooted native, the rustic producer of basic necessities of life, the artist who creates a deeply meaningful work of art as a form of genuine self-expression. The first is clever and learned. This spiritual prototype operates by dint of a talent that expresses itself through intellect. The creative power of such an artist is of a kind that can be grafted onto any cultural body. It will take root there and flourish. The second spiritual prototype has a creative power, which expresses a singular human character that is integrated in organic fashion into the particular culture in which it operates, rendering its creations authentic expressions of that culture. Artists that embody the first spiritual prototype utilize the achievements of the culture in which they operate to claim them for themselves. Artists that embody the second spiritual prototype create new cultural assets and bestow them upon others. The first are artificial, the second authentic. The first are sophisticated, the second primitive. The first cannot be geniuses, the second can.

In Wittgenstein's reflections on these ideas, emancipated Jews affiliate themselves with Western culture by learning to follow its social and aesthetic rules and judgments. However, they do not engage this culture through the sensibilities, dispositions, and attitudes toward life that provide for its spirit. They do so by relying on their Jewish sensibilities, dispositions, and attitudes, which are predominantly intellectual. In doing so, they remain spiritually alien to this culture, while their effect on it is to change it into a modern, artificial, intellectual, characterless expression of their human spirit, which now emerges as being embodied by modern civilization.

Five

GENIUS, TALENT, CHARACTER, AND INTELLECT

To clarify the spiritual difference between the cultural pathways of Jews and non-Jews, Ludwig Wittgenstein makes special use of four keynote concepts: intellect, character, talent, and genius. These concepts have an extensive philosophical pedigree, as in the intellectual discourse of Western Europe they have been used to provide edifying insights into the creative spiritual forces that underlie cultural affairs. Their role in that discourse and the particular insights that Wittgenstein brings to them to clarify the concepts of cultural creativity and the spirit of Jews merit special attention.

1. The Concept of Genius in Myths, Religion, and Philosophy

The first thing that should be noted about the concept of genius is that both in the received philosophical discourse and in Wittgenstein's remarks that express his reflections on it, genius is an ability to create a work of art that is original and of profound human significance. Genius is not a matter of high intelligence quotients. It is not a trait demonstrated by admittance to a university computer department at the age of twelve. Genius is a spiritual quality that enables those endowed with it to create within their cultural milieu as though they are laying a foundation for the establishment of a new culture. It is to create a unique mode of expression for a basic facet of human experience—one that addresses people and moves them to express themselves in the spirit of that work. Therefore, in the stereotyped conception of Jews that he both employs and undertakes to clarify, genius is a quality that human beings possessing a Jewish spirit never attain.[1]

The conception of genius outlined here explains Wittgenstein's formerly quoted obscure remark about Jewish saints, namely: "The saint is the only Jewish 'genius.' Even the greatest Jewish thinker is no more than talented. (Myself for instance.) . . . ." The term "genius" is bracketed in his remark, signifying that he is using it according to received philosophical discourse. Since the Jewish religion does not espouse the existence of saints, the reference to a Jewish saint is unclear. Perhaps he is thinking of certain esteemed Hasidic figures. Beginning in 1906 and until 1924, Martin Buber published several books in German with the sayings of eminent Hasidic figures. They are referred to in Hebrew by the title *Tsadik*, meaning a just (or virtuous) person. Unlike Jewish scholarly religious discourse based on the Talmud, the sayings of *Tsadiks* are spontaneous, personal, and anecdotal. They express religious insights drawn from ordinary examples and illustrated through everyday events, transforming them thereby into spiritual symbols that manifest important religious meanings. Buber describes these anecdotes as instantiating what he calls a "legendary" discourse that expresses "a legendary reality." Another way of expressing this idea would be to say that the discourse expresses a spiritual conception of reality that lends ordinary events an expressive religious symbolic mystical meaning.

In my reading of Wittgenstein's remark on a Jewish saint, he likens such an expressive symbolic form of religious discourse to an artistic creation. He notes in this connection that Jewish religious thinkers who do not operate within this tradition of discourse are not geniuses. From the fact that he includes himself in that category, it follows that such thinkers encompass not only Jewish scholars, but also most philosophers. Against the background of this assessment, he expresses his formerly mentioned desire to join philosophy with original artistic expression, writing "philosophy only as one writes a poem." In contrast to this artistic ideal, which would transform philosophy into an expressive discourse that provides insightful perspectives on language and meaning, "a thinker is very similar to a draughtsman. Who wants to represent all the interconnections."[2]

The philosophical conception of genius underlying Wittgenstein's remarks about Jews and genius goes back to ideas first raised in European literary and philosophical circles in the middle of the eighteenth century. It reflects the philosophical interest generated at the time in the very concept of culture, as manifesting the creative, inspired, expressive spiritual nature of human beings. It is a conception of human spiritual nature that was also used to oppose philosophical ideologies about the inherently rational nature of human beings, which provided for the proclaimed political and moral "historical progress" achieved in the modern period. Geniuses, it might be said, are the creative heroes of a culture, as saints and prophets are its religious heroes, great statesmen are its political heroes, leaders of revolutions are its social heroes, inventors of new devices are its technological heroes, discoverers of new explanations are its scientific heroes, courageous soldiers are its war heroes, sport champions are its athletic heroes, and so forth. Geniuses create original, innovative cultural steppingstones for a culture's spiritual advancement from one inspired expressive adventure to the next.

However, the use of the word "genius," in which these ideas were encapsulated, has more archaic origins. In its ancient etymological roots in both Greek and Latin; "gene" referred to giving birth and the ancestral origins of tribal groups. In myths and legends, it came to mean a guiding spirit or deity allotted to people at birth and guarding over certain places. Apparently, this is also the mythical and linguistic source of influence for the Arabic word *jinni* that in legends refers to a demon or spirit possessing supernatural powers. Ironically, the title of "genius" was first conferred on human beings possessing extraordinary spiritual powers in Jewish scholarly tradition during the sixth century CE. It was the outstanding spiritual title bestowed on eminent rabbinical scholars who headed prominent *Yeshivot* (schools of religious study) in the Middle East and were considered to possess extraordinarily deep insights into religious matters. This ability enabled them to prescribe new religious practices and to interpret ancient religious scriptures in new ways, with a singular religious authority. The word used in this connection is the Hebrew word *gaon*, which in its new usage came to mean genius, perhaps because of its close resemblance to the Latin and Greek word for genius. It is derived from the Hebrew word signifying a magnificent and powerful demeanor, such as the deportment of a lion or the surging of a river with a powerful force of its own.

During the eighteenth century in Europe, this humanized concept of genius was also extended to secular cultural affairs pursued by non-Jews. Describing the way it took over the imagination of Europeans in the modern period, Ben-Ami Scharfstein writes the following:

> the old word *genius*, meaning "guiding spirit," was undergoing a marked change. By degrees it was applied to one's nature or particular gift or spiritual characteristics; and there were or came to be nuances that made the word usable for a person's spontaneous inventiveness or, in contrast to reason, the person's natural spontaneity. Diderot was preoccupied with the idea of geniuses, who would always be, he said, the glory of their nations and the benefactors of mankind. He found genius, mysteriously beyond judgment and beyond even imagination . . . .
>
> The belief in Genius was a disbelief in the usefulness of imitation and sometimes of academic studies. Edward Young's *Conjectures on Original Composition,* which was published in 1759 and immediately translated, with great effect, into German, attacked the "meddling ape imitation," guessed that there had been many geniuses innocent of both reading and writing, and claimed that "genius sometimes owed its greatest glory" to the absence of learning.[3]

In Scharfstein's edifying description of this line of thinking, the Romantics, especially, took up the idea of genius. A German philosopher—who is not usually identified as a supporter of Romanticism—but who also took up this idea was Immanuel Kant. In his third critique he offered the following thoughts on genius:

> Genius is the talent (natural gift) that gives the rule to art. Since the talent, as an inborn productive faculty of the artist, itself belongs to nature, this could also be expressed thus: Genius is the inborn predisposition of the mind (*ingenium*) through which nature gives the rule to art.[4]

Kant also claimed that the first feature of genius is originality. Genius, he explained, is the complete opposite of imitation. Since originality may also be a feature of silliness, absurdity, and madness, genius must result in a product that embodies an ideal achievement. Kant said, furthermore, that persons of genius could not explain how they achieve their results. It is nature that works through them. He also claimed that genius is manifested only in art, not in science. Science, he suggested, is a product of rational thought and reasoning, not nature. The philosophical background to these claims was the emerging dispute between followers of the Enlightenment and followers of the Romantic Movement. The first stressed the role of rational thought (sometimes referred to as "Reason") in providing human beings with understanding and knowledge. The second stressed the role of culture in providing human beings with created and observable customs that cater to attitudes, emotions, and imagination.[5] (Kant's solution to this dispute was to divide human existence between the two. Cultural affairs pursued through the arts are a product of the imagination, aesthetic ideas, and the faculty of judgment. Knowledge of natural laws and universal truths is the domain of rational thought.)

Arthur Schopenhauer, who regarded Kant's philosophical achievement with great esteem, was struck by the very idea of genius. He applied it not only to the realm of art, but also to philosophy and other cultural activities, distinguishing therein between geniuses and talented creators. He also claimed that genius stems from will, talent from intellect and reasoning. In his view, talented artists and philosophers lack the originality and penetrating intuition of the genius. However, they are able to clarify and elaborate the creative genius's intuitive insights. He also claimed that talent is a feminine, reproductive capacity that is connected with the faculty of reason, which "merely conceives but does not generate." Genius, by contrast, is tied to the faculty of understanding, which "is masculine."[6] Subsequently, he claimed that the normal person has two-thirds will and one-third intellect, the genius two-thirds intellect and one-third will.[7]

2. Talent and Character

As may be seen from Wittgenstein's remarks on Jews, he turns to reflect on these ideas by considering Schopenhauer's and Weininger's claims about genius and talent. His first move is to consider the relationship between influence and creative artistic power:

> Every artist has been influenced by others & shows (the) traces of that influence in his works; but what we get from him is all the same only his own personality. What is inherited from others can be nothing but egg-shells. We should treat the fact of their presence with indulgence but they will not give us Spiritual nourishment.[8]

According to this insight, there is nothing wrong with artistic expressions that are produced within a given style and show the influence of some great artist, as long as one expresses one's own personality and character through them.

Wittgenstein's next move is to clarify what genius involves by amalgamating Schopenhauer's and Weininger's remarks, rendering genius into a special talent embedded in strong character. "The measure of genius," he writes, "is character—even if character on its own does *not* amount to genius. Genius is not 'talent *and* character,' but character manifesting itself in the form of a special talent."[9] Character manifests a spiritual disposition posited in contradistinction to another spiritual disposition, namely intellect. This spiritual contrast is of crucial importance to what he is trying to express in these remarks and requires some further elaboration.[10] Underlying it is the insight that character is a basic natural core in human beings, through which what is singular and authentic about an individual manifests itself. In a way, character is just a particular, singular, human *nature*, manifested in the emotions, imagination, personal attitudes, and aesthetic sensibilities from which a person's actions ensue in a natural and uninhibited fashion. In a work of genius, something that belongs to a person's basic and singular nature is expressed in an authentic and unique way. And so, "genius is talent in which character makes itself heard."[11]

Hence, even a person as talented as Karl Kraus lacked genius: "Kraus has talent, an extraordinary talent, but not genius."[12] For Kraus created only through his Jewish spirit and as a result through intellect only. His work, therefore, was a "mere intellectual skeleton," and not what results from a talent that expresses itself through character: "a complete human being." In works of art that express character, as opposed to works of art that are intellectual abstractions, real human life is manifested in a singular way.

As emerges from these remarks, character is one's singular spiritual nature. It is what enables each human being to be unique and authentic. It is also what enables human beings to live their lives with integrity, by being true to themselves and who they really are. Hence, it is also what brings about tragedy when, like a tree that cannot bend before the wind, human beings remain true to themselves and their nature and do not accommodate themselves to the turn of events. Intellect, on the other hand, is what enables human beings to formulate and grasp things in a general and abstract way. Its effect on nature, human or otherwise, is to tame it. It enables us to accommodate ourselves to events, to survive. Intellect is something that all human beings possess (to a greater or lesser degree) *in common*. It is not a feature of human life through which real, unique, singular human lives manifest themselves. It does not provide a basis for the emergence of either different human beings or different cultures. It is not part of the basic individuating nature of either of these. (Indeed, it is not part of "nature" at all. It is, rather, the "stuff" of which Pure Reason is made.) What makes human beings both real and unique in an individual way results from the fact that their lives and their personalities are an expression of their singular character.

Hence, a person's character is what he or she *is*. Intellect is what he or she *has*. The intellect with which a person is endowed is a product of logic. It is manifested by acquiring scientific knowledge and by an ability to think abstractly and critically about all sorts of things. It is a feature of life that cuts across individuals and cultures. At the most, it is a basis for the emergence of human life in what Spengler calls civilization, not culture. Therefore real, concrete human life emerges only within a culture and as an expression of character. Through intellect, human life emerges merely as an abstract generalization.

The resulting distinction places culture and character on one side of the divide, and civilization and intellect on the other. The first is natural, real, singular, and authentic, the second contrived, abstract, imitative, and artificial. The idea is that, just as people are differentiated by their different characters, so, too, human societies are differentiated by their different cultures. Character is what lends an individual a singular spiritual nature. Culture is what lends a human society its singular spiritual nature, manifested in what is sometimes referred to as its *ethos*. It is short step from this idea to the idea of national character. Of course, the idea of national character is not new. In his *Politics*, Aristotle discusses the character of the citizens in the state. He notes in this connection that different nations (referred to as "races") have different character.[13] Indeed, prior to the Second World War, the idea of national character was deemed obvious. (The question discussed in this connection was whether national character derives from culture, or vice versa.)

In emphasizing the concept of character, Wittgenstein is following one of the central themes of the Romantic Movement in its opposition to the philosophy of the Enlightenment, as expressed also in the philosophical tradition of both empiricists and rationalists.[14] Human beings are set apart from each other by their different natures (or characters), just as human societies are set apart from each other by their different natures (or cultures). Attempts to reduce human beings and human cultures to a common denominator by universal generalizations, regarding both human nature and the nature of human societies, necessarily ignore the different characters of people and the different cultures of human societies. Explanations of this sort regard human beings as if they were merely intellectual creatures devoid of character and lacking any culture. An explanation that ignores the difference that character and culture make for human life, by producing different cultured human beings and different cultural communities, is bound to miss all that is singular in human life and spiritually meaningful. It is typical of an intellectual mode of thought that seeks abstraction. It makes all human beings appear equal and all cultures seem the same. (It is demonstrated, for example, by the way in which philosophers try to determine principles for human behavior "in a rational manner," when attempting to take a view of human affairs in the light of a hypothetical social contract.) Trying to determine human nature and the nature of human societies in this way alienates human beings and their society from nature and misses the crux of the matter on two counts. It misses what sets human beings and human societies apart from each other: character and culture. It also misses what human beings have in common within different cultures: in that they are creatures possessed of a basic common human spiritual nature, which is (only) manifested differently through different cultures; a spiritual nature that enables human beings both to partake of culture and to express themselves in a singular cultural way.

3. The Characterless Features of the Jewish Spirit

Within this conceptual context of discussion regarding the nature of the human spirit, the concept of Jewish spirit signifies a spiritual disposition marked by intellectual features of talent and cleverness only. As such, it is divorced from the deep spiritual and natural forces of life that shape the concrete lives of human beings and give rise to culture. It manifests a mind that lacks a creative nature of its own, a spirit of something other than that which provides for culture. The Jewish spirit, being an intellectual force only, is like a civil society with no culture of its own, or a clever person lacking a distinct personality. In order to flourish and create in a meaningful cultural manner, this spirit must first settle upon some cultural habitat and acquire a distinguishing human nature. It must lodge within somebody else's culture, and its possessors must reflect someone else's character. But because of its intellectual spiritual nature, because it does not derive from a real, genuine, natural force that shapes a culture, it is incapable of creating in a manner that authentically expresses the spirit of that culture.

So much for conceptual clarifications pertaining to the human spirit in general. In a more detailed way, Wittgenstein seems to find proof of what he has said about the nature of the Jewish spiritual disposition in the works of a few renowned artists of Jewish origins—like himself. Thus Felix Mendelssohn, being a Jewish artist, is judged to be a characterless artist. Therefore, he tries to reflect the spiritual nature of others—those into whose culture he has stumbled. Mendelssohn, it can be said, does speak a language that stems from a basic spiritual disposition, and in which human beings of non-Jewish spirit speak among themselves: music. He even speaks it with great skill and talent, but with a foreign (spiritual) accent nevertheless, for he speaks it through the intellect.

As noted earlier, a similar fate awaits another artist of Jewish origin, Karl Kraus. Thus, it is typical of Kraus to write a play for masked theatre and it is typical of Jews to have a liking for that sort of theatre. For in masked theatre, various human *types* are presented onstage, rather than *real*, *singular people* of unique character. This way of abstracting the nature of human beings is a mode of representation typical of those endowed with Jewish spirit.

In Wittgenstein's reflections on language, these insights resonate in the distinction he makes between understanding the "meaning of a word" and understanding the "soul of a word." In the first instance, to understand a word is to understand the grammar of its use in the stream of life. In the second instance, to understand a word is akin to understanding music. It demands acquiring the linguistic sensitivity particular to a given linguistic culture, which enables its affiliates to tell why a particular word is more appropriate than another that has the same meaning:

> It may be that if it is to achieve its effect a particular word cannot be replaced by any other; just as it may be that a gesture cannot be replaced by any other. (The word has a *soul* and not just a meaning.) No one would believe that a poem remained *essentially unaltered* if its words were replaced by others in accordance with an appropriate convention.[15]

Nonetheless, there might be a language in which this distinction between the meaning of a word and its soul is lost. Such a language would not bear the unique spiritual marking of a particular culture. Its expressions would be linguistically grammatical, but lacking character. Others could replace them just as well, as long as they were in proper grammatical form. We might think in this connection of invented "languages" used in codes.

> There might also be a language in whose use the "soul" of the words played no part. In which, for example, we had no objection to replacing one word by another arbitrary one of our own invention.[16]

At this point, it may be worthwhile to recall what Rudolf Carnap has related about his first meeting with Wittgenstein.[17] At that meeting, Morris Schlick, the founder of the Vienna Circle who instigated the encounter, mentioned Carnap's interest in Esperanto. Carnap writes that Wittgenstein expressed strong opposition to Esperanto with a vehemence that astounded him. Wittgenstein stated that a language that has not "grown organically is despicable." Indeed, later, Wittgenstein himself writes: "Esperanto. Our feeling of disgust, when we utter an *invented* word with invented derivative syllables. The word is cold, has no associations & yet plays at 'language.'"[18] In view of things said previously about Jews, Esperanto, the brainchild of a Jew by the name of Ludovic Zamenhof, constitutes an example of a language that has no authentic cultural foundation. Esperanto is a language invented by the intellect. It is an example of what a cultural work based on the intellect alone looks like: an abstraction of language, in which no character is manifested and no culture is expressed; a language in which words have a semantic and even a pragmatic meaning, but no soul. It is a distinct product of the Jewish mind: a pseudo-cultural work of art that is invented by intellect when trying to reproduce a language. Esperanto, it may be said, is a language of masked theatre. In Wittgenstein's view, it may now be said, Esperanto is the language of civilization in the age of modernity. It is the abstracted, skimmed-off formal features of many genuine languages with which it has no authentic cultural ties and to which it bears no spiritual allegiance. It is only the mask of a language, one in which modern, emancipated, scientifically oriented Jews and their contrived and sophisticated kind speak among themselves.

Six

STEREOTYPES, SYMBOLS, AND IDEOLOGIES

It is useful to differentiate among several philosophical issues that merit discussion in vis-à-vis Ludwig Wittgenstein's remarks on the spiritual nature of Jews. The first is the validity of Oswald Spengler's distinction between culture and civilization, as both a historical and a metaphysical distinction. The second is the validity of the Romantic distinction between talented artists and geniuses, as either a metaphysical or a cultural distinction. The third is the validity of the metaphysical distinction drawn by Otto Weininger between the spiritual nature of Jews and other people. The fourth is the validity of the historical view that emancipated Jews in Europe are the spiritual catalysts for the emergence of modernity in culture from the end of the nineteenth century. However, all these issues are beyond the scope of my present study. My concerns at this point are three concepts underlying Wittgenstein's remarks on Jews and their relationship to cultural ideologies: stereotype, national character, and symbol.

1. The Spiritual Character of Nations and their Stereotypes

To begin exploring this subject, it might be noted that Wittgenstein's remarks on the spiritual nature of Jews, like those of Weininger's, are derived by succumbing to the stereotyped conceptions and views about Jews that were circulating at the time in their culture. Therefore, what I propose, first, is to place Wittgenstein's clarifications of the concepts of the Jew, Jewish spirit, Jewish character, and Jewish mentality in the context of the general use made of concepts that promote stereotyped conceptions. To elucidate this point, it may be useful to begin by noting some of the particular features of this conceptual category.

There are, of course, all sorts of stereotypes in circulation. There is the stereotyped concept of the Scotsman as a miser, of the Englishman as restrained and unemotional, of the Italian as overly emotional, of the German as pedantically undeviating from the law, of the Romanian as a sharp operator, of the Irishman as hotheaded. There is a stereotyped concept of the Rugged Individualistic Cowboy, the Dejected Housewife, the Bigoted Southerner, the Ignorant Blue-Collar Worker, the Shrewd Lawyer, the Independent Bedouin, the Meek Clerk, the Absent-Minded Professor, the Hot-Tempered Redhead, the Passionate Widow, and so on. These stereotypes serve to represent different types of human beings possessing different human natures, dispositions, inclinations, temperaments, characters, attitudes, values, and perspectives on life, all of which manifest a different human spirit out of which they engage life. To regard actual people only through a concept that classifies them as a particular type of human being, be it English, Housewife, or Farmer, is to miss out on their human individuality. That is the case whether the concept used for typing them is an ordinary one or a stereotyped conception of it.

One of the hallmarks of stereotypes is the way they embody particular conceptions within the concepts to which they are attached. Stereotypes overcome the conceptual distinction between idea, judgment, viewpoint, and concept, by merging them. Stereotypes, it might be said, are highly enriched, "thick" concepts, not deflated, "thin" ones. They inflate ordinary concepts used to differentiate types of human beings with enriching conceptions that provide edifying viewpoints of their inherent nature.

From the outlook on both human nature and culture dictated by present liberal ideology, to conduct our everyday social affairs and judgments of people by leaning on stereotypes is to be unjustifiably prejudiced. To lend credence to this ideological stance, it is sometimes argued that the use of stereotyped considerations in actual life is irrational, as it is unsupported by evidence. We would do well to remember in this connection that, prior to World War II, the description and analysis of various national stereotypes was widely accepted within both political and academic discourse. The concept of national character was evoked in political manifestoes calling for national self-determination. It was given credence in academic discourse that discussed the different characters of contending nations. Indeed, the use of stereotyped conceptions of people may still serve many of us in our everyday social affairs in instances of puzzlement or possible strife, when we lack proper information about those whom we encounter. (Thus, we may find ourselves trying to ascertain whether the irksome driver behind us is a man or a woman, young or old, of some particular racial or ethnic identity, a blue- or white-collar worker.)

A characteristic feature of stereotypes is the way in which they are constantly proven true for those who entertain them. This is not because they are put to an empirical test that inductively confirms them to be the case. They are not scientific theories. They are conceptual ways of seeing things that underlie dogmatic judgments and beliefs that are formed through them. It is useful to note that stereotypes are not the only dogmatic ways of acquiring beliefs and judgments. They share this feature with worldviews and ideologies, the unscientific logic of which is the same. They, too, are ways of perceiving and regarding things that are not based on empirical methods of confirmation or falsification. In philosophical discourse, the response to them is often of two kinds: either to justify or deny their claims in a rational discourse. Thus, liberal ideology denies the validity of all stereotypes, but seeks to validate ideological claims about universal human rights that emerge from it. Nazi ideology denies the validity of ideological claims about universal human rights, but justifies the validity of national stereotypes. Nonetheless, to simply judge both of these features of human discourse as simply unfortunate, irrational ways of acquiring beliefs and judgments about life and world is to miss two important conceptual points in their connection. The first is their usefulness in bestowing meaning on what confronts us in the stream of human life. The second is the way in which they provide a spiritual basis for shared attitudes toward life and what it encloses that underlie different cultures.

2. Stereotypes as Symbolic Figures

Unlike worldviews and political ideologies, stereotypes are concrete forms of representation that stand proxy for a whole class of things. They are conceptual, linguistic, cultural, representational products that offer visual aid, furnishing those who embrace them with a picturesque, insightful, concrete, symbolic means of understanding and demonstration. They awaken associations, stir memories, direct our point of view and aesthetically evince an idea or point of view, which is to be instilled in us for our edification. In their ability to represent certain features of human life in a concrete and powerful manner, stereotypes are akin to similes and metaphors. Equally, fictitious animals and human beings are depicted in moralistic parables, legends, and myths, personifying through a concrete figure some significant way in which human beings engage life. "A good simile," writes Wittgenstein, "refreshes the intellect."[1] A well-turned parable or apt metaphor or striking simile revitalizes what was previously only an "intellectual skeleton." It enriches an abstract intellectual mode of discourse by means of a concrete example, instilling life in what the intellect has contrived. In doing so, it enables us to rise above the need to explicate things by displaying the heart of the matter in a striking, concrete, enriching, and enlightening fashion that provides us with immediate insight. The same, it seems, holds also for stereotypes. All of these are powerful, expressive conceptual devices that are rendered into the spiritual heritage of culture when they are embraced and shared with others. As such, to relinquish the hold of such an expressive concept on us is not unlike breaking out of some of our culture's spiritual hold on us.

In the way in which we distinguish between literal and metaphorical use of words, we might distinguish between ordinary (use of) concepts and stereotyped conceptions used to enrich them. Accordingly, someone may be familiar with the ordinary (use of) concepts that refer to Scots and Germans, as to people who are of different nationalities, but not with (the use of) these same concepts to refer to stereotypical Scots and Germans, as embodying different psychological traits. An important conceptual feature of stereotypes is their use to represent the nature or essence of certain types of people and kinds of animals. Cultural stereotypes, it might be said, are figurative cultural essences. They lack any individuating contingent features, possessing only essential features. The German stereotype as a pedantic human being, just like the Scot stereotype as a miser or the Jewish stereotype as a clever person, has no individuating human features that are not intrinsic to it as a cultural type. Therefore, to respond to individual human beings only through the cultural stereotype through which they are identified is to miss out on their human individuality.

As may now be seen, the philosophical extension of stereotypes is their transformation into ideal representations of classes of beings. These representational ideals are what Wittgenstein refers to as "prototypes." A curious linguistic feature of both stereotypes and prototypes is the tendency to refer to them through a definite article. We speak in this connection of "the Cat," "the Dog," "the Pole," "the Englishman," "the Farmer," "the Housewife," and so forth. The definite article used in these cases is divorced from any particular empirical context. In empirical contexts, it is used to pick out a particular exemplar out of a class of things, such as "the cat next door" or "the Jew living in the upper apartment." It is used therein as an individuating description to refer to a particular individual out of a class of similar individuals. In both symbolic discourse and philosophy it is used to refer to a symbolic individual that represents the entire class itself.

In this regard, it is useful to distinguish two different kinds of identifying (or defining) features that are ascribed to these beings. One kind is physical and instrumental. A lion is a wild animal that has a certain shape and outward demeanor, by which it is recognized and differentiated from other wild animals, such as tigers or monkeys. An Englishman is a male human being from England who is affiliated with English culture. As such, he is differentiated from other human beings that are from other countries and are affiliated with other cultures. However, we also ascribe to different creatures different dispositions, attitudes, and natures out of which they engage life. Sometimes these are rendered into spiritual dispositions, characteristic attitudes, and natures. Thus, we may hold lions to be majestic, snakes to be conniving, Englishmen to be restrained, Americans to be boisterous, and housewives to be dejected. These latter features are stereotypical features of these beings, investing their possessors with a particular psychological nature. As these two different kinds of features emerge from two different categories of identification, there is no contradiction in telling a story about a cowardly lion, a hot-tempered Englishman, a quiet American, or a happy housewife.

When the dispositional or spiritual features that are ascribed to living creatures that fall under a given concept are well integrated into the way in which they are regarded and considered, these creatures are sometimes used as a symbol for the features they are held to represent. Accordingly, it is but a short step from holding lions to be majestic, tigers to be ferocious, dogs to be loyal, cats to be self-centered, and pigs to be gluttonous, to rendering lions, tigers, dogs, cats, and pigs, respectively, into symbols for majesty, ferociousness, loyalty, self-centeredness, and gluttony. It is important to note that symbols are not signs. Both symbols and signs have a meaning, but in a somewhat different way. To bring out the difference between symbols and linguistic signs in particular, it is helpful to note that in the above examples, it is not merely the names of the animals that are endowed with a symbolic meaning, but the animals themselves.

Note that someone who knows the linguistic meaning of the words used to name certain animals may not be aware of the symbolic meaning that these animals acquire for a given cultural community. Such a person does not then share in the symbolic meaning of the language. Some would say that such a person does not partake of its cultural spirit. Just as knowledge of various facts relating to these events and figures may not bring about understanding of their symbolic meaning for a cultural community, knowledge of the meaning of linguistic signs may not suffice for understanding the symbolic meaning of the entities to which they refer. Part of what is involved in breaking out of and going beyond the spiritual boundaries of our predecessors' culture is that their symbols no longer have any meaning for us, or that they no longer appeal to us. This can happen despite the fact that we still share the same (non-symbolic use of the) language.[2] Thus, the use of the locution "to Jew" someone, as to obtain something by means of deceitful transaction, may be common in some cultural linguistic setting, lending instrumental and ordinary life to a particular conception of Jews, but neither among Jews themselves, nor various cultures (for example, Chinese) for whom Jews have little significance.

The distinction I am marking here between symbolic and ordinary (or instrumental) use of language is not always maintained as separate modes of speech. If I speak about the "Vain Raven" described in a fable or the "Stingy Scotsman" described in a joke, it is clear that I am not referring to actual ravens and Scotsmen, but to fictitious figures, which symbolize particular human traits. If I say that ravens are inherently vain birds or that Scotsmen are inherently stingy people, I am making an empirical generalization in which I apply symbolic features of discourse to actual ravens and Scotsmen, expressing my stereotypical conception of them. Indeed, stereotypes seem to be marked by this discursive feature in particular, as they are symbols that have attained ordinary instrumental use. So that while a discourse that makes use of human stereotypes may be closely related to a symbolic discourse, it is not limited to a symbolic context of expression. Stereotypes, it may now be said, are symbols that have acquired instrumental life within the linguistic and social space of a particular cultural community, bequeathing their predetermined prejudicial spiritual essence to ordinary uses of language, human perspectives and conceptions of actual people.

Despite the analogy I have been exploring here with other symbolic and stereotyped uses of language, there is, of course, a great difference between the stereotypical symbolic use of such concepts and images and the stereotypical symbolic use Wittgenstein makes of the concept of the Jew. The stereotypical and symbolic use of national characterizations, like those previously mentioned, focuses on different psychological traits. There are many such traits that human beings possess and using them to stereotype the nature of people belonging to different cultures and having different national and ancestral origins does not divide humanity into two exclusive possible kinds of human beings. In ordinary affairs, stereotypes are used mainly in telling jokes, deriding and insulting people, explaining someone's behavior, prejudging someone, warning of the impending danger of dealing with certain people, legislating against them, and so forth. In contrast to such socially practical uses, Wittgenstein uses the concept of the Jew in a stereotypical way to draw a conceptual dichotomy between two fundamentally different kinds of cultured human beings manifesting two different kinds of spiritual natures that underlie cultural affairs in the West. Indeed, not only does his use of the stereotypical concept of the Jew take place within the framework of a conceptual inquiry about the spiritual forces underlying culture, but the purpose of the inquiry itself is to clarify the conceptual essence of stereotyped Jews.

The idea that a stereotyped concept harbors an important conceptual distinction about the spiritual character of various nationalities and the spiritual forces that provide for their cultures, as well as the idea that it is the philosopher's task to expose and clarify these, are difficult for many of us to take seriously nowadays. The wish to make use of the stereotyped conceptions and symbolic images of Jews, or any other people, in philosophical inquiry, let alone to draw an important conceptual distinction between two spiritually different kinds of cultured human beings, today seems bigoted, ethically reprehensible, and philosophically picayune to many of us. It is worthwhile to recall that this was not always the situation within Western intellectual discourse in the modern period.

3. Jewish Stereotypes in Anti-Semitism, Zionism and Liberalism

An important matter associated with Wittgenstein's remarks on the spiritual nature of stereotyped, symbolic, prototypical Jews relates to their historical and cultural context. None of the stereotyped concepts mentioned previously has been accompanied by a phenomenon analogous to anti-Semitism and what transpired because of it in the history of Europe. The phenomenon of anti-Semitism, which expresses, provokes, enhances, and builds itself upon a disparaging conception of Jews, which Wittgenstein both adopts and seeks to clarify, has to serve as an historical cultural background for any philosophical discussion that makes use of a concept of Jews as spiritually deviant human beings.

Without seeking to outline its complicated and appalling historical tributaries, it is useful to note that the stereotype of Jews draws on attitudes and images that have shifted over time, societies, and discourses. It has different manifestations in religious, political, national, cultural, and artistic discourse. It is also important to note that, in most of them, this is not merely a stereotypical conception of the so-called Other, as it is used to define a spiritual dichotomy that is not applied to other nationalities and religions. In looking at some of its historic manifestations, it can be noted that the metaphysics of religious anti-Semitism, which holds the Jews to be inherently deviant and evil, mirrors in an inverted way the religious narrative that underlies the ancient Jewish faith, namely that Jews are distinguished from all other people for having been chosen by God to follow the holy Torah. In religious versions of anti-Semitism, this sanctifying predicament that has fallen to the lot of Jews is turned around. It is rendered into a conception of Jews, according to which they are a human species unique among all others in their inherently deviant character and evil spirit. In the history of the West, this outlook on Jews was first instantiated in the religious stigmatization of Jews as the ancient rejecters and evil crucifiers of Christ, which is the reason why Jews should be despised. This religious outlook on Jews as inherently deviant and evil, coupled with their being perceived as an alien, mysterious, and powerful human element, possessing secretive intellectual abilities accruing from their Talmudic studies and strange rituals, was enhanced in the modern period during the time of national self-determination and developed into a new conception of Jews. They were now regarded (as previously discussed) as a people lacking universal human values and esteemed ethical ideals and attitudes, subsisting by means of their inherent egotistical nature and their cunning ability to wheel and deal. Upon seeking to assimilate, they were perceived as settling in cultures that others had created, using their sharp intellect to profit from the genuine cultural creations of others.

In late nineteenth- and early twentieth-century Vienna, as in Germany earlier, blatant anti-Semitism also took on the guise of intellectual discourse about cultural roots, spirituality, authenticity, and artistic creativity.[3] The "parasitic nature of Jews," which was formerly ascribed to the Jews' economic mode of subsistence, as a people who profit from what others labor to produce, was now also extended to describe their special mode of involvement in the arts.[4]

A powerful metaphysical influence on this conception was, as noted earlier, that of Romanticism. In contrast to the Enlightenment's conception of historical progress and universal humanism, Romantic thinkers stressed the emergence in human history of different cultures and their spiritual impact on the lives of people. They noted in this connection that cultures, like people, are apt to differ from one another. Each has its own distinct character and spirit. According to Romantic conceptions of human life, cultural affiliation and identity are essential features of human existence and understanding.[5]

In describing the political impact of Romantic conceptions of human cultural existence on views about Jews, George L. Mosse has stressed the role played by new German Romantic ideologies from the mid-nineteenth century.[6] In these ideologies, each culture was typified by a cherished living space, a cherished language, a cherished history, and cherished rituals and arts. Such shared cultural features of human existence were held to imbue human lives with a particular cultural spirit, which in the modern period manifests national self-identity. Out of this spirit, the historical destinies of nations are molded. Mosse describes the views on human cultural modes of existence that emerged as "Volkish" ideology. The individual was tied to the *Volk*, which was the repository of a communal spiritual "life force." From it, people drew spiritual sustenance for their lives and to express themselves in arts, religion, politics and economic practices. Mosse stresses the role played in such cultural ideologies by the pantheistic conception of nature, which provides a life force corresponding to the emotions, rather than to ways of reasoning. Nature was defined as landscape: those features of the environment peculiar and familiar to the members of one's *Volk*, and alien to others. The landscape thus becomes a vital part of the definition of the *Volk*, sustaining the self-identity of its members. The glorified environment for human cultural aspirations turned not on the city, but on nature and the countryside. The term "rooted" was employed to convey the image of a person who has an authentic cultural way of life. In similar fashion, authentic cultural expressions were considered to emerge from the spirit of the *Volk*. Thus, "rootedness" both in nature and in *Volk* history came to be a mark of a proper cultural style of living and expression in the arts.

In this ideology, the Jews were described as having lost their connection with the ancient Hebrews and as not having true roots in German culture. They were a fossilized people, a living example of a spirit that has run dry. Being spiritually barren, they were deemed incapable of becoming truly German. As such, they were often portrayed as conspirators against the Gentile world. Stereotypical anti-Semitic descriptions of Jews stressed the link between Jews and money. As may now be seen, this metaphysical conception of Jews underlies anti-Semitic ideologies. (In racial ideology it merely acquires the semblance of a biological explanation.) Accordingly, the question now arises whether the metaphysics of spirit in cultural ideologies provides a fundamental justification for existing anti-Semitic attitudes toward Jews, or whether anti-Semitic attitudes toward Jews arise out of such metaphysical conceptions and cultural ideologies. The answer, I believe, is that the relationship, as in many forms of conceptual metaphysics and cultural ideologies, is reciprocal. Reason not only is (and ought to be) a slave to the passions, as David Hume claimed, but in the form of vibrant cultural ideologies and alluring metaphysical views about the spiritual nature of a people, it also provides an enhancing, edifying intellectual support for such passionate cultural attitudes.

It is tempting to suppose that disparaging stereotypes manifest the way a people's national character and spirit are grasped by other nationalities. However, the influence of anti-Semitic conceptions of Jews is not limited only to how non-Jews relate to Jews. They have also affected the way some Jews regard themselves. There is a powerful ideological strand in Zionism, particularly in the ideology of its so-called labor movement that echoes the disparaging attitude toward Jews expressed in anti-Semitic ideologies. It calls on Jews to return to the Land of Israel to develop authentic cultural roots and establish themselves on sturdy cultural foundations: to return to speaking and writing in Hebrew, settle on the land, work in agriculture and industry, and create a culture of their own that is not dependent on the religious traditions that evolved in the "Diaspora."

Foremost among these ideals is the creation of an independent state and a military defensive force.

One way of overcoming a disparaging stereotype is to transform our attitude toward it, responding to it as to a valued human trait and cultural disposition. A way of doing so is to incorporate it into a cultural ideology or ethos that renders it an esteemed cultural trait. Accordingly, in contrast to the disparaging stereotype of Jews emerging out of national ideologies, lately there has been an attempt to resurrect the very stereotype of a Jew on which they built a liberal ideology, however, this time, by rendering it as a positive evaluation of the Jews' spiritual character and their cultural role in the emergence of modernity.

This is expressed, for example, in a powerfully narrated historical discourse by Yuri Slezkine in his *The Jewish Century*. In it, he rediscovers this stereotyped conception of Jews and their influence on modernity, albeit often without seeming to notice that this is what he is doing. He does that by placing it in an intellectual narrative about the role of Jews in the cultural history of the twentieth century and the emergence of liberalism as the central ideology of the West. Accordingly, in a provocative and highly spirited opening to his book he notes, "the modern age is the Jewish Age, and the twentieth century, in particular, is the Jewish Century." He explains this tantalizing pronouncement not in connection with either the holocaust or the creation of the state of Israel, but in terms of universal Jewish manifestations of modernity:

> Modernization is about everyone becoming urban, mobile, literate, articulate, intellectually intricate, physically fastidious, and occupationally flexible. It is about learning how to cultivate people and symbols, not fields and herds. It is about pursuing wealth for the sake of learning, learning for the sake of wealth, and both wealth and learning for their own sake. It is about transforming peasants and princes into merchants and priests, replacing inherited privilege with acquired prestige, and dismantling social estates for the benefit of individuals, nuclear families, families, and book reading tribes (nations). Modernization, in other words, is about everyone becoming Jewish.[7]

He might also have said that his own attempt to transform a previously disparaging stereotype of Jews into an esteemed cultural stereotype that nourishes a liberal culture, typifies a Jewish intellectual spirit of reinterpreting a given cultural discourse.

4. Self-Clarification in the Land of anti-Semitic Stereotypes

The relationship I have been tracing here between cultural stereotypes and cultural ideologies is interesting in its own right. In the particular case at hand, it is reason enough for taking an interest in Wittgenstein's cultural attitude towards real, flesh-and-blood Jews, when he utilizes a disparaging conception of Jews, promoted by anti-Semitic ideologies, to draw a spiritual distinction between them and all other human beings. The fact that those remarks are also directed at their author, himself, does not change the matter. It is no different from a desire to clarify the point of telling a Jewish joke in certain social circumstances. A Jewish joke that illustrates the stereotyped nature of Jews in an amusing way acquires a different meaning when told with self-mockery in congenial surroundings, as happens among Jews themselves, than when told by non-Jews in hostile surroundings to berate Jews. (Take by way of example the remark that Jews are just like everyone else, only more so; or the statement that an anti-Semite is someone who hates Jews more than they deserve. Consider such jokes asserted by Jews among themselves, and then asserted by non-Jews.) The phenomenon of anti-Semitism justifies such a desire, and there is no reason to compromise over it.[8]

Read today against the background of anti-Semitism and what transpired because of it, these remarks of Wittgenstein about the spiritual nature of Jews no longer appear to be merely innocent clarifications of a stereotyped concept used to describe the prototype of the Jew, which does not refer to real human beings. He not only clarifies this concept, but uses it to describe the spiritual nature of actual Jews, expressing his disparaging attitude towards Jews, his discontent and criticism of their impact on his culture, and his disappointment at possessing this spirit himself. In doing so, he appears to give credence to both anti-Semitic views and what has been described as "conservative ideology."[9] Moreover, it is not clear what could constitute a form of conceptual criticism that does not implicate real life. With anti-Semitism as background, the fact that these remarks are also self-directed does not alter this perception. It only makes them expressions of what Theodor Lessing has described as "Jewish self-hatred."[10] In this case, it also takes the form of spiritual self-hate, manifesting a yearning for a different spiritual nature than the one the writer possesses, a yearning for a non-Jewish spiritual nature.

However, my interest in this matter is not to explore Wittgenstein's conflicts with his self-identity, spiritual, cultural, or otherwise, for its own sake. Nor is it to explore the way in which his esteem for what he views as a (masculine) non-Jewish spirit embodies his desire to purge what he views as his (feminine) Jewish spirit. My concern here is with the way in which the conceptual distinction that Wittgenstein draws and strives to clarify between the spiritual nature of Jews and other people manifests an acute philosophical problem that is a deep personal difficulty for him and how, in the processes of overcoming it, he transforms his entire way of dealing with philosophical problems.

Seven

FROM PROTOTYPES TO FAMILY RESEMBLANCES

Ludwig Wittgenstein's reflections on the spiritual nature of Jews, along with his use of a stereotyped image of Jews for clarifying the concept of a Jew, came to an end at the beginning of the thirties. (The last remark on this subject in *Culture and Value* was written in 1931.) However, as I will show, the ideas that he expressed about two different kinds of spiritual dispositions that underlie cultural creation in the West were never abandoned. He expressed them in several different ways for many years afterwards—however, without making any further mention of the Jewish aspect. What lay behind this change in the formulation of his ideas? Though knowledge on this matter is lacking, the known facts add up to provide a biographical, historical and philosophical background against which the change in his style of expression becomes intelligible, pointing along the way to an important personal and philosophical issue that underlies it. It can help explain what might have made him realize at the time that he had to change both his former phrasing and the focus of the discussion to something other than Jews, enabling us to see in this change an expression something that was of profound philosophical and personal importance to him. As I will also show, it is a change that was part of a striking transformation that also took place in his philosophy.

1. Prototype versus Family Resemblance

The political and social turmoil that began to be felt in Europe during the early thirties, as fascism took hold and anti-Semitism became more virulent, were among the factors that may have induced Wittgenstein to recognize a required change in phrasing. He may also have been influenced at this time by changes of a profound significance in his philosophical outlook that took place concurrently. These, as I shall now show, point to more than just a change in phrasing. In this regard, I want to point out two keynote concepts that occupied him at the time and how, in his exchange of one for the other, an explanation can be found for the change in the phrasing of his ideas and for his having ceased to formulate conceptual clarifications of Jews and their spiritual nature. It also explains the change in his entire philosophical approach. These are the concepts of "prototype" and "family resemblance."

In a remark written in 1931, the year in which he wrote most of his remarks on the spiritual nature of Jews, Wittgenstein tries to distinguish the difference between a discussion relating to prototype and a discussion relating to family resemblance:

> [Oswald] Spengler could be better understood if he said: I am *comparing* different periods of culture with the lives of families; within the family there is a family resemblance, while you will also find a resemblance between members of different families; family resemblance differs from the other sort of resemblance in such & such ways, etc.. What I mean is: We have to be told the object of comparison, the object from which this approach is derived, so that prejudices do not constantly slip into the discussion. Because then we shall willy-nilly ascribe what is true of the prototype of the approach to the object to which we are applying the approach as well; & we claim "it *must always be* . . ."
> This comes about because we want to give the prototype's characteristics a foothold in the approach. But since we confuse prototype & object we find ourselves dogmatically conferring on the object properties which only the prototype necessarily possesses. On the other hand we think the approach will lack the generality we want to give it if it really holds only of the one case. But the prototype must just be presented for what it is; as characterizing the whole approach and determining its form. In this way it stands at the head & is generally valid by virtue of determining the form of approach, not by virtue of a claim that everything which is true only of it holds for all the objects to which the approach is applied.
>
> One should thus always ask when exaggerated dogmatic claims are made: What is actually true in this. Or again: In what case is that actually true.[1]

In this passage, Wittgenstein is comparing claims asserted in connection with the idea of a conceptual prototype to Spengler's claims asserted in connection with the idea of family resemblance. Spengler describes the creative achievements of a given culture in different fields, art, technology, war, and everyday life as having a family resemblance. He also describes different historical periods during the life span of a culture in a manner analogous to the life stories of several succeeding generations of a family. In Spengler's view, the resemblance between innovations emerging within a culture in different fields and in its different historical periods derives from their being different manifestations of the same idea or conception of life that underlies that culture.

Wittgenstein's first comment concerns the familial analogy. Resemblances are found, he claims, not only among members of the same family, but also among members of different families. It all depends on how they are viewed, by means of which concept. In the same way, resemblances can be found not only among succeeding generations of what is perceived as a single culture, but also among different cultures. The resemblance we see among what we perceive as different manifestations of the culture is, in his opinion, a function of our perceiving all of them by means of a particular representational entity: a particular cultural prototype. So family resemblance is the resemblance we see when we look at things through an idealized representation—a prototype. Later, the concept of family resemblance will come to signify a resemblance seen among things without making use of any entity that represents them, as there is no single essence behind them. Later, the concept of family resemblance is destined to replace the concept of prototype, as all that stands behind conceptual distinctions. Later, it will completely "determine the discussion." But not at this juncture.

The next comment is that we must distinguish between a (conceptual) discussion concerning the nature of a certain prototype as a mental representation and an (empirical) discussion concerning the nature of actual things the prototype represents. The conceptual discussion concerning the prototype must ignore actual properties of the things it represents. A discussion of the prototype does not concern them. It is a purely conceptual discussion. Wittgenstein formulates the conceptual requirements for such a discussion in the following statement:

> But the prototype must just be presented for what it is; as characterizing the whole approach and determining its form. In this way it stands at the head & is generally valid by virtue of determining the form of approach, not by virtue of a claim that everything which is true only of it holds for all the objects to which the approach is applied.
>
> One should thus always ask when exaggerated dogmatic claims are made: What is actually true in this. Or again: In what case is that actually true.[2]

Two aims can be discerned behind these words. The first is to distinguish between a conceptual discussion, which pertains to something ideal, operating as a representational entity, and an empirical discussion, which pertains to something actual. The aim of a conceptual discussion is to characterize the nature of the prototype through which we represent things by describing properties it *necessarily* possesses. The prototype has no other properties. The historical, or empirical, discussion deals with the properties of things, which we see in the light of one prototype or another. Actual things have properties that accrue to them *contingently*.

Here, Wittgenstein is trying to draw a line between the (supposedly) metaphysical context of Otto Weininger's claim (and his own purported conceptual claims) and the historical context of Spengler's claims about the spiritual nature of different cultures. Spengler is engaged in a historic, therefore empirical, discussion. He compares different innovations emerging in different fields and periods of the same culture according to the (family) resemblance they share, by instantiating the same idea; a resemblance that is a function of his viewing them through the lens of their cultural prototype. But Wittgenstein's discussion (like Weininger's) is supposed to be conceptual. He wants to define the (spiritual) essence of a culture, not the way in which it is manifested as historical fact in different fields and in different periods. He wants to describe and clarify the conceptual nature of various spiritual efforts that are manifested through Western culture in the modern period.

The second aim behind these remarks is to draw a line between (conceptual) generalizations of the kind Wittgenstein makes about Jews and racist generalizations pronounced by anti-Semites. Racism is expressed by "dogmatically conferring on the object properties which only the prototype necessarily possesses."[3] It is to regard actual people as necessarily possessing the properties of a conceptual prototype through which we perceive them. Such a dogmatic view of people is prejudiced and racist. It seeks necessity in the realm of contingency. It claims that Jews are always so and so, that Jews are *necessarily* so and so.

As opposed to this "dogmatic" attitude, the validity of his conclusions is supposed to stem from their being formulated only in a conceptual context that determines "the form" of the discussion, and not because actual Jews always evince the properties found in the spiritual prototype of the (ideal) Jew. In this way, Wittgenstein seeks to convince himself that, in speaking of Jewish mentality and Jewish spirit, he refers only to the spiritual prototype of the Jew and that this is not to be confused with anti-Semitic comments made about actual Jews. His remarks, in contrast to dogmatic, anti-Semitic pronouncements, are made only in the context of a conceptual discussion. Therefore, within such a context, "This is not to allege a vice & everything is all right as long as what is being done is quite clear."[4]

But it does not work. The attempt to place the (Spenglerian) concept of family resemblance alongside the concept of a spiritual prototype and to distinguish between empirical remarks based on one and conceptual remarks based on the other, is insupportable. These are not remarks that pertain to two different matters—one empirical and one conceptual. These are remarks that pertain to the very same thing and in the very same context!

2. Overcoming the Metaphysical Spell

The idea that we are able to see a family resemblance between actual things is Wittgenstein's insightful resolution of the ancient philosophical problem regarding the metaphysical status of universals. It grants us this conceptual ability without assuming the need to make use of a representational entity such as a prototype. In his critique of his own former metaphysical assumption about the existence of such an entity, he notes that the argument for its existence "is based on the notion that what is needed to justify characterizing a number of processes or objects by a general concept-word is something common to them all." However, he now concludes that this way of confronting the problem is "*too primitive*":

> What a concept-word indicates is certainly a kinship between objects, but this kinship need not be the sharing of a common property or a constituent. It may connect the objects like the links of a chain, so that one is linked to another *by intermediary links*. Two neighboring members may have common features and be *similar* to each other, while distant ones belong to the same family without any longer having anything in common. Indeed even if a feature is common to all members of the family it need not be that feature that defines the concept.
>
> The relationship between the members of a concept may be set up by the sharing of features which show up in the family of the concept, crossing and overlapping in very complicated ways.
>
> Thus there is probably no single characteristic which is common to all the things we call games. But it can't be said either that "game" just has several independent meanings (rather like the word "bank"). What we call "games" are procedures interrelated in various ways with many different transitions between one and another.[5]

He formulates his conclusions by placing the metaphor of family resemblances at the heart of his philosophical discussion about conceptual distinctions:

> I can think of no better expression to characterize these similarities than "family resemblances"; for the various resemblances between members of a family: build, features, colour of eyes, gait, temperament, etc. etc. overlap and criss-cross in the same way.—And I shall say: "games" form a family.
>
> And for instance the kinds of number form a family in the same way. Why do we call something a "number"? Well, perhaps because it has a—direct—relationship with several things that have hitherto been called number; and this can be said to give it an indirect relationship to other things we call the same name. And we extend our concept of number as in spinning a thread we twist fibre on fibre. And the strength of the thread does not reside in the fact that some one fibre runs through its whole length, but in the overlapping of many fibres.[6]

Overcoming the metaphysical need to stipulate the existence of a common feature that is the essence of things falling under the same concept renders the idea of a prototype (that represents this essence) redundant. It opens the way to a different, non-metaphysical way of clarifying our ability to make use of concepts. The idea that various things falling under a common concept have family resemblances, rather than one thing common between all of them, is the idea that we are able grasp them as such, despite not representing them as having anything in common between all of them. Thus, it is an idea that what joins them together is our ability to grasp them as falling under a common concept. Acquiring use of a concept is acquiring the ability to grasp things as the same. Such an ability is anchored in ordinary abilities to recognize resemblances between things:

> Anyone with an eye for family resemblances can recognize that two people are related to each other, even without being able to say wherein the resemblance lies. (Think of the case of the calculating-genius.)[7]

Hence, there is no longer a need to regard concepts as representational entities that are entertained in the mind through their prototypes. We can see family resemblances among actual things directly, despite that they have nothing essential in common: by way of neither a mental representation nor some other metaphysical incarnation. This realization is the beginning of a great change in his former philosophical outlook and method, in particular in his philosophical approach regarding the nature of concepts and their relationship to the world. From here on, the concept of family resemblance assumes a pivotal role in determining the discussion, with Wittgenstein relinquishing any idea of conducting a conceptual investigation according to some presupposed representational entity that embodies the essence of things.

Abandoning the idea that any such entity exists, along with the idea that a conceptual clarification is directed at it only and not yet at the way our concepts embody our grasp of actual things, is a great change in Wittgenstein's understanding of where the lines are drawn between metaphysical assumptions, conceptual clarifications and ethical demands. Interestingly enough, he foregoes using the concept of prototype in conducting his conceptual clarifications at the same time that he foregoes either using the stereotyped concept of the Jew or seeking to clarify it.

Is this simultaneity coincidental? I think not. It seems to me that Wittgenstein found that he could no longer hide behind the claim that he was merely conducting a conceptual discussion about Jews when he spoke of Jews as he did. He was speaking of the way in which he perceived and regarded actual Jews, by making use of the stereotyped concept of the Jew prevalent in his society. As the very concept of a prototype had turned into a nonsensical metaphysical assumption, he was not referring thereby to some representational entity, but to real Jews. He now had to acknowledge that even a conceptual distinction does not arise out of the void, pertaining only to a purported prototype that does not refer to real, living human beings. The reference to such an entity is merely a fictitious explanation, arising from our ability to perceive resemblances between the things that make up our world. Since we are able perceive resemblances between the things that make up our world without any reference to such an entity, it is a useless metaphysical assumption. But if so, then the features ascribed to the representational prototype are features that we perceive in actual things. In that case, they concern the way in which he regards and perceives the spiritual nature of actual Jews and their cultural works, not merely some purported prototypical representation of them, and not merely some metaphysical incarnation of their kind.

Given the above understanding, it might thus have become clear to Wittgenstein that, in speaking about Jewish mentality and character, he was speaking about the way he regarded actual Jews, not merely what is enclosed in some prototypical conceptual representation of them. He could now see that he had been making use of the ways in which his culture regarded Jews and their spiritual nature, by making use of its stereotypical symbolic discourse. He was thus partaking of a shared critical attitude towards Jews and expressing the anti-Semitic metaphysical outlook emerging out of his culture. In doing so, he was also associating himself with a social attitude and ideology hostile toward Jews. In seeing this, he could now realize that what "determined the form of the discussion" was a stereotypical picture of Jews that had become encapsulated in his metaphysical view regarding the existence of conceptual prototypes as representational entities. He could now realize that he had been held captive by a metaphysical picture painted with stereotyped imagery to which he had succumbed. He could now also see that in clarifying the concept of a Jew in the way he did, he was expressing his personal attitude toward Jews, and that he was doing so by succumbing to the stereotypical image of them propagated in his culture.

The interesting question, and one that remains a mystery to me, is which came first. Was it the realization Wittgenstein had that he had succumbed to the stereotyped image of Jews propagated in his culture that made him abandon the metaphysical idea of our needing a representational prototype in his conceptual discussions and rest his case on the (new) idea of family resemblance from here onwards? Or was it the other way around: did abandoning the metaphysical idea of needing a representational prototype and its replacement with the idea of family resemblance lead him to a realization of the anti-Semitic attitude he had been expressing all the while toward actual Jews?

3. Conceptual Clarifications of Cultural Practices

From here on, Wittgenstein's criticism of his former view of linguistic meaning and its logical grammar begins. In the opening paragraph of *Philosophical Investigations*, he presents it as a criticism of Augustine of Hippo's view of meaning, suggesting that it gives us "a particular picture of the essence of human language." According to this picture:

> individual words in language name objects—sentences are combinations of such names. In this picture of language, we find the roots of the following idea: Every word has a meaning. This meaning is correlated with the word. It is the object for which the word stands.[8]

The object that supposedly constitutes the meaning of a word is what in philosophical discourse is called a concept and it is represented in the mind by means of a certain prototype. The metaphysical view of linguistic meaning he is criticizing here is not merely that of Augustine. It was both his own view and that of Gottlob Frege and Bertrand Russell, who first raised the idea of a logical analysis of language that reveals the meaning of words by displaying their hidden conceptual essences. Language was explained as a system of signs used for representing states of affairs in propositions.

In contrast to the above view of linguistic meanings, Wittgenstein now begins to describe language as an assortment of shared practices used for all sorts of purposes. From here on, the use of language itself "determines the discussion," not logical forms and not logically incarnated signs that give it meaning. In this approach, to reveal the grammar of language is to reveal what users of language mean through it. To do so, we need to describe how they use it. In the philosophical insight that underlies this approach to language, the ability of human beings to use words according to their different meanings manifests an ability to understand and use words according to shared linguistic practices, which are cultural practices. By rendering the use of words into a practical cultural normative enterprise, Wittgenstein disengages our use of language from its former mooring in logical forms that provide a transcendental basis for representing states of affairs in propositions. Language is a cultural phenomenon and culture is a normative, social framework that embodies shared normative ways of engaging and understanding life.

To help with this philosophical insight, Wittgenstein evokes his fictitious cultural tribes, noting that different cultural "tribes" might not only speak in different languages; they might also possess through these languages different concepts, some of which are also different from ours. He asks us to "imagine a use of language (a culture) in which there was a common name for green and red on the one hand and yellow and blue on the other."[9] Similarly:

> We could also easily imagine a language (and that means again a culture) in which there existed no common expression for light blue and dark blue, in which the former, say, was called "Cambridge," the latter "Oxford." If you ask a man of this tribe what Cambridge and Oxford have in common, he'd be inclined to say "Nothing."[10]

In still another place, he evokes an imaginary tribe that has a different concept of pain from ours. They are unfamiliar with the concept of "simulated pain."[11] In still another place, he imagines the following:

> A tribe has two concepts, akin to our "pain." One is applied where there is visible damage and is linked with tending, pity, etc. The other is used for stomachache for example, and is tied up with mockery of anyone who complains.[12]

In such fictitious philosophical examples, "to imagine a concept" is to "imagine a use of language," and to imagine a use of language is "to imagine a culture."

In the philosophical overview of the concept of culture that thus emerges, it is manifested in a linguistic community, possessing all sorts of concepts, embodied in shared ways of communicating, of doing things, of expressing themselves, of understanding and valuing things. In my reading of Wittgenstein's insight on this matter, the acquisition (and creation) of concepts is a cultural phenomenon. It is manifested in the use of all sorts of shared practices, some of which are instantiated in the common use of words for various purposes that endow them with linguistic meaning. As such, like the use of shared practical techniques for hunting and cooking, and like the observance of social customs regarding marriage and private property, language is a cultural phenomenon, manifesting cultural affiliation through the ability to use and understand all sorts of linguistic practices. Thus, our ability to use words according to their meanings embodies our linguistic ways of partaking in cultural norms, which manifest our understanding of linguistic meanings that underlie our concepts.

Given this insight, which renders language into an assortment of practices that provide for a culture, the philosophical puzzlement over our ability to understand the very concept of a linguistic norm is overcome by rendering such norms into shared practices and forms of life, manifesting common judgments by their users. Accordingly, he now suggests, "the use of a word in the language is its meaning."[13] This is to say that the use of words is like the uses of utensils and practical techniques. Hence, to the extent that a tribe of users of words shares these uses, it manifests shared, cultural, linguistic practices.

Following the above new overview of language and linguistic meanings, it becomes clear that the concept of a Jew that Wittgenstein was undertaking to clarify manifested the way Jews were typed, grasped, and regarded in his culture. To clarify the use of this concept in his culture, by noting how it is based on the way the spiritual nature of Jews is manifested and experienced, was to affiliate himself with an antagonistic attitude toward people identified as "Jews." He could no longer shrug this off as implicating just its representational entity. And so Wittgenstein abandoned it.

Eight

WITTGENSTEIN CONFRONTS HIS ATTITUDE TOWARD JEWS

A major factor that may have induced Ludwig Wittgenstein to discard his philosophical project of clarifying the concept of a Jew concerns political developments in Europe at the beginning of the thirties. With the surging tide of anti-Semitism, his reception and employment of a conceptual distinction between the spiritual natures of Jews and non-Jews took on great significance. He could no longer ignore the fact that it expressed a negative attitude toward Jews. In the context of emerging political realities, it was difficult for Wittgenstein to delude himself that he was only drawing an important conceptual distinction, pertaining only to the concept of Jew and not to actual people identified as Jews. There were partners to this distinction who obviously were not to his liking. And this conceptual partnership may have made him aware of other possible affinities of perception and attitude toward real Jews, of which he now wished to free himself.

1. Two Significant Events

Two events that occurred at this time shed some light on Wittgenstein's emerging self-consciousness about his past attitude toward Jews. The first is an incident that Norman Malcolm has related, which occurred at the time of their acquaintanceship in Cambridge:

> One time, when we were walking along the river, we saw a news-vendor's sign, which announced that the German government had accused the British government of instigating a recent attempt to assassinate Hitler with a bomb. This was in the autumn of 1939. Wittgenstein said of the German claim: "It wouldn't surprise me if it were true." I retorted that I couldn't believe that top people in the British government would do such a thing. I meant that the British were too civilized and decent to attempt anything so underhanded; and I added that such a deed was not in keeping with British "national character." My remark made Wittgenstein extremely angry. He considered it to be a great stupidity and also an indication that I was not learning anything from the philosophical training that he was trying to give me. He said these things very vehemently, and when I refused to admit that my remark was stupid he would not talk to me anymore and soon after we parted.[1]

Later, in a letter written to Malcolm in the autumn of 1944, Wittgenstein comments on this incident:

> You & I were walking along the river towards the railway bridge & we had a heated discussion in which you made a remark about "national character" that shocked me by it's primitiveness. I then thought: what is the use of studying philosophy if all that it does for you is to enable you to talk with some acceptable plausibility about some abstruse questions of logic etc., & if it does not improve your thinking about the important questions of everyday life, if it does not make you more conscientious than any . . . journalist in the use of *dangerous* phrases such people use for their own ends. You see, I know it is difficult to think well about "certainty," "probability," "perception," etc. But it is, if possible, still more difficult to think, or to try to think, really and honestly about your life & other people's lives. And the trouble is that thinking about these things is not thrilling, but often downright nasty. And when it's nasty, then it's most important.[2]

Keeping in mind Wittgenstein's own use of the concepts of Jewish character and Jewish mentality in the past, this last passage is most impressive. His outburst at Malcolm's remark is an indication of a new awareness and a greater sensitivity to the subject at this time. Accordingly, his criticism of Malcolm can also be seen as a criticism of his own use of a stereotypical concept and, particularly, the *attitude* toward Jews manifested in the stereotyped concept of the Jew. For obviously, Wittgenstein was not merely clarifying the stereotyped concept of Jews manufactured and marketed in his culture. He was making use of it to clarify his own attitude toward the spiritual nature of Jews and what he deemed to be the effect of Jews on his culture. He was not like someone who merely notes that the concept of a witch is of a woman who possesses supernatural powers. He was more like someone engaged in distinguishing witches from ordinary women for the purpose of "clarifying" the debasing effect of witchcraft on society. Thus, it must have dawned on him that in his clarifications of the concept of a Jew, he was expressing a social attitude hostile toward real Jews that he had shared and from which he now wanted to disassociate himself: an attitude that was enhanced by blatant ideologies hostile to Jews. Much later, he expressed this realization as a general injunction against drafting philosophy into the service of an ideology: "(The philosopher is not a citizen of any community of ideas. That is what makes him into a philosopher)."[3] However, it is not always easy to tell when clarifications of our use of concepts end, and when ideological conceptions that build on them begin.

The incident with Malcolm and the interpretation I have given it can also render certain aspects of the affair of his confession more understandable. In 1937, while at Cambridge, Wittgenstein confessed to some of his closer acquaintances about several matters in his past over which he felt ethical remorse—mostly for having acted disingenuously or without proper courage. Apparently, this was not his first confession about these matters. According to Maurice O'Conner Drury, in 1931, Wittgenstein had lived for a while in his hut in Norway. On his return to Cambridge, he told Drury that he had done no philosophical writing, but had spent his time in prayer. He had written a confession of those things in his past of which he was most ashamed. He asked Drury to read it. He also asked G. E. Moore to read it.[4] Neither of them disclosed what it included. However, Malcolm surmises that it "was possibly the same confession" that he made orally to some of his acquaintances in 1937.[5]

One of the matters about which Wittgenstein confessed orally concerned his Jewishness. Fania Pascal, who taught Wittgenstein Russian, was one of the people to whom he made his oral confession in 1937.[6] She recalls that she was busy at the time with family matters, but Wittgenstein insisted on coming, saying it was urgent. When she learned of the purpose of his visit, she became annoyed. Her annoyance was aggravated by the stiff and remote manner in which he set about it. It was not an emotionally charged confession of sins in Russian style, with kneeling on the ground, crying and gnashing of teeth, such as is enacted by Fyodor Dostoyevsky's troubled heroes. According to her recollections, Wittgenstein told her in the first part of his confession that most people tended to regard him as non-Jewish, for he was supposedly three-quarters Aryan and only one-quarter Jewish. However, the proportions were reversed. But, he claimed, he had never done anything to prevent this misunderstanding.

Pascal remarks with sarcasm that given Wittgenstein's ancestry and his family's conversion to Christianity, her (Jewish) grandmother would have remarked, "some Jew."[7] She also recalls her reluctance to discuss the problem with him, perhaps because he did not strike her as a Jew at all. "I had no idea whether he knew that I was a Jewish girl from the Ukraine, who had been through pogroms during the Civil War, whose childhood was darkened, branded by the anti-Semitism of Tsarist Russia," she writes. "I understood too well the agony a Jew might endure if he was taken for a gentile." She, therefore, tried to reach out to him as one Jew to another, offering her own confession of a similar experience as a comforting gesture of shared social fate and agony. She told him:

> "I am Jewish and I have often missed the chance to come out with it in time to stop others from revealing their profound dislike of Jews in general. Anyhow, the English are shrewd. I assume they know about me, they probably know about you . . . ." I was moved to see that he looked hopefully.[8]

2. Reflections on Wittgenstein's Confession

Reviewing Pascal's recollection of Wittgenstein's confession, Rush Rhees writes:

> in what he told Mrs. Pascal in 1937 there was something to suggest that he had failed to make plain to himself or to others what was Jewish in his character and in what he wrote; and she found it hard to see what he was getting at.[9]

On Rhees' interpretation of Wittgenstein's confession, it had to do with deceiving himself about his own spirit. He claims that, unlike Otto Weininger, Wittgenstein did not hold the Jewish character that one recognizes in oneself as something to be deplored. It was not a defect. Thus, he was seeking in his confession to acknowledge what he regarded, in accordance with Weininger's view, as his Jewish character. He was concerned with a spiritual matter, having to do with self-deception, whereas Pascal understood it as a social matter, having to do with being accepted by others. In the interpretation Rhees puts on Wittgenstein's confession, he was following Weininger's remarks about the need for a "gifted" person (genius) to reach spiritual self-understanding by judging his own character in a completely honest fashion, doing so in the context of meaningful experiences that shape one's life. Rhees explains the point of Weininger's view that was important to Wittgenstein in the following way:

> There is an (internal) connection between being gifted and the quality of the man's remembering—the way in which he remembers (not the matters he learned in the secondary school, but) the experiences which from his early childhood, have been for him significant; in other words, have made his life what it is. . . . The man who is gifted has a vivid interest in certain things he has experienced, and also a vivid sense of what they "mean" for his life. They determine what he can produce that is in any sense original or is *his*.[10]

Rhees maintains that this kind of self-scrutiny promotes an attitude of piety toward one's life. In this interpretation, Wittgenstein was trying to transform his attitude toward his life by relinquishing his former desire to possess a non-Jewish character, accepting with humility the Jewish character that he had formerly tried to disown. Rhees describes what I have called our "attitude" toward our lives in Wittgenstein's words as "the feeling we have for our life." He relates this attempt by Wittgenstein to change his attitude toward his life to Wittgenstein's previous attempts to change his attitude toward his life. In this regard, he mentions Wittgenstein's putting himself in life-threatening danger during the First World War, giving away his inheritance, and trying to settle in Russia. He might have mentioned other examples as well. He also mentions in this connection Wittgenstein's recurring appeal to change himself, to become a different and better person than he was.

Rhees' interpretation of Wittgenstein's confession is edifying. It clarifies it as a personal, ethical, spiritual act of humility, through which Wittgenstein sought to come to terms with himself, to both acknowledge and accept his Jewish spirit, which in his view precludes being a genius, and to relinquish his aspiration for a non-Jewish spirit. Indeed, nine years later, he writes:

> Are all people great human beings? No.—Well then, what hope can you have of being a great human being! Why should something be given you that is not given your fellows? To what purpose?!—If it isn't your wish to be rich that makes you think you are rich, then it must be some observation some experience that shows you it! And what experience do you have (except that of vanity)? Simply that you have a *talent*. And my *conceit* of being an extraordinary human being is of course *much* older than my experience, of my particular talent.[11]

However, Rhees' interpretation of Wittgenstein's confession is too one-sided and bereft of any historical context. First, it does not mention the anti-Semitic climate in Europe, which in 1937, at the time of Wittgenstein's second confession, had become even more pronounced, providing an ominous social context to both his former remarks on Jews and his confession of not having acknowledged being Jewish. The question whether one was Jewish and in what proportions, was about to become a question of life and death in central Europe, not merely a personal spiritual problem. Indeed, Rhees himself mentions that, after the Nazis took over Austria, Wittgenstein left "to Vienna, where his sisters were having trouble with the German (National Socialist) authorities." Afterwards, "he and their German lawyer went from Vienna to Berlin, and from there they went directly to New York."[12] He does not mention what this trouble with the authorities was or what was the purpose of these excursions.

In point of fact, Wittgenstein was involved in the transfer of his family's fortune to the Nazis, which enabled them not to be declared Jews.[13] In narrating about these events in his edifying biography of Wittgenstein, Ray Monk reflects, "the irony of bribing the Nazis to accept a lie about the very thing to which he had confessed just two years previously can hardly have escaped him."[14] Second, while Wittgenstein did not condemn Jews as Weininger had, he did express a critical evaluation of Jewish influence on modern Western culture. Third, Rhees does not note that, from 1931, the year of his first confession, Wittgenstein stopped commenting on Jews and their character. Presumably he realized that he was using "dangerous phrases," which expressed and promoted a view of Jews that had dangerous social implications. Fourth, Rhees does not note the change in Wittgenstein's philosophy that had already begun to take place in 1931, which also included his inability to support Weininger's metaphysical claims about the existence of Platonic ideal cultural types that are divorced from actual attitudes toward real human beings.

The differing interpretations by Pascal and Rhees of the meaning of Wittgenstein's confession to them may be labeled "the social interpretation versus the ethical-spiritual interpretation," or "the Jewish interpretation versus the non-Jewish interpretation." Having described them both, I find that there is no reason to choose between them, as they are two sides of the same coin. Indeed, it can be said that Weininger's demand of real Jews to acknowledge their Jewish character was merely a philosophical strand in the tangle of anti-Semitism that Wittgenstein finally recognized when he referred to dangerous phrases used in Western discourse about its spiritual underpinnings. Thus, his confession can be seen as an attempt both to acknowledge his Jewish spirit and to renounce his previous critical attitude toward Jews, so as to distance himself from the anti-Semitic ideology that had now overtaken central Europe. For, as he wrote at the time of his first confession, "a confession has to be part of one's new life."[15] Part of this new life was to acknowledge that he was a Jew himself and to declare it to others. In so doing, he adopted a humbler attitude toward his life, philosophical aspirations and achievements. He also sought in this way to distance himself from the anti-Semitic ideologies that were engulfing Europe.

On the philosophical interpretation that I am putting on Wittgenstein's confession to being a Jew, he saw himself as having been enthralled by a metaphysical picture about the spiritual nature of cultural beings, which had been drawn by the use of the stereotyped conceptions of Jews in his culture. It was a picture that had determined his attitude both toward himself and toward Jews, one from which he now wanted to break free. To disentangle himself from it, he acknowledged being a Jew. In doing so, he sought to resolve the metaphysical problem that had turned into an existential difficulty for him: how to live when one is critical of one's spiritual nature on metaphysical grounds? The solution was to turn a metaphysical problem into an ethical difficulty that could be overcome through an act promoting an attitude of humility: by acknowledging his Jewish spirit to himself—in public.

Curiously, even in acknowledging himself a Jew by declaring it to others, Wittgenstein did so in an ambiguous fashion—not unlike the ambiguous duck-rabbit picture that he used later to demonstrate two different possible aspects of perception. A confession is a traditional Christian practice of acknowledging and renouncing a committed sin, which Wittgenstein now employed to acknowledge his Jewishness and renounce his past attempts to hide it. (Was it this discrepancy between form and content that made Pascal unsympathetic to his confession?) Indeed, in declaring himself a Jew, he acted counter to the "secretive and cunning" spiritual nature that he had formerly ascribed to Jews, demonstrating "courage" and integrity that he had formerly ascribed to persons possessing a non-Jewish spiritual disposition.

His acknowledgment and declaration of being a Jew may also have expressed his desire to draw a clear line between himself and Weininger regarding Jews, particularly as he had once expressed admiration for Weininger to his friends. Weininger was a Jew who had succumbed to his culture's disparaging stereotyped conception of Jews, becoming a metaphysical anti-Semite and choosing to convert to Christianity. He, Wittgenstein, is not an anti-Semite, neither a metaphysical anti-Semite, nor a self-hating Jewish anti-Semite. Thus, in contrast to Weininger, who sought to renounce his Jewish identity, he affirms his Jewishness. Of course, the comparison I am drawing here between Wittgenstein's public acknowledgement and Weininger's public rejection of their Jewishness has its other side as well. The metaphysical irony of the matter is that what Weininger's conversion to Christianity expressed—more than anything else—was what he had typified as constituting "Jewish (and "feminine") character." It embodied his lack of an integral, spiritual core of his own, his susceptibility to the influence of the (anti-Semitic) social and cultural environment in which he lived, to the extent of adopting an anti-Semitic attitude himself and converting. This is the paradox of the self-hate induced for lack of a self-sustaining character, which Weininger could not solve, even by committing suicide.

Much later, Wittgenstein tries to explain (away) this paradox in Weininger by remarking, "it is not unheard of that someone's character may be influenced by the external world (Weininger)."[16] Yet in his own case, the solution to this paradox took an opposite direction. By both acknowledging and declaring himself a Jew, he refused to let the disparaging stereotypical concept of the Jew have any influence upon him. He was thus withstanding the social pressure and the metaphysical temptation to renounce his Jewish origins and spiritual nature. In so doing, he acted like a person of "strong character" and demonstrated spiritual integrity. He also gave expression in this way to what he formerly would have described as "a non-Jewish mind."

Moreover, in confronting his past desire to possess a non-Jewish spirit, he was following Weininger's suggestion as formulated by Rhees, namely, that a gifted person "has a vivid interest in certain things he has experienced, and also a vivid sense of what they 'mean' for his life." This is because it is in relation to them that what he creates "is in any sense original or *his*."[17]

Thus, in acknowledging being Jewish, he was confronting the meaning of his past desire, as a "gifted" person, who possesses a non-Jewish spirit, does.

Conceptual distinctions that rely on stereotypes (just like those that rely on metaphors, similes, and symbols) are cultural artifacts. As such, they draw their vitality from the social and cultural background in which they are embedded. During the thirties this background in Europe became overtly anti-Semitic. Wittgenstein's renunciation of the use of his culture's stereotyped conception of the Jew, as expressed in both its ordinary and metaphysical discourse, manifests a desire to divorce himself from a social attitude toward Jews that underlies the story of anti-Semitism in Europe. It was an attitude that, in the modern period, was expressed in critical ideologies, then became socially hostile, and finally turned blatantly violent, taking the form of a ruthless systemic extermination of Jews. It also manifests a realization that a stereotyped concept is not merely an innocent conceptual entity the conceptual features of which can be clarified without indulging in its use. It is a concept that expresses and enhances our attitudes toward and the perspectives from which we look upon actual human beings. Since a stereotype is such a concept, we are required to take an ethical stance on its continued use. Nonetheless, Wittgenstein's ambivalence toward this issue in the case of the Jews' impact on European culture and his own spiritual creative abilities remained. In a cryptic remark, he finally attempts to sum up both his ambivalence about the subject of Jews and his awareness of what is nevertheless required:

> If you cannot unravel a tangle, the most sensible thing you can do is to recognize this; & the most decent, to admit [anti-Semitism]. What you should do to cure the evil is not clear. What is *not* permissible is clear from one case to another.[18]

Apparently, one of those particular cases concerned his continued use of the stereotyped concept of the Jew in philosophical discourse, and so he abandoned it.

3. Weininger's Metaphysics Reconsidered

As may now be seen, Wittgenstein's reflections on Weininger and Jews manifest not only his concerns with his own spiritual nature and attitude toward Jews and their influence on cultural affairs, but also express his concerns with philosophy and the way in which philosophical problems are to be overcome and philosophical insights are to be derived. During the early thirties, after returning to Cambridge University, he recommended Weininger's *Sex and Character*[19] to some of his undergraduate friends and to G. E. Moore, once his teacher and now his colleague and friend. Their response was cool. The book, which had excited the pre-war Viennese intellectual community, offering a metaphysical theory about the spiritual nature of men and women that expressed hostility to women and was steaming with anti-Semitic feelings, may have looked bizarre to them. Wittgenstein tried to explain. He wrote to Moore:

> I can quite imagine that you don't admire Weininger very much, what with that beastly translation and the fact that W. must feel very foreign to you. It is true that he is fantastic but he is *great* and fantastic. It isn't necessary or rather not possible to agree with him but the greatness lies in that with which we disagree. It is his enormous mistake, which is

great. I.e. roughly speaking if you add a "~" to the whole book it says an important truth.[20]

This strange and cryptic remark reflects the way in which Wittgenstein's ways of thinking in philosophy began to take shape during the thirties. As I interpret it and particularly the negation sign that he wishes to place on the book, there is, indeed, a difference between the spiritual disposition with which Jews and women engage life and the spiritual disposition that underlies metaphysics in Western philosophy. Only Weininger got it wrong when he maligned the former two and praised the latter. In the pursuit of philosophical insight, the practical, everyday, social, spiritual disposition toward life and the affairs of culture exhibited by Jews and women is the correct one. Whereas the spiritual disposition underlying Western metaphysics, which includes also his own earlier attempt to base language on logic, propositional forms, and prototypes that represent states of affairs in propositions divorced from the actual flow of life and the practical use of language, is a deceptive philosophical illusion. Thus understood, the remark points to the way Wittgenstein now sought to deal with what he perceived, along with Weininger, as a Jewish, feminist, non-metaphysical approach to life in relation to a non-Jewish, masculine, metaphysical approach. He now affirmed the non-metaphysical approach, turning it into a central method of discourse in his own philosophical investigations: one that in the stereotyped terminology he had used before, he might have described as "Jewish."

In the context of Weininger's distinction between Jewish and feminine spirit, on the one hand, and non-Jewish and masculine spirit, on the other, Wittgenstein allies his new philosophical ways of thinking with what he took to be the Jewish (and feminine) spirit. Philosophy, as he now engages in it, does not aspire to find a metaphysical voice of its own, not even an empty logical one. At most, it provides perspicuous representations of linguistic norms and cultural forms of life created and observed by human beings. The remarks he offers are mostly deflationary and critical. Their aim is to demolish metaphysical castles in the air, including the one that he himself built on the misleading picture of the sublime scaffold of logical form, encasing propositions and states of affairs. They often take the form of a dialogue between himself as an aspiring metaphysician and himself as deflationary critic.

This is nothing akin to the grand philosophical style of Gottlob Frege that he admired, nor to the poetic, high style of the imposing pronouncements that make up Wittgenstein's earlier *Tractatus Logico-Philosophicus*, which presents the essence of language, world, and life as given to a solitary person invested with sublime logic. The earlier philosophical venture may be said to have provided a masculine, poetic, non-Jewish overview of linguistic meaning, in which logical form, substances, propositions, pictures, and prototypes "determine the form of the discussion." It expresses an attempt by the author to affiliate himself with something eternal and sublime that transcends the limits of human experience, social forms of life, and culture.

By contrast, *Philosophical Investigations* is a Jewish (and feminine) philosophical discourse, in which forms of life, family resemblances, language games, and shared practices underlie the existence of human beings. The aim of its discourse is to deflate metaphysical assumptions about the essence of language, meaning, understanding, mind, reading, and following rules. It seeks to replace such grand illusions by calling our attention to ordinary human activities and everyday uses of language. Instead of the grand edifice of logic that is the *Tractatus-Logico Philosophicus*, which captures the world and language in its net, we now get an album of various uses of language, conjoined to critical remarks directed at the conjuring philosophical tricks that attempt to consolidate them into a single vision, which typifies *Philosophical Investigations*.

Instead of logic constituting the transcendental foundation for language, the relationship is now reversed. Logic is an abstracted, skimmed off, normative aspect of the actual use of language by human beings within the practical and social stream of everyday life. In this approach, articulated conceptual distinctions are merely "grammatical remarks," for the use of words by a linguistic community. Their normative status derives from the fact that they manifest shared uses of words that provide for linguistic forms of life, rather than sublime logical forms.

Nine

IN SEARCH OF LESS "DANGEROUS PHRASES"

1. New Metaphors for Old Insights

Although he stopped distinguishing between Jews and other human beings in his remarks on the spiritual underpinnings of culture, Ludwig Wittgenstein kept returning to the idea he had been trying to express by it, diffused now of both its prior hidden metaphysical presuppositions and its anti-Semitic ways of expression: namely, that a distinction can (and should) be made between two spiritually different kinds of creative efforts discernable in the cultural affairs of the West. The need to express this idea continued to haunt him, as he tried time and again to clarify it through new similes, metaphors, and symbols.

In 1939, while trying to evaluate his own creative powers, Wittgenstein utilizes the images of seed and soil. "My originality (if that is the right word) is, I believe, an originality that belongs to the soil, not the seed. . . . Sow a seed in my soil, & it will grow differently than it would in any other soil."[1] Ten years later, he adds, "there are remarks that sow and remarks that reap."[2] At other times, he again attempts to distinguish between these two kinds of artistic effort by using the concepts of genius, talent, character, and intellect. "Genius," he writes, "is talent in which character makes itself heard."[3] It is manifested through "strong character." A strong character is demonstrated by the "courage" that the artist exhibits: presumably his willingness to express in his artistic efforts his singular human nature, and to do so in his own authentic way, without covering it up with intellectual frivolity and without relying on well established ways of expression. He once again distinguishes between those who have good taste and cultural manners and those who have true creative power. "The faculty of 'taste' cannot create a new organism,"[4] he writes. Taste can only make adjustments in structures that already exist:

> Taste loosens screws & tightens screws, it doesn't create a new original work. Taste rectifies, it doesn't give birth . . . (Hence, I think, a great creator needs no taste: the child is born into the world well formed.) . . . The *most refined* taste has *nothing* to do with creative power.[5]

About himself: "I *cannot* judge whether I have only taste, or originality as well. The former I can see distinctly, but not the latter, or only quite indistinctly";[6] and another image: "Within all great art there is a WILD animal: tamed."[7] Once again, Felix Mendelssohn's name comes up:

> Not, e.g., in Mendelssohn. All great art has primitive human drives as its ground bass. They are not the *melody* (as they are, perhaps, in Wagner), but they are what gives the melody *depth* & *power*. In *this* sense one may call Mendelssohn a '*reproductive*' artist.[8]

Another example of this reproduction is Wittgenstein's work in architecture. The house he built for his sister is said to be:

> the product of a decidedly sensitive ear, *good* manners, the expression of great *understanding* . . . . But *primordial* life, wild life striving to erupt into the open—is lacking. And so you might say, *health* is lacking (Kierkegaard). (Hothouse plant).[9]

As may be noted, the distinction that Wittgenstein formerly drew between two different spiritual forces discernable in Western culture, Jewish and non-Jewish, has not been rejected, but merely transformed into several contrasting distinctions regarding two different kinds of creative efforts in the arts, which are expressed in several similes and metaphors. On one side, then, are similes and metaphors for creative effort that manifests character, originality, potency, wildness, and primacy. On the other side are similes and metaphors for creative effort that manifests understanding, taste, refinement, good manners, sophistication, reproduction and tameness.

2. Philosophy as Poetry

At this point, a long deferred question intrudes: Why all these similes and metaphors? (Of course, this question concerns not only Wittgenstein's remarks discussed here, but most of his writings.) The answer has to do with Wittgenstein's anti-metaphysical viewpoint and poetic aspirations in philosophy. From this viewpoint, it is impossible to explain the deep spiritual meaning of things to us by means of philosophy. Initially, worldviews and ethical ideas are supposed to provide a metaphysical foundation for both representing and grasping life from some such spiritually meaningful, value-laden viewpoint. However, Wittgenstein sees such explanations as ways of bewitching us by intellectual magic:

> Compare the solution of philosophical problems with the fairy tale gift that seems magical in the enchanted castle and if it is looked at in daylight is nothing but an ordinary bit of iron (or something of the sort).[10]

Immanuel Kant argued that such views and ideas, which hold that God created the world for humanity or that there is an afterlife, are useful for regulating our lives despite our inability to justify them as providing genuine items of knowledge. In Wittgenstein's response to this solution, such ideas may express the way in which we both experience and give spiritual meaning to our lives, despite not being able to explain them in a conceptually meaningful way. When we try to do so, they become meaningless metaphysical intellectual expressions of our personal attitudes toward life. Although he claimed that they are what is important, nonetheless, in philosophy, we must pass over them in silence. We must suffice with expressing them in our ways of living rather than in ideological and philosophical claims.[11]

A corollary to this view, which Wittgenstein derives from the Viennese cultural critic Karl Kraus, is that art and religious rituals are more successful in this matter than philosophy. That is because the profound spiritual aspects of human life are expressible in art and religious ritual, but not explainable in philosophy by means of a formulated metaphysical theory or worldview. Thus, a work of art is an expression that shows something that cannot be meaningfully asserted and explained by means of metaphysics: the manner in which an artist perceives the world and experiences it as spiritually meaningful. It manifests the artist's attitude toward life by expressing the way in which life and what it encompasses is experienced in a personally meaningful way.

A second philosophical corollary to this view is that philosophy can partake in such an effort by providing insightful similes and metaphors in which how we experience things in a meaningful way is shown rather than explained. Thus, it is a philosophical stance that manifests a preference for using a striking artistic creation to gain philosophical insight over the use of an intellectual explanation. It expresses a preference for insights that derive from potent artistic creations, which demonstrate "courage" and are original, authentic, and primary, over sophisticated, intellectual, theoretical explanations. For metaphors and similes are basic, primary, singular, authentic, poetic modes of expression, conveying a powerful, immediate, and rich insight into a given matter.

As such, metaphors and similes created in the course of drawing an insightful philosophical distinction enable us to achieve two things at once. They can provide us with an authentic expression of our human experience, and they can afford striking artistic insight into the matter at hand. It is these poetic measures, and not abstract formulations, that enable us to create a real "human being" rather than an "intellectual skeleton" when pursuing philosophical ideas. Note, however, that inventing metaphors and similes to embody an idea is an aesthetic form of (philosophical) expression characteristic of what Wittgenstein had previously described as a non-Jewish mind and spirit. It is an attempt to express a thought from a spiritual disposition similar to that which he takes to be at the foundation of culture. It demonstrates originality and shows real "character." In contradistinction, abstract philosophical formulations and explanations express an intellectual spiritual disposition, one which Wittgenstein had previously identified with a Jewish mentality. Thus, this philosophical stance can now also be seen to express Wittgenstein's former metaphysical yearnings to create through what he had described then as a "non-Jewish spirit."

Having come this far, we can now note some resemblances and differences between these new similes and metaphors and his previous use of the stereotypical concept of the Jew. The first thing that emerges is the great similarity to what he had written previously. In the same way as before, these similes and metaphors are meant to distinguish between two kinds of artistic endeavors through which the human spirit finds expression in culture. This distinction, however, is now made twice, each time by presenting pairs of opposing images and concepts. The first distinction differentiates between works of genius as opposed to works of talent, original works as opposed to reproductive works, works that express courage as opposed to works that merely express good manners and show good taste. The second distinction differentiates between works of culture that spring from an intense spiritual force, works that are imbued with a primordial human element as opposed to domesticated works, which are formulated through the intellect and express cleverness and sophistication.

These two distinctions are reducible to two similes that Wittgenstein now propounds. The first can be reduced to the simile of the artist who is like a seed which propagates of itself, as opposed to the artist who is like a seed that grows in the soil. The second distinction can be reduced to the simile about a spiritual force that resembles a wild animal merely tamed as opposed to a spiritual force that resembles a domesticated animal, or the simile of the wild plant as opposed to the hothouse plant. (These new similes are mostly an extension of similes previously used by Oswald Spengler. Wittgenstein simply divides each of Spengler's similes into two cases.)

It seems, then, that the conceptual spiritual distinction Wittgenstein had previously made by contrasting Jews with the rest of humanity has been transformed into a set of aesthetic distinctions, which are drawn by means of several different images and symbols. The concept of the Jew as a spiritual force that adapts to any culture and makes use of its achievements is replaced by the simile of a seed that grows out of the soil. The concept of the non-Jew as a spiritual force endowed with originality is replaced by the simile of a seed that propagates of itself. The concept of the Jew as a spiritual force that functions through intellect and displays cleverness and sophistication is now replaced by the similes of the domesticated animal and the hothouse plant. The concept of the non-Jew as someone who demonstrates spiritual courage and strong character is expressed by the similes of the wild animal and the wild plant. Nevertheless, it seems that none of these new similes—not the seed that propagates of itself as opposed to the seed that grows out of the soil, nor the wild animal as opposed to the domesticated animal, nor the hothouse plant as opposed to the wild plant—can successfully encompass the entire matter. They are good similes that refresh the intellect. However, they do not give us the broad perspective of the matter that is possible with the use of the stereotyped concept of an artist of a Jewish mind as opposed to an artist of a non-Jewish mind, given the rich stereotypical images associated with these concepts once they become cultural symbols. None of the new similes conveys as rich a load of cultural associations as those accompanying the previous stereotyped concepts. None of them therefore clarifies or demonstrates the spiritual distinction he is trying to draw with the same philosophical and aesthetic clarity. However, in the context of the political and social situation in Europe, any attempt to continue using the former stereotyped concept of the Jew was like trying to tell a Jewish joke before an anti-Semitic audience. And so Wittgenstein stopped using that concept.

But suppose things had been different. Suppose the use of the stereotyped concept of the Jew had not been accompanied by the hostile anti-Semitic attitude and violent social background, which (rightfully) required that it be dropped. Suppose also that we had at our disposal a shared cultural image of the Jews' way of life in Europe over centuries as a people who make their living in the homelands of others, residing in what for them is always an exile: an image of Jews as people who trade in what others produce and who live in a complicated and sophisticated way; an image of Jews as a people who regularly transforms the loftiest metaphysical ideals into everyday practices, cultural sensibilities, personal and social commitments, communal attachments, and banal reminders; an image of Jews as a clever and industrious people who, in the Modern Age, upon leaving the ghettoes, have turned to operating within Western culture in Europe as they previously operated within Europe's economy (and even earlier in their own religious thought, by rendering God's awe-inspiring Biblical pronouncements into a Talmudic, reason-based, intellectual, argumentative, interpretive discourse), employing their intellectual talents to partake of a culture that others have created, becoming, in the process, outstanding figures in various fields of this culture, in music, languages, journalism, theatre, literature, painting, architecture, science, and philosophy. We would then have, on the one hand, an incisive picture of the Jews' spiritual path through Western culture, particularly in the Modern Age, and, on the other, a striking simile for a cultural force of life that expresses a sophisticated, intellectual, socially oriented spiritual disposition, characteristic of that which underlies Western civilization in the Modern Age. It would be a simile by means of which an insightful distinction could be made between two different ways of engaging Western culture, and perhaps also any culture that attains maturity.

Such a simile could have clarified in a symbolic and stereotypical manner two different spiritual dispositions and attitudes shaping the cultural affairs of human beings in the modern period. Such a simile might have refreshed the intellect and provided greater understanding of the cultural nature of human beings, by pointing to two telling different ways in which the human spirit is embodied in human cultures.

But, of course, events did not turn out that way. The hostility toward Jews in Europe prevailed, turning any such description of the Jews' involvement in social and cultural affairs into "dangerous phrases." It eventually submerged even the stereotyped concept of the Jew in Jewish blood, rendering it unfit for philosophy.

Second Study

THE SPIRITS OF CULTURE AND CIVILIZATION

Alongside his remarks on language, mind, and mathematics, Wittgenstein wrote several scattered remarks on art and culture. He also discussed various manifestations of these concepts in conversations and in his lectures. In what follows, I first disclose and then discuss a pivotal theme regarding the different spiritual natures of that to which he refers as "culture" and "civilization" that runs through many of them. Finally, I reflect on the standing of this theme, both as a metaphysical distinction and as a personal spiritual expression, formulated as a conceptual clarification.

One

ANNOUNCING "THE DISAPPEARANCE OF A CULTURE"

In 1930, in a draft of a foreword to a book now published as *Philosophical Remarks*, Wittgenstein declared his spiritual allegiance and set forth his cultural standpoint:

> This book is written for those who are in sympathy with the spirit in which it is written. This spirit is, I believe, different from that of the prevailing European and American civilization. The spirit of <u>this civilization</u> the expression of which is the industry, architecture, music, of present day fascism & socialism, is <u>a spirit that is alien & uncongenial</u> to the author. This is not a value judgment. It is not as though I did not know that what today represents itself as architecture is not architecture & not as though he did not approach what is called modern music with the greatest mistrust (without understanding its language), but the disappearance of the arts does not justify a disparaging judgment on a whole segment of humanity. For in these times genuine & strong characters simply turn away from the field of the arts & towards other things & <u>somehow</u> the value of the individual finds expression. Not, to be sure, in the way it would at a time of Great Culture. Culture is like a great organization which assigns to each of its members his place, at which he can work in the spirit of the whole, and his strength can with a certain justice be measured by his success as understood within that whole. In a time without culture, however, forces are fragmented and the strength of the individual is wasted through the overcoming of opposing forces & frictional resistances; it is not manifest in the distance travelled but rather perhaps in the heat generated through the overcoming of frictional resistances. But energy is still energy & even if the spectacle afforded by this age is not the coming into being of a great work of culture in which the best contribute to the same great end, so much as the unimposing spectacle of a crowd whose best members pursue purely private ends, still we must not forget that the spectacle is not what matters.
>
> Even if it is clear to me then that the disappearance of a culture does not signify the disappearance of human value but simply of certain means of expressing this value, still the fact remains that I contemplate the current of European civilization without sympathy, without understanding its aims if any. So I am really writing for friends who are scattered throughout the corners of the globe.[1]

These dark and gloomy pronouncements of Wittgenstein are cryptic and yet strangely moving. They convey a feeling of deep personal distress over a profound spiritual loss ("the disappearance of a culture"), intertwined with a powerfully expressed disdain for what has replaced it ("the spectacle afforded by this age"), the reason for and precise nature of which are not clearly explained. The uninformed reader may, therefore, be somewhat baffled as to *what* exactly Wittgenstein is bemoaning and disdaining about culture and European civilization here—let alone *why* he is doing so. This difficulty in understanding is no accident. The ideas conveyed through these gloomy pronouncements are, to an extent, coded. The reason Wittgenstein himself gives for thus concealing them is that since the "book has been written for only a few readers . . . [it] must automatically separate those who understand it & those who do not." Hence, "the foreword too is written just for such as understand the book," that is, those who are "in sympathy with its spirit." All others are to be kept out. As he elaborates: "If you do not want certain people to get into a room, put a lock on it for which they do not have the key."[2] But how do you devise a lock for a book that will allow only some readers to open it? How can you restrict its readership without any glaring preconceived prejudice? Wittgenstein's solution is ingenious: "The decent thing to do is: put a lock on the doors that attracts only those who are able to open it & is not noticed by the rest."[3]

A foreword to a book is a door to a room. The draft of the foreword quoted above is a door devised by Wittgenstein, with a concealed lock that can be seen only by those who possess a key to open it. In what follows, I first identify this lock and then both provide a key that will fit it and comment on the difficulty of using it.[4]

Two

A LOCK CONSTRUCTED FROM A CONCEALED SPIRITUAL DISTINCTION

1. The Intellectual Backdrop

Expounding his views on the nature of culture, the Viennese cultural critic and writer, Karl Kraus, once offered a ribald illustration. He remarked that he and his Viennese compatriot, the architect Adolf Loos, despite their different pursuits, were engaged in the same endeavor. Both of them, Loos practically and he "grammatically," had done nothing more than show that there is a distinction between an urn and a chamber pot and that it is this distinction, above all others, that provides culture with elbow room. The others, those who fail to make this distinction, are divided into those who use the urn as a chamber pot and those who use the chamber pot as an urn.[1]

Wit and sarcasm aside, Kraus was attempting to provide insight into the essence of culture as an expressive spiritual enterprise, by contrasting a ceremonial cultural artifact with a practical utensil belonging to the amenities of civilization. The aim of the contrast is to illustrate what in philosophical discourse we are apt to classify as "a metaphysical difference" in two kinds of activities pursued by human beings, which is exemplified in this case by the use of certain manufactured utensils. It is described by Kraus as a "grammatical" distinction that is embodied in the concepts of culture and civilization. In drawing it, Kraus was expressing a philosophical desire to discriminate clearly between two central features of human life, manifested respectively as the spiritual and the material, the aesthetic and the functional, the ceremonial and the practical, or the ethical and the instrumental. The aim of this endeavor on his part was twofold. First, to demonstrate that an important difference emerges between practices and objects in human life that have religious, artistic, emotional or ethical value and purpose, and practices and objects, the value and purpose of which lies in their being useful and helpful in some practical or instrumental sense. Second, to castigate cultural trends and innovations that blur this important difference.

The oblique manner in which the distinction between culture and civilization is illustrated through an insightful and humorous aphoristic example, as well as the way in which it is described as a "grammatical" rather than a "metaphysical" difference, both demonstrate Kraus's injunction that the profound spiritual meaning of various aspects of human life can be expressed in art and religious ritual, but not explained through philosophy by means of a formulated metaphysical theory. Thus, a work of art—which demonstrates how an artist experiences the world and interprets it in a personally meaningful way—is an expression of something that cannot be meaningfully asserted and explained by means of metaphysics. It manifests the artist's spiritual attitude toward life and what it encloses. Hence, the grammatical distinction between objects and practices to which Kraus refers as "culture" and those that he refers to as "civilization" is not abstract. It is not formulated through some philosophical explanation of a metaphysical difference between the spiritual features of life that embody culture and the instrumental features of life that embody civilization. Instead, it is *shown* by means of a striking example that provides what later, in the context of his remarks on the meaning of words, Ludwig Wittgenstein calls "a perspicuous representation" of the "grammar" of our language.[2]

In this way, by providing immediate philosophical insight, the illustration of the contrast is rendered into both a philosophical and an artistic achievement. It demonstrates a metaphysical difference between spiritual practices that provide for culture and instrumental practices that provide for civilization. This difference is perceived at once, without its having been explicitly stated.

The philosophical advantage of this aphoristic method of demonstrating the distinction between the concepts of culture and civilization is obvious. For, of course, once we try to state the distinction in an explicit way, we are forced to explain and support it. It may then become apparent that instrumental practices and objects are often conjoined to aesthetic ones, as may be seen in styles of building houses, making furniture, fashioning clothes, etc.—all this despite Kraus's doctrinaire efforts to separate the artistic from the instrumental, due to concealed metaphysical assumptions about the spiritual essence of cultural practices.

Oswald Spengler distinguished between culture and civilization in a different way.[3] His distinction was drawn within a metahistorical discourse, where it played a central role in what turned out to be a very ambitious attempt to formulate a new historical overview (or grand theory) of human life. This view emerges by comparing different historical periods in that to which he referred as "the great cultures" that human beings have created. In Spengler's view, a great culture is the spiritual orientation of an historical group of people which achieves a unitary conception of its world, oriented on a distinctive conception of the physical space in which the people live and act. This orientation informs all their activities: in art, religion, philosophy, science, politics, economics, and ways of waging war. The conceptual scheme put forward by Spengler purported to provide a grand historical overview, regarding different periods of spiritual development through which such great cultures inevitably pass. He claimed that, like the seasons of the year, they divide into four consecutive periods. Of these, the first three are different subperiods of culture, the last one a period of civilization.

Periods of culture, according to the view expounded by Spengler, are a spiritual stage distinguished by creative, artistic, religious, and scientific endeavors that arise in a dynamic, spontaneous, and very forceful fashion. The spiritual forces that operate at this stage of development in the history of a community, he claimed, are very basic and powerful, close in nature to those manifested in actions. Contrariwise, civilization is a stage of maturity. Spengler claimed that when an historical community eventually passes into such maturity, its culture has begun to stagnate. Civilization is a period of spiritual decline; a period characterized by the absence of new, powerful, creative spiritual innovations. In civilization, the early achievements of a culture are reworked and elaborated upon in a more sophisticated manner. The spiritual forces manifested in civilization are more technical and intellectual.

Culture, Spengler suggested, is soul. Civilization is intellect. Thus, the Greek world, according to Spengler, provides an example of a culture, the Roman world an example of that culture having turned into a civilization. In the context of his historical overview, Spengler noted that, in the modern period, the West is now in its last spiritual stage of evolvement. As such, it has been transformed from a viable and innovative culture that provides for powerful and original creations into a declining and feeble civilization that can only reprocess its received inheritance through intellectual efforts.[4]

2. Wittgenstein's Reflections on the Culture Civilization Distinction

I have begun this discussion of Wittgenstein's views on the spiritual nature of practices and innovations that embody what he calls "culture" in contrast to those that embody what he calls "civilization" by referring to views put forward by Spengler and Kraus. I do so because they provide an intellectual backdrop for many of his reflections on these issues. Although he notes their influence on his thinking, this fact is sometimes glossed over, or not sufficiently stressed when discussing his work.[5] One reason may be that Wittgenstein does not often acknowledge the philosophical sources of influence on his thinking. Another reason is that he has a unique way of transforming and deepening these sources in what he describes as his "work of clarification."[6] One way in which he often pursues this work is by creating what he calls a "perspicuous representation" of the grammar that underlies our use of words. In it, he aims at bringing philosophical insight to what is puzzling us about their meaning by means of edifying examples. Accordingly, it may be said that his remarks on the different spiritual manifestations of culture and civilization are aimed at clarifying the distinction, by both describing and contrasting various expressive examples of it.

Still another reason, perhaps even more telling, is an inclination on the part of many readers to divorce Wittgenstein's remarks on art, religion, and ways of living from those about language, mind, and mathematics. They tend to be judged as a curious, somewhat unfortunate, but ultimately unimportant supplement to his discourse on language, mind, and mathematics. The extent to which he himself saw them as conjoined may be inferred from the fact that the remarks on which I am focusing here precede a book that is on the fundamentals of language and mind.

Of course, Wittgenstein's clarification of the different spiritual manifestations of culture and civilization begins by setting up these concepts in contrast to one another. In doing so, he uses these concepts as insightful symbols to mark what he categorizes as two spiritually different kinds of creative effort, which underlie arts and ways of living in the West in the modern period. For unlike such paired concepts as true and false, night and day, or left and right, culture and civilization are not contrasting concepts wedded to each other from their linguistic birth and used as such. The word "civilization" is derived from its Latin use, which refers to a social condition of the citizen (*civis*). In Roman times, it was used to distinguish their own way of life, which was contrasted to what they regarded as barbarian ways of life. In present usage, the term often refers to societies that have developed technical, political, and urban modes of living. As an adjective or adverb, it is used to describe refined, courteous behavior, referring to it as "civil" behavior.

The word "culture" is also derived from its Latin use (*cultura*), which refers to the practice of cultivating land. In that context, it was used to differentiate between cultivated and uncultivated plots of land—the latter being described as natural (*natura*). Used in social, intellectual, and artistic contexts, it was initially a metaphor referring to the cultivation of human sensibilities and abilities. According to Raymond Williams' account, this modern use of the term "culture" developed predominately from the late eighteenth through the late nineteenth centuries.

Broadly, the concept was developed in four ways, all of which still affect its meaning. First, culture came to mean "a general state or habit of the mind," with close relations to the idea of human perfection. Second, "a general state of intellectual and moral development in a society as a whole." Third, "the general body of the arts and intellectual work." Fourth, "the whole way of life, material, intellectual, and spiritual, of a given society."[7]

Reflections on culture as an expressive spiritual endeavor came to preoccupy writers, predominantly those inclined toward Romanticism. Eventually, it also motivated some to contrast this spiritual conception of culture with the technical, political and social achievements of civilization, by way of distinguishing the spiritual aspects of a cultural endeavor. Wittgenstein clarifies this particular way of instantiating the distinction between culture and civilization by remarking on the difference between the concepts of building and architecture: "Architecture is a gesture. Not every purposive movement of the human body is a gesture. Just as little as every functional building is architecture."[8] Wittgenstein takes this "grammatical" insight all the way to its origins. He thus echoes Kraus's criticism of the spiritual confusion of the age and its conflation of the expressive values of culture with the amenities of civilization and heeds his injunction that the profound and inspiring spiritual aspects of life can be experienced and expressed in art and religious ritual, but not explained by philosophy. He contrasts the effect of dismal modern city surroundings on our spirit with an experience that disposes us to seek a lofty religious expression of something that transcends our existence:

> It is very *remarkable*, that we should be inclined to think of civilization—houses, streets, cars, etc—as separating man from his origin, from the lofty, eternal, etc. Our civilized environment, even its trees & plants, seems to us then cheap, wrapped in cellophane, & isolated from everything great & from God as it were. It is a remarkable picture that forces itself on us here.[9]

As may be noted, this remark was written sixteen years after the previously quoted draft of a foreword to *Philosophical Remarks*. In my reading of this remark, Wittgenstein is attempting here to clarify the distinction between culture and civilization by exhibiting what he experiences as the desultory and spiritless character of human life in Western civilization in his time. He does so by focusing on an ordinary modern city environment. He notes how its bland, mundane, and artificial instrumental surroundings completely fail to produce in us the kind of inspired experience that in the past inclined human beings to express themselves in a grand and lofty cultural manner, by reaching out to something eternal. To pursue this insight, we might compare the mundane experience afforded us by an ordinary modern city environment with the stirring experience of some ordinary natural phenomenon, such as the stars shining in the sky, clouds gathering before a storm, a silent and barren desert, or the renewal of spring after winter. We might also compare it with the deeply meaningful way in which we experience ordinary natural events that touch us personally, such as the birth of a new child in the family or the suffering and death of someone dear to us. The way we tend to experience such natural events evokes in us attitudes of awe, wonder, and mystification at life, often prompting us to reach out to something lofty and eternal.

In the context of these comparisons, the physical amenities that go into making our mundane civilized world can be experienced as completely devoid of anything deeply meaningful that beckons us toward something lofty and eternal. For Wittgenstein, they are perceived as actually hindering us from experiencing anything deeply meaningful that could inspire us in such a way. In his experience of a mundane city environment, even trees and plants appear tame and domesticated, whereas in a natural setting they incline us to see their growth and blossoming as "the miracles of nature," motivating us to refer to nature as "Creation" and to wonder about its "Creator." It is his insight that in civilization, a similar fate befalls trees and plants and human beings. They too are tamed by it, becoming in the process contrived and artificial human beings, who no longer seek to express anything lofty and eternal in their artistic expressions.

Wittgenstein draws this insight from the impact of a modern city environment on his consciousness. The philosophical slogans of modernity, such as Humanism, Enlightenment, and Historical Progress, are only intellectual expressions of our modern, superficial, instrumental, civilized, contrived, ways of living and habitats that alienate us from everything lofty and eternal, "from God as it were." Thus, he sees in the very physical manifestations of our modern cities, an embodied philosophical "picture that forces itself on us," a picture of artificial and desultory life that renders us susceptible to modern worldviews and the shallow spiritual attitudes toward life that grow out of them. In its very physical incarnation, civilization estranges us from anything spiritually lofty and eternal that transcends our individual human lives, as was once experienced and expressed in religion and art in an age of true culture.

So it is not merely the contrast between instrumental amenities, on the one hand, and artistic and ceremonial objects, on the other, which provides for a spiritual difference in the kinds of pursuits that underlie culture and civilization. At the present time, even when human beings engage in cultivated artistic endeavors, they do so from a different spirit than that which sustained their efforts in a time of true culture. For Wittgenstein, civilization has won the day (which means that Spengler was right). The age of culture is over. The spirit of modern human beings (that "informs the vast stream of European and American civilization in which all of us stand") is that of civilized human beings. It is at once contrived and sophisticated, lacking in depth and lofty inspiration, removed from both nature and God. It is a spirit that is all intellect and no soul.

With the above insight as a backdrop, Wittgenstein contrasts the spirit in which his book is written with that which belongs to "the main current of European and American *civilization*" (emphasis added). He suggests also that "the book in my opinion has nothing to do with the *progressive civilization* of Europe and America."[10] It is in the emerging hegemony of this latter spirit (of civilization) over human life that he perceives "the disappearance of a culture." Against the background of these reflections, he then formulates the final version of the foreword to his book, describing in it once again what he experiences as a spiritual difference between human life as it emerges and is given expression, in a period of culture versus a period of civilization. In clarifying this difference, he suggests that the spirit of civilization "expresses itself in an onward movement, in building ever larger and more complicated structures." By contrast, the spirit of culture expresses itself "in striving after clarity and perspicuity in no matter what structure. The first tries to grasp the world by way of its periphery—in its variety; the second at its center—in its essence. And so, the first adds one construction to another, moving on and up, as it were, from one stage to the next, while the other remains where it is and what it tries to grasp is always the same."[11]

In my reading of these remarks, an authentic creative effort in a period of culture is one that seeks to "clarify," as Wittgenstein describes his own philosophical endeavors, the central conception (or idea) of life that embodies the spirit of the culture in which it is made. That is in contrast to a creative effort in an age of civilization, which endeavors to express the spirit of its creator only, and to do so in a contrived and sophisticated way that squanders this central conception (or idea) of spiritual life on peripheral matters.

Experiencing the spirit of the time in which he lives as one of civilization, not culture, Wittgenstein declares that he does not want to ally his book with it. He wants the book to be associated with the spiritual attitude and effort that once provided for culture and had enabled cultured human beings to experience and express something lofty and eternal in their lives and creative work. "I would like to say," he declares, "'this book is written to the glory of God,' but nowadays that would be chicanery, that is, it would not be rightly understood."[12] Such declarations had been made in the past by artists working within a cultural tradition that strove to supplement a religious tradition of worship by expressing the human spirit in a grand and lofty manner through the arts.

Cultured people who appreciated such works of art expressed their experience of them in similar terms, asserting that they were "divine." As emerges from Wittgenstein's desire to evoke this declaration, he would like to conjoin his book to such an expressive spiritual effort. However, in his perception of how human life is experienced and expressed in modern civilization, this lofty, creative, spiritual attitude, which, in the past, had inspired artistic expressions (and perhaps also works in mathematics and logic), no longer does so. A completely different spirit manifests creative efforts and their expressions in his times. The spirit that in the past inspired all sorts of expressions embodying a shared high and lofty spiritual attitude toward life and its meaning has disappeared. Thus, all that remains for him is to say instead that "the book is written in good will,"[13] manifesting his own spirit only.

The idea that there is an important spiritual difference (to be noted and clarified) between two kinds of artistic expression, technical innovation, social practice, and ordinary ways of life, namely those that manifest "culture" and those that manifest "civilization," underlies Wittgenstein's thinking about human ways of life. It is also the idea that human beings may be possessed by either of these two different kinds of spirits, depending on their engrained spiritual nature, the historical circumstances in which they are placed, and their upbringing. As may be also seen now from the draft of his book, he believed that, in the modern period, most human beings in the West were possessed by the spirit of civilization. Only a small, dispersed minority were still possessed by the spirit of culture.

3. Clarifications of a Spiritual Dichotomy

One of the difficulties in following Wittgenstein's remarks on culture and civilization as manifesting two different spiritual attitudes toward life and what it encloses is that he is wary of falling into metaphysical explanations. He aspires to follow Kraus' injunction about this matter against wanting "to make the *spirit explicit*"[14] when discoursing on the expressive and creative aspects of human life, as Hegel, for example, did. Instead, he seeks to *clarify* the spiritual meaning of various human practices, activities and attitudes toward life, which he does by describing in an insightful way how he experiences their expressive meaning.

As in the draft of the foreword to his book, Wittgenstein's remarks on spirit commence by drawing on our shared expressive, nonphilosophical uses of the concept. In this framework, we speak of spirit in a number of circumstances and with a number of meanings. We speak of spirit in connection with a vital force or principle that animates people and is behind their activities and efforts, such as will, attitude, inclination, feeling, mood, or emotional state. We say that a person is in high or low, good or bad spirits and ascribe this state also to sports teams and nations. We speak of spirit in connection with the real sense or significance of some endeavor, as well as with what is the essential aspect of a given effort or practice. We say that free elections embody the spirit of democracy and war, the spirit of human aggression and violence. We speak of spirit in connection with the ethical nature or value of various ways of pursuing life, such as the spirit of a given religious holiday or the spirit in which a game is played.

It is within such ordinary contexts of using the concept of spirit that I have described above that Wittgenstein seeks to clarify the spirit of various expressive and creative achievements in the West in the modern period and the attitudes toward life and its meaning that they embody. In doing so, he is seeking to clarify what he grasps as the two essentially different kinds of spiritual endeavors in the West, "culture" and "civilization." As may be seen, this attempt permeates many of his remarks (particularly those offered in *Culture and Value*, "Remarks on Frazer's Golden Bough," and *Lectures and Conversations on Aesthetics*), providing a focal point on which many of them can be seen to turn.[15]

In my reading of Wittgenstein's remarks in these matters, the spiritual difference between culture and civilization emerges from the different shared attitudes toward life and its meaning, attitudes that are expressed through various human practices and innovations. Shared attitudes toward life are not a set of collective opinions that are entertained about life through some formulated worldview. They are expressed in how we approach and engage our lives, manifesting how we experience what is valuable and meaningful to us therein—both what deeply concerns us about our life and the way in which our deep concerns are experienced. Such attitudes toward life are the spirit in which we approach our lives and engage in various activities. When these attitudes are shared with others, we speak of pursuing life in the same spirit. For example, we might compare the different spirit in which a game of football may be played by different players, such as to beat the other team and win, to earn a living, to have fun, or for the sake of health. Given these different attitudes toward the game, we might say that although the game is played by following the same rules, it has a different meaning to the players in each of these cases and is invested by them with a different value. We might also say that they approach games with different attitudes toward sport and, therefore, that they play them in a different spirit. Thus the concepts of spirit, attitude, value and meaning are often joined together in a common linguistic endeavor, the aim of which is to draw our attention to important differences that may obtain between ways of engaging life through the same practices.

From an historical perspective, the suggestive idea that human practices and innovations that provide for culture and those that provide for civilization manifest different spiritual attitudes toward life and what it encloses aligns Wittgenstein's philosophical thinking on these matters with the Romantic Movement and conservative ideologies. Both scorned the idea of "historical progress," supposedly achieved in modernity. At the same time, it also bears his unique philosophical stamp manifested through his clarifications of the spirits of culture and civilization.

In my reading of the draft of his foreword, the special hidden lock Wittgenstein has put on the door to his book lies in the cryptic formulation of the idea that there is an important spiritual difference between culture and civilization. But, at the same time, it is also an idea that, in its exposition and elucidation, provides a key to this lock—and perhaps to most of his other work as well. What remains to be examined is just how this key needs to be turned to open the lock to his thinking on these matters. One way of doing so, I believe, is to focus carefully on his scattered remarks regarding the different spiritual manifestations of culture and civilization. In most of what follows, I undertake to do just that, finally dwelling on how they are conjoined to the main body of his work and why, nevertheless, it may be difficult for us to make personal use of them.

Three

CULTURE AND ITS SPIRITUAL MANIFESTATIONS

1. Culture as Observance and Creation

A key concept used by Ludwig Wittgenstein to clarify the concept of culture is *observance.* "Culture," he remarks, "is an observance. Or at least it presupposes an observance."[1] "Observance of what?" is the question that immediately comes to mind. Well, to begin with, why not observance of *anything?* For in one use of the concept, culture consists in the observance of ways of behavior regarding just about anything: observance of ways of dressing, building shelter, farming, cooking, calculating, dining, worshipping, celebrating, dancing, painting, playing music, and so on. In short, all the varied and multiple ways in which activities that go into the making of human cultures are practiced and observed.

At first sight, this way of filling out the notion of observance appears extremely uninformative. For if that is the case, what then in shared human practices and customs is *not* a cultural practice or custom? Now, in a way, this is quite to the point. For to say that culture is the observance of certain practices is to say that they are created, normative, ways of doing things, manifesting shared conceptions of right and wrong, good and bad, and so on. As such, the concept of observance highlights a very telling feature of the human effort that goes into a culture. For although cultured human beings may engage in private practices, the concept of cultural behavior emerges against the background of created and shared practices. By observing certain created practices, we both adopt and share them with others. Moreover, cultural practices need to be adopted and observed, because they are created and shared ways of behavior rather than natural ways of behavior. It is through their observance that created ways of behavior become shared cultural practices and customs. It is through acculturation to them that we are transformed into cultural beings.[2]

Nature can take care of itself. Culture requires the creation and observance of shared practices to emerge. In line with these conceptual insights, it may now be said that noncultural beings may have all sorts of *common* practices and ways of behavior. Cultural beings have created and shared practices and ways of life, which emerge from the effort they make into observing them. Indeed, all sorts of human practices, customs, and ways of life may emerge within different human cultures, based on the same human nature, due to the efforts of creation and observance. As such, the spiritual nature of human beings, which is manifested in created and observed shared practices and customs that constitute a culture, is a cultural nature.

To note that cultural practices are the product of observance is not to say that whenever we engage in cultural behavior we are making a conscious effort to observe some cultural practice. Having adopted and mastered the use of a given cultural practice, no special effort would then be required to observe it, as it has become what Wittgenstein calls a "form of life" for us. Nonetheless, we can still note how a culture is based on observance of its practices. We might remind ourselves of how our ability to communicate in a given language, dress, use a fork, drive a car, or dine testifies to the success of our acculturation. We might remind ourselves of the effort we make to acculturate our children, by helping them master and cherish its various practices and ways of life. We might also contemplate the possibility of various practices becoming outdated and discarded, as new technologies and concepts are introduced, as social customs change, and as even the language that serves us is replaced by another.

On the conceptual insight that thus emerges, two seemingly different kinds of abilities on the part of human beings go into the making of cultural practices and customs. The first is an ability to adopt shared practices, observe customs, and follow rules. The second is an ability to create and invent new and original forms of behavior. The first enables human beings to partake of a given culture and, in the process, to acquire a particular shared cultural way of engaging the world and expressing human nature. The second enables human beings to do things on their own and, in the process, to lay down the foundation for new cultural ways of engaging the world and expressing human nature.

Observance of customs, adoption of shared practices, and following of rules are participatory forms of behavior that provide for spiritual bonds among human beings. They demonstrate an attempt to adhere to a common path, to comply, and conform. They also constitute forms of behavior that manifest an attitude of submission to authority. When successful, this both sustains and provides for tradition in a culture. The second ability that human beings bring to the making of a culture, namely creating new ways of behavior, allows them to do things on their own, to go all the way by themselves. By this means, they express a desire to blaze a trail rather than follow one. This kind of behavior may seem to other members of the cultured community as deviating from accepted norms and as breaking with cherished tradition. When successful, it contributes to the spiritual progression of a culture.

What unites these two different spiritual paths into one common enterprise is the cultural backdrop against which they emerge, for they are both dependent, and in the same way, on affiliation with a culture in order to become culturally significant. In the case of cultural observance, such significance is accomplished by joining in. In the case of cultural creation and invention, it is accomplished by attracting others. Whether one endows a human endeavor with cultural significance by becoming a follower or by acquiring a following, it is always dependent on the existence of and acceptance by a community of cultured human beings possessing similar dispositions, judgments, attitudes, and ways of behavior. By interacting with them in various ways—either by expressing their value and meaning to them through deeds, or by paying them such linguistic compliments as "meaningful," "true," "beautiful," "insightful," "moral," or "revolutionary"—they render them culturally significant to themselves.

Obviously, a culture cannot be sustained unless human beings are able to share certain practices, observe common customs, and agree in some of their judgments and attitudes toward various kinds of behavior and their consequences. However, a culture can neither arise, nor change and continue progressing, unless human beings also manage to forge innovations which, when adopted and followed by others, become culturally significant achievements. Thus, to ask what turns human beings into the cultural species that we are is to ask what makes possible both kinds of cultural endeavor—creation and invention, on the one hand, and observance and participation, on the other; and to ask that is to note that they are basic cultural forms of behavior expressive of our cultural nature.

2. Culture as Tradition

A complementary concept to observance, which Wittgenstein employs to highlight the spiritual features of culture, is that of tradition. An important part of culture consists in observing practices and customs that go back in time and connect us with other human beings who existed before us and observed them. Such traditional practices and customs may include ways of communicating in a given language, of working, of dressing, of preparing food and eating. They may include ordinary shared social gestures of greeting people, welcoming guests, giving presents on birthdays, celebrating the end of the school year, dining with family and friends, and the like. They may include rituals of celebrating the birth of new children, marriage, burial and mourning, ways of commemorating special historical dates, and of religious worship, prayer, and blessing. Such traditional shared rituals and customs are often accompanied by ancient stories that enrich and deepen their meaning for those who observe them. When we grow up on traditional practices and customs and integrate them into our cultural ways of life, they may be prized as ancient family heirlooms, which we also seek to pass on to our decedents.

Wittgenstein clarifies the way in which tradition requires acculturation to become personally meaningful for us in the following way: "Tradition is not something that anyone can pick up, it's not a thread, that someone can pick up, if & when he pleases; any more than you can choose your own ancestors."[3] Of course, people sometimes find a foreign cultural tradition appealing and adopt it. Yet the concept of such adoption or conversion already demonstrates the problem involved in trying to "pick up" some tradition. To convert is, first of all, to change. In the context of tradition, converting means to exchange one cultural inheritance for another. This entails replacing what has become meaningful to us in a given cultural tradition through time and upbringing with an alien tradition that we now seek to buy into. It is to want to change our cultural identity and nature by rational choice. For tradition is dependent on observance, and observance is a way of engaging in shared practices and customs instilled in us by shaping our attitudes, developing our skills, and cultivating our aesthetic sensibilities so as to conform to the cultural customs and practices, which provide for a given cultural tradition. Thus, when we observe a certain tradition, it is our very nature that has been molded to fit the culture of which we partake. Therefore, tradition is neither a feature of cultural life that may be picked up at random nor a feature of cultural life that may be invented, as is a new style of dress or some new mechanical device. It develops and matures over time, and requires acculturation on the part of human beings to find meaning in it.

In the Romantic tradition in which I am thus seeking to place Wittgenstein's thinking on culture, an attempt is made to provide an outlook on human life that allies culture with human nature, albeit without reducing cultural modes of existence to natural ones. The idea is to provide a conception of culture in which it is not viewed as an artificial or contrived mode of existence that is the product of intellect and reasoning. Wittgenstein manages this realignment of culture as a universal human mode of existence by rethinking the spirit of human beings. The idea is that the spirit of human beings, when not yet spoilt by intellect and reasoning, is a natural force of life. It promotes the creation and observance of shared human practices and customs, out of which a culture both arises and is sustained in a very organic and powerful fashion.

The philosophical setting for this idea is the Romantic conception of the human spirit—predominantly as articulated earlier by Oswald Spengler. In this line of thinking, there are two fundamentally different spiritual pathways along which human beings can live their lives: one contrived, sophisticated, and artificial, the other primitive, basic, and natural. The contrived way is guided by intellect and is a function of thought. It comes about by thinking things out according to devised rules or general principles for procuring certain rational goals. The more basic way results from adapting to certain shared traditional ways of doing things that are thus experienced as invested with spiritual meaning. This is accomplished through the acquisition of skills, habits, tendencies, inclinations, likes and dislikes, all of which enable us to observe a way of life, acquire an aesthetic taste, or develop a religious attitude by engaging in shared practices and customs that are deeply meaningful to us. A cultural tradition remains vital and operates as a strong spiritual force in our lives when our cultural sensibilities and skills play a major role in the observance of a way of life. Through the observance of customs and practices, then, the human spirit is expressed in a powerful and meaningful fashion, culminating in the acquisition of a lofty spiritual attitude toward life rather than some mundane opinion about it. In this way, a culture can now be seen as providing human beings with shared forms of life that, through acculturation into traditional practices and observance of cherished customs, manifest an inspired attitude toward life that is infused with a lofty spirit.

3. Culture as *Kultur*

Nothing said so far about the spiritual nature of culture and the beings who partake in it seems to give just cause for Wittgenstein's gloomy pronouncement regarding "the disappearance of a culture" or the advent of "a time without culture." Western civilization is still inhabited by people who, in their various communities and social interchanges, employ in their everyday affairs languages that are authentic cultural forms of life. People still observe various cultural ways of greeting friends, eating, dressing, working, and raising families. Holidays are still celebrated in many communities. Rituals that give spiritual expression to events that have important personal meaning for human beings, such as birth, marriage, and death are still observed. Arts and sports are still being pursued and cultivated with the same interest and intensity as before. Even God is still worshipped within the cultural traditions of various religious practices and customs.

Of course, there is nowadays a relaxing of standards in many of these practices and customs. There is also a discernible mixing of customs from various cultures in the exercise of all these activities. Still, it is not as though all the traditional cultural practices have been completely abandoned or that no past customs are now observed. Indeed, it is not clear how there could be a human society that is entirely devoid of tradition and which does not cultivate the observance of any cultural ways of behavior. Wittgenstein's announcement regarding "the disappearance of a culture" seems to have been either exaggerated or premature.

I think the thing to note here is that when Wittgenstein writes of a time without culture or the disappearance of a culture, he is bemoaning the disappearance of a particular way in which he feels that certain things were once cultivated, observed, and cherished. His despair is over the disappearance of *a* culture—not of every aspect of a cultural form of life. The culture that he takes to have disappeared is closely connected with what he also describes as "the disappearance of the arts." The initial difficulty here may be due to the fact that the term "culture" in English does not always convey the same meaning that *Kultur* does in German.

Kultur, I believe, is a concept much more closely related to the arts than is the English term "culture," with its anthropological reference to "human cultures." The culture to which Wittgenstein referred when speaking of "a time without culture," is akin to that which a "cultured person" is said to possess. A closely related expression—and one that Wittgenstein also uses to announce the disappearance of culture in his time—is that of "great culture." This expression was formerly used by Spengler to describe several historical cultures that provided a potent conception of life through its shared practices and customs. A slightly different expression, which Wittgenstein also uses in connection with *Kultur*, is "high culture."

The concept of a great or high culture has an expressive meaning, manifesting a value laden judgment. As a simple thesaurus notes, "great" is not merely big. It is synonymous with "distinguished, impressive, noble, lofty, imposing, grand, exalted, splendid, majestic, and wonderful." As such, the concept of a great and high culture is posited in contrast to a "low, coarse, vulgar, common, boorish, unrefined, awful, horrendous, horrible, depleted, degrading" culture. An example of the latter is the use of slang and profanities in speech as contrasted with refined, grammatical uses of language and expressions based on an esteemed literary tradition.

The concepts of high culture and great culture bring us somewhat closer to understanding what Wittgenstein means when he speaks of a time without culture or the disappearance of a culture, but only as long as we note that even the expression high culture is not used by him merely as a contrast to what is referred to as "low" or "popular culture." The concept of high culture, as Wittgenstein uses it, is not just, say, opera versus folksong, or the *New York Review of Books* as against the *Reader's Digest*. It is a concept of culture manifesting a powerful and serious effort directed at expressing the human spirit in what he describes as "a grand and lofty manner."

A high and great culture is distinguished both by the spiritual goal at which it aims and by the way in which this goal is pursued. As such, it may permeate many aspects of human life, not only religious and artistic practices. The Greeks, for example, thought that through the agony of competition and perseverance in sport tournaments, one not only attains perfection in sports but of spirit. One is thus able to experiences either victory or defeat, resulting from doing one's utmost, as the perfection of one's character and, therefore, as having ethical value. In this insight, a high and great culture may be manifested in many different practices that are created and observed in many different societies, in Wittgenstein's grand and lofty manner.

In his *Lectures and Conversations on Aesthetics*, Wittgenstein suggests an example of what he perceives as such high and great culture in the West:

> You can get a picture of what you may call a very high culture, e.g., German music in the last century and the century before, and what happens when this deteriorates. A picture of what happens in Architecture when you get imitations or when thousands of people are interested in the minutest details. A picture of what happens when a dining-room table is chosen more or less at random, when no one knows where it came from.[4]

The paradigm, then, of a culture that has disappeared is a cultivated artistic tradition that merged with a cultivated way of life to form a high and great culture. It presents an idealized picture of a community that devoted itself to expressing the human spirit in a grand and lofty manner, by carefully cultivating and developing its tradition of creation and observance in the arts and crafts, as well as in the various practical details of its ways of life. Presumably, in a culture such as this, human beings were still in touch with their spiritual origins. They were still capable of expressing themselves in a profound and inspiring way by reaching out for "what is lofty and eternal," even when engaging in everyday practices and ordinary ways of life. They were not "isolated from everything great and from God as it were." An idealized image of such spiritually inspired ordinary human ways of life seemed to him to be described in a few lines written by Henry Wadsworth Longfellow:

> In the elder days of art
> Builders wrought with greatest care
> Each minute and unseen part,
> For the gods are everywhere.[5]

Wittgenstein was so impressed by these lines that he considered using them as a motto for *Philosophical Investigations*.[6] Norman Malcolm recalls in this connection how, on Wittgenstein's visit to his home in Ithaca, New York, Wittgenstein criticized the way ordinary devices are produced in the United States:

> At Trinity College, Wittgenstein had taken me to look at one of the toilets in order to inspect its sturdy construction, and now he commented unfavorably on the construction of ours. He always had a keen appreciation of sound workmanship and a genuinely moral disapproval of the flimsy or the slipshod. He liked to think that there might be craftsmen who would insist on doing their jobs to perfection, and for no reason other than that that was the way it ought to be.[7]

In the insight that emerges from these remarks, a high and great culture manifests a committed spiritual effort to both observe a given tradition and create in the context of a given tradition. It is a shared human form of life in which, through the diligent and inspired observance of traditional practices and the creation of inspiring new ones on their basis, the activities of those who partake in it are infused with a grand and lofty spirit. We sometimes describe such an inspired and committed way of pursuing a cultural tradition by saying that it is pursued "religiously" or in a "religious manner." Indeed, in Wittgenstein's idealized description of the high and great culture of the West, it was an artistic tradition that manifested the same committed and lofty spiritual attitude toward life that had previously been expressed in religion. Like religion before it, it provided for the creation and observance of all sorts of spiritually inspiring practices in which people could share in many different ways, and through which they could express themselves in an inspired and lofty manner. In Wittgenstein's insight, the difficulty in describing what made the activities in the past able to provide for a great and high culture stems from the fact that they were a conglomeration of a myriad of practices, all of which, while interacting with one another, nonetheless manifested the same spirit of trying to do things in a grand and lofty manner. When that happened, a way of life and an artistic tradition emerged that supported each other, manifesting a spiritual attitude toward life embodying a great and high culture.

4. Describing a Great and High Culture

To get an inkling of what is involved in rendering certain human practices into the expression of such a high and great culture, consider what a culture needs to be composed of, so that choosing a dining room table, say, might manifest the spiritual attitude toward life that a high and great culture embodies.[8] To begin with, there first needs to evolve a distinction between dining and eating. For this, table manners have to evolve, and alongside them customs of dress for dining. Then there has to evolve a tradition of dining in one's home and not just outside it. This, in turn, requires a tradition of designing homes and constructing them in certain ways, all of which brings about a need for a tradition dictating how dining rooms are supposed to be constructed, decorated and furnished. And we have yet to speak of the dining room table itself: of the tradition that goes into designing dining room tables, the tradition of craftsmanship which goes into their making. We must then consider how all of this is created, refined, taught, acquired, observed, and cherished, by the makers and buyers of dining room tables who are engaged in cultivating the art of making and buying an appropriate dining room table.

What the above clarification of the concept of a high and great culture suggests is that, in describing the cultural sensibilities—judgments and skills—that manifest themselves in the tradition of a high and great culture, what needs to be described are insightful aspects of the various activities and practices in which these are embodied and of the committed effort that goes into observing them and creating from within them. It suggests, as Wittgenstein writes, "in describing musical taste you have to describe whether children give concerts, whether women do or whether men only give them, etc. In aristocratic circles in Vienna the people had [such and such] a taste, then it came into bourgeois circles and women joined choirs, etc. This is an example of tradition in music."[9]

The aim of this sort of description of the past cultural environment of music in Vienna is not simply to disclose the role of music in the history of Europe. Nor is it to offer a sociological explanation of how the refined artistic culture of the aristocracy came to be adopted by the middle class. It is to clarify the way in which cultured tastes and traditions are manifested and pursued in the arts within a great and high culture. It does so by focusing on a particular paradigmatic cultural environment that displays the kind of committed effort that goes into a high and great culture, as well as the way aesthetic taste and judgments are manifested in such a culture by its affiliates.

> In what we call "the Arts," a person who has judgment develops. (This does not mean a person who says "Marvelous!" at certain things.) If we talk of aesthetic judgments, we think, among a thousand things, of the Arts. When we make an aesthetic judgment about a thing, we do not just gape at it and say:
>
> "Oh! How marvelous!" We distinguish between a person who knows what he is talking about and a person who does not...of a person who does not know meters but who is overwhelmed, we would say he doesn't know what's in it. In music this is more pronounced. Suppose there is a person who admires and enjoys what is admitted to be good but can't remember the simplest tunes, doesn't know when the bass comes in, etc. We say he hasn't seen what's in it. We use the phrase "A man is musical" not so as to call a man musical if he says "Ah!" when a piece of music is played, any more than we call a dog musical if it wags its tail when music is played.[10]

Of course, taste, judgments, and appreciation of cultural works are not limited to the arts. They extend to ways of speaking, writing, dressing, designing, decorating, building, celebrating, and more:

> If a man goes through an endless number of patterns in a tailor's [and] says: "No. This is slightly too dark. This is slightly too loud," etc., he is what we call an appreciator of material. That he is an appreciator is not shown by the interjections he uses, but by the way he chooses, selects, etc. Similarly in music: "Does this harmonize? No. The bass is not quite loud enough. Here I just want something different . . ." This is what we call appreciation.[11]

Note that in Wittgenstein's description of how taste, judgment, and appreciation are manifested in the behavior of cultured human beings, nothing is explained about their essential constituents. The behavior which manifests cultured taste, appreciation, and judgment emerges within a specific context and against a particular cultural background. It is expressed in many different ways, depending on the cultural practice and background in which it emerges. The essential constituents of cultured taste, appreciation and judgment as such, or even of a particular instance of them, are left out of the description of their manifestations. Indeed, the point of these suggested examples of the application of cultured taste, appreciation and judgment is to remind us both how they are manifested in various instances and that this is all that is accessible to description.

On Wittgenstein's insight in this matter, "it is not only difficult to describe what cultured appreciation consists in, but impossible. To describe what it consists in we would have to describe a whole environment"[12]—an entire culture in which appreciation of a given practice is embedded and through which it is manifested in the judgments, taste, and understanding of its affiliates.

5. Cultured Appreciation as Based on Reasons, Not Causes

A conceptual point Wittgenstein seeks to clarify is that cultured taste or appreciation is a form of judgment that manifests cultured understanding. As such, it does not fall under the category of a mental state that directs us:

> There is a kind of general disease of thinking which always looks for (and finds) what would be called a mental state from which all our acts spring as from a reservoir. Thus one says, "The fashion changes because the taste of people changes." The taste is the mental reservoir. But if a tailor to-day designs a cut of dress different from that which he designed a year ago, can't what is called his change of taste have consisted, partly or wholly, in doing just this?
>
> And here we say "But surely designing a new shape isn't in itself changing one's taste,—and saying a word isn't meaning it,—and saying that I believe isn't believing; there must be feelings, mental acts, going along with these lines and these words."—And the reason we give for saying this is that a man certainly could design a new shape without having changed his taste, say that he believes something without believing it, etc. And this obviously is true. But it doesn't follow that what distinguishes a case of having changed one's taste from a case of not having done so isn't under certain circumstances just designing what one hasn't designed before. Nor does it follow that in cases in which designing a new shape is not the criterion for a change of taste, the criterion must be a change in some particular region of our mind.[13]

As emerges from the above remarks, the concept of cultured taste is not the concept of a mental state that enables us to dress or design new clothes that show taste. If it were, the criterion for a change of taste would "be a change in some particular region of our mind" or brain. In point of fact, we do not ascribe a change of taste on the basis of changes in mental states. We do it on the basis of what people say and do. But does not what they do and say in this connection emerge out of a certain mental state that provides for cultured taste? Wittgenstein does not elaborate why this explanation is misleading, but this can be filled in. To have cultured taste in dressing is not akin to being in a bad mood or to experiencing depression or joy, which are examples of mental states that are apt to lead to certain kinds of behavior. It is not a mental state that a person is in that has genuine duration, can be experienced, and in which fluctuations and changes can be noted and described.[14] It is no more a mental state than to be intelligent or to be able to ride a bicycle is to be in a certain mental state.

As becomes clear from our use of the term "mental state" in the stream of life, it concerns mostly our moods and emotions that we experience. In philosophy, on the other hand, it is used to explain the nature of all aspects of mental life, including pains, thoughts, beliefs, intentions, wishes, and judgments. Wittgenstein claims that the inclination in philosophy to posit such "mental states" by way of explanation for conceptual distinctions that serve us in the stream of life is the inclination to reify them. He notes, for example, that there seems to be something mysterious about a thought:

> because we misunderstand its grammar and feel the lack of a tangible substance to correspond to the substantive. (It is almost like hearing a human voice coming from in front of us, and seeing nobody there.)[15]

He also notes the following:

> The questions "What is length?" "What is meaning?" "What is the number one?" etc., produce in us a mental cramp. We feel that we can't point to anything in reply to them and yet ought to point to something. (We are up against one of the great sources of philosophical bewilderment: a substantive makes us look for a thing that corresponds to it.)[16]

He thinks that this is because in philosophy, we often use a confusing picture to reflect on our use of concepts.

> The confusing picture is this: that we observe a substance, its changes, states, motions; like someone observing the changes and motions in a blast furnace. Whereas we observe and compare the attitudes and behaviour of human beings."[17]

Because we are unable to specify what cultured taste is, we are apt to think that it is some mental or physical state that directs us in our judgments.

Wittgenstein objects to an explanation that identifies cultured taste with such a state because cultured taste is expressed in reason-based judgments. To judge because of some causal mechanism that induces us to judge as we do is not to do so out of a cultivated aesthetic reason. In the same way, to appreciate a given cultural work, just as to have cultured taste, requires the development of proper cultured sensibilities. This is not akin to developing an allergy or to becoming sensitive to the sun's glare, which may be explained through the emergence of some physical state of the body that is the cause of certain bodily symptoms. Wittgenstein claims in this connection that the philosophical inclination to explain cultured taste as a mental state that promotes cultured behavior derives from what he describes as the conflation of reasons with causes:

> We are talking here of the grammar of the words "reason" and "cause": in what cases do we say we have given a reason for doing a certain thing, and in what cases, a cause? If one answers the question 'Why did you move your arm?' by giving a behavioristic explanation, one has specified a cause. Causes may be discovered by experiments, but experiments do not produce reasons. The word "reason" is not used in connection with experimentation. It is senseless to say a reason is found by experiment . . . .[18]

The conceptual distinction between reasons and causes is also used by Wittgenstein to clarify the difference between a psychological investigation and an aesthetic one:

> In aesthetic investigation the thing we are *not* interested in is *causal connections*, whereas in psychology we are. This is *the main point* of difference. To the question "*Why* is this beautiful?" we are accustomed to being satisfied with answers which cite *causes* instead of reasons. To name causal connections is to give an hypothesis. Giving a cause does not remove the aesthetic puzzle one feels when asked what makes a thing beautiful. It is useful to remind yourself of the answers given to the opposite question, "What is wrong with this poem or melody?" for the answer to the first question is of the same kind. The answer to "What is wrong with this melody?" is like the statement, "This is too loud," not like the statement that it produces sulphur in the blood.[19]

In the above clarification, to answer a question posed in an aesthetic context "What is wrong with this melody?" by saying that it is too loud is to judge its aesthetic value. It is not merely to express our irritation on its being played too loudly, since some melodies need to be played loudly. One way of reading the above remark is to note that aesthetic remarks express aesthetic judgments. An investigation of their meaning is not an investigation of psychological responses and their causes. Theoretical remarks in science, about causal mechanisms underlying our psychological responses, do not express aesthetic judgments and attitudes. Furthermore, when we call into question people's aesthetic judgments, we are calling into question their aesthetic understanding. We are making normative assertions: "The sort of experiment we carry on to discover people's likes and dislikes is not aesthetics. . . . In aesthetics the question is not 'Do you like it?' but 'Why do you like it?'"[20] This holds true not only for sophisticated discussions about art, but also for our basic aesthetic experiences:

> A statement about a visual or auditory impression, as against what causes it, need not be psychological. That a sorrowful face becomes more sorrowful as the mouth turns downward is not a statement of psychology. In aesthetics we are not interested in causal connections but in descriptions of a thing.[21]

Sorrow is expressed in the face of human beings. Creatures that have no faces are incapable of expressing sorrow as humans do. Moreover, human beings who are unable to recognize sorrow in the face of another person are lacking a fundamental human ability on which human communication and social relations are constructed. This ability is expressed also in painting, sculpting, and acting. The ability to recognize sorrow in the face of another person is not a scientific ability to theorize from empirical data, just as the ability to express sorrow is not a technological ability. Aesthetics is not divorced from our natural expressions and our natural human abilities; it manifests them. Indeed, it may be said that our ordinary uses of psychological concepts to ascribe sorrow, depression, elation, or pain to human beings on the basis of their expressive demeanor manifests a descriptive, expressive, nontheoretical psychological discourse, which is also at the basis of various aesthetic practices that are manifested in them. Wittgenstein notes in this connection that just as to use everyday psychological concepts is not to theorize, reasons given in aesthetic judgments are not theoretical explanations about psychological causes:

> The reasons are further descriptions. Aesthetics is descriptive. What it does is to *draw one's attention* to certain features, to place things side by side so as to exhibit these features. To tell a person "This is the climax" is like saying "This is the man in the puzzle picture." Our attention is drawn to a certain feature, and from that point forward we see that feature.[22]

To note that "aesthetics is descriptive" is to clarify the conceptual nature of aesthetic assertions. They are not theoretical explanation of what brings about satisfaction or dissatisfaction. They are more like ways of drawing attention to significant aspects of a given work, which subsequently determine how we experience it: such as that the face in the drawing looks sad, happy, angry, serene, bemused, and the like. Their conceptual character is akin to giving reasons that elucidate the point of certain actions, such as exclaiming to someone that you have to run now, because it is getting late. They are not ways of offering a hypothesis about a cause for behavior. Aesthetics is not a branch of theoretical psychology:

> The reasons one gives for feeling satisfied have nothing to do with psychology. These, the aesthetic reasons, are given by placing things side by side, as in a court of law. If one gave *psychological* reasons for choosing a simile, those would not be reasons in aesthetics. They would be causes, not reasons. Stating a cause would be offering a hypothesis. Insofar as the remedy for the disagreeable feeling of top-heaviness of a door is like a remedy for a headache, a question concerning what remedy to prescribe is not a question of aesthetics. The aesthetic reason for feeling dissatisfied, as opposed to its cause, is not a proposition of psychology. A good example of a cause for dissatisfaction which I might have, say, with the way someone is playing a waltz, is that I have seen the waltz danced and know how it should be played. This does not give a reason for my dissatisfaction. The person who plays it, and I, have a different ideal of the waltz, and to give the reason for my dissatisfaction demands a *description*. Similarly, if a composition is felt to have a wrong ending.[23]

Note that this clarification is not about the subsequently debated metaphysical issue as to whether "reasons" for actions are "causes." It concerns the difference between giving an aesthetic reason for a given judgment and theorizing about a psychological cause for the judgment. This is why "In aesthetic investigation the thing we are not interested in is causal connections, whereas in psychology we are." (Therefore, the question whether certain brain mechanisms are underlying causes for artistic judgments is not at issue here.) To have an aesthetic reason is to possess aesthetic judgment. In the example Wittgenstein gives, the cause for this judgment is the fact that he has seen the waltz danced and knows how the music should be played accordingly. However, to express an aesthetic judgment about the way the music is played is not to theorize about the cause for his aesthetic satisfaction or dissatisfaction with it. It is an expression of his cultured judgment of significant features of it.

6. Cultured Ways of Understanding and Cultured Experiences

When clarifying the concept of understanding in the arts, Wittgenstein reconsiders the conceptual nature of cultured taste and appreciation. He notes in this connection that cultured taste, appreciation, and judgment in arts manifest artistic ways of understanding. However, as noted before in connection with these concepts, understanding is not a state, neither a mental nor a physical state. It is an ability:

> We are trying to get hold of the mental process of understanding which seems to be hidden behind those coarser and therefore more readily vis-

> ible accompaniments. But we do not succeed; or, rather, it does not get as far as a real attempt. For even supposing I had found something that happened in all those cases of understanding—why should it be the understanding? And how can the process of understanding have been hidden, when I said "Now I understand" *because* I understood?![24]

Elsewhere, Wittgenstein adds the following remark: "Understanding is like knowing how to go on, and so it is an ability: but 'I understand,' like 'I can go on,' is an *utterance*, a signal."[25] He might also have said that it is an expression of understanding. However, note that just as in the case of riding a bike or baking a cake, which are activities often accompanied by certain experiences, our understanding of artistic practices in which we engage is often accompanied by certain experiences. At this point, we might be tempted to suggest that certain kinds of experiences underlie cultured understanding. Wittgenstein considers this suggestion in two contexts, providing a kind of negative phenomenology to the philosophical attempt to identify cultured understanding with certain sensations and feelings that we might experience, albeit without denying that it may be manifested in certain experiences:

> What does it consist in: following a musical phrase with understanding? Observing a face with a feeling for its expression? Drinking in the expression on the face?
>
> Think of the demeanour of someone who draws the face with understanding for its expression. Think of the sketcher's face his movements; what shows that every stroke he makes is dictated by the face, that nothing in his sketch is arbitrary, that he is a *delicate* instrument? Is that really an experience? I mean: can we say that this expresses an *experience?*
>
> Once again: what does it consist in, following a musical phrase with understanding, or, playing it with understanding? Don't look inside yourself. Ask yourself rather, what makes you say that's what *someone else* is doing. And *what* prompts you to say *he* has a particular experience? Indeed, do we ever actually say that? Wouldn't I be more likely to say of someone else that he's having a whole host of experiences?
> I would perhaps say: "He is experiencing the theme intensely'; but ask yourself, what the expression of this is?[26]

To "ask yourself" this question in philosophy is not to use the expression "experiencing the theme intensely" in ordinary discourse about the experience of hearing music. Rather, it is to attempt to find by introspection a particular experience, which is that of "experiencing the theme intensely." Wittgenstein notes that this attempt never even leaves the ground:

> If I now ask, "What do I actually experience then, if I hear the theme & hear it with understanding?" nothing but inanities occur to me by way of reply. Such as images, kinaesthetic sensations, thoughts and the like.[27]

Nonetheless, Wittgenstein concludes that appreciation of music that manifests an understanding of music is a kind of experience:

> The understanding of music is neither sensation nor a sum of sensations. Nevertheless it is correct to call it an experience inasmuch as this concept of understanding has some kinship with other concepts of experience. You say "I experienced that passage quite differently." But still this expression tells you *"what happened"* only if you are at home in the special conceptual world that belongs to these situations. (Analogy: "I won the match.")[28]

In the above insight, enjoyment of certain music, liking some material for clothing or fancying a given dining room table, do not of themselves manifest cultured appreciation, taste, judgment, and understanding. They are merely the causal effect of certain cultural practices on us. They are experiences that someone who is a complete stranger to the culture might experience, albeit without really understanding it. A dog might find pleasure in hearing a given piece of classical music that we judge highly. But it does not appreciate it in a musically meaningful way; nor does it reveal thereby musical taste, judgment, or understanding. Similarly, a person might like a piece of clothing or fancy some furniture without knowing anything about it and its role within a given culture of dressing or dining. In choosing these artifacts, such a person would not be expressing cultured taste, appreciation, or judgment and would not be showing cultured understanding:

> Appreciation of music is *expressed* in a certain way, both in the course of hearing & playing and at other times too. This expression sometimes includes movements, but sometimes only the way the one who understands plays, or hums, occasionally too parallels he draws & images which, as it were, illustrate the music. Someone who understands music will listen differently (with a different facial expression, e.g.), play differently, hum differently, talk differently about the piece than someone who does not understand. His appreciation of a theme will not however be shown only in phenomena that accompany the hearing or playing of the theme, but also in an appreciation for music in general.[29]

In my reading of these remarks, they show that we come to understand music by acquiring musical sensibility in the form of musical taste, judgment, and appreciation, and vice versa. In this insight, when we become acculturated

rated into music we learn *how* to value it in a cultured manner: not as the manifestation of some aesthetic idea or as a source of pleasurable experiences, but by becoming more musically discriminating through our experience of hearing music. A way of exploring this suggestion is to reflect on how we would go about explaining what understanding music is, to someone who has no appreciation for music at all. Such a person would be removed from a central aspect of human life that underlies human cultures. To explain how this is managed is not to acculturate that person into a musical culture. To acculturate is to bring about understanding that takes the form of appreciation, taste, and judgment. Wittgenstein reflects on this point in the following way:

> Appreciating music is a manifestation of human life. How could it be described to someone? Well, above all I suppose we should have to describe *music*. Then we could describe the relation human beings have to it. But is that all that is necessary, or is it also part of the process to teach him to appreciate it for himself? Well, developing his appreciation will teach him what appreciation is in a *different* sense, than a teaching that does not do this. And again, teaching him to appreciate poetry or painting can be part of an explanation of what music is.[30]

I take it that to teach someone to appreciate poetry, painting, or music, just like teaching someone to appreciate sports, cooking, or architecture, is to acculturate that person into these practices. It thus emerges that this is a way of coming to understand a culture from within, by partaking in it and thus sharing its meaningful expressions. Trying to understand it without being acculturated into it is to approach it from outside: through a theoretical stance, as we would a scientific subject. Whatever is learned in that approach, it does not suffice for transforming us into cultured affiliates of the practice. It does not provide a way of understanding a culture from within, by bringing about a spiritual alliance with the cultured judgments and experiences of its practitioners and the way in which their practices are experienced by them in a culturally meaningful way.

7. Culture as a Great Organization

Focusing on the practices through which a strong, spiritual commitment to some particular tradition is manifested in a great and high culture, by observance and creation of shared practices, yields a picture of a community organized for the purpose of producing what Wittgenstein calls a "great work of culture." Examples of such undertakings can be seen, perhaps, in the communal efforts that, in the past, had gone into the building of monumental places of worship or commemoration, such as the Pyramids, the Temple in Jerusalem, or the Cathedral of Notre Dame in Paris. In Wittgenstein's view, culture itself is in the nature of a great work that is constructed by a communal effort through many generations and through many different kinds of practices and ways of life. Hence, the initial claim:

> Culture is like a great organization which assigns to each of its members his place, at which he can work in the spirit of the whole, and his strength can with a certain justice be measured by his success as understood within that whole.[31]

The simile of a great organization is supposed to convey two important ideas about a culture. The first is that a culture is in the nature of a communal endeavor, one in which each person, while devoting him or herself to his or her own specific task, contributes to the advancement of something larger. Wittgenstein alludes to such a sketch of such an "organization" in his (former) description of the culture that gives rise to musical taste. We can envision that in such a culture, music is performed in various cultural settings; musical instruments are designed and manufactured; music is written down and styles and formats of playing music emerge; children are taught to play musical instruments by teachers of music who are themselves professional musicians; adults both listen to music and play music themselves; concerts are performed in solemn gatherings; concert halls are constructed; and so on. All these different activities may be pursued in different ways, but are nevertheless united through "the spirit of the whole" by their contribution to the observance and advancement of a cultural tradition, devoted to expressing the human spirit in a grand and lofty manner through music.

The second idea expressed through the image of a culture as a great organization is that a person's "power" needs to be assessed with respect to the "contribution" he or she is able to make to a cultural tradition. Power is the basic spiritual ability that human beings possess and bring with them to a culture, when they take part in it. In the context of culture, "power" is the spiritual ability with which a person is endowed. Wittgenstein clarifies the nature of this ability in connection with cultural creativity. He distinguishes two kinds of spiritual power—in parallel to two kinds of artists operating in a culture.[32] There are talented artists and there are geniuses. The first are said to possess "good manners" or a refined cultural "taste." They are, as it were, the observers, preservers, consumers, cultivators, developers, and enhancers of their cultural heritage. They may even elaborate, enrich and refine the cultural contributions that others before them have made. But they lack the ability to advance their culture's tradition in *new* directions:

> The faculty of "taste" cannot create a new organism, only rectify one that is already there.

> Taste loosens screws & tightens screws, it doesn't create a new original work.
>
> Taste rectifies, it doesn't give birth.
>
> Taste makes ACCEPTABLE.
>
> (Hence, I think, a great creator needs no taste: the child is born into the world well formed.) . . .
>
> The most refined taste has nothing to do with creative power.[33]

The explanation Wittgenstein gives for these claims is that artistic taste is merely a cultural manifestation of an expressive power to which we refer as "talent." He judges talent alone, no matter how great, as insufficient to produce an original and profound creation in a culture. Something more than great talent is needed to create a profound artistic expression that is culturally significant and not merely an aesthetic rearrangement of already given elements. In the context of cultural creation, cultured taste is a supportive spiritual force. It only enables cultured human beings to develop and refine what others before them have created.

The second kind of cultural power is the spiritual force that is manifested in genius. Geniuses have the ability to contribute to the spiritual progression of a culture by creating within its cultural tradition original and innovative works of art that are both powerful and deeply meaningful, which talented artists then disseminate, refine and elaborate on. It is through the constant interchange between the respective contributions to a culture of its artistic geniuses and talented artists that the observance and progression of a spiritual tradition in a culture takes place. And it is with respect to the contribution people make toward either the observance or the progression of their culture that their (spiritual) power needs to be evaluated.

It is worth noting here that the distinction Wittgenstein makes is between geniuses and talented innovators, not between cultural revolutionaries and cultural conformists. In his conception of genius, both talented innovators and creative geniuses are observers of tradition. The difference is that geniuses have the capacity to devise new inspiring ways of expressing human nature on the basis of their cultural tradition. Like talented innovators, though, they do not break with tradition.[34]

Wittgenstein is not suggesting that the value of human beings arises only from the fact that they contribute to the making of a culture, or that all human values arise from the contribution people make to their cultures. He grants, after all, that "the disappearance of a culture does not signify the disappearance of human value." But it is also obvious that he was "without sympathy" for the way in which human value was being expressed in "the current of European civilization," noting that he was "without understanding [for] its aims if any."

8. Culture as an Epic

The image of culture as a big organization, while often insightful, is apt to mislead in certain ways, for it is likely to suggest a somewhat static spiritual way of life, geared toward the preservation of tradition and the cultivation through observance of cherished cultural practices and customs. But a living culture is a very dynamic spiritual venture. It is manifested through a communal enterprise that constantly progresses and changes as innovations are made and certain old practices are discarded. It is a spiritual venture, which, despite the changes and shifts it undergoes, enables its observers to share in a common spiritual effort and to experience it as such.

To describe this dynamic, constantly changing feature of a culture, Wittgenstein uses the image of an epic: "the development of this culture," he writes when reflecting on Western high and great culture, is that of "an epic."[35] This image is intended, I believe, to express two major ideas. The first is that such a culture is in the nature of a heroic spiritual journey. It is one that unites different people in different places and at different times in a shared cultural pursuit: to express the human spirit in an inspired and lofty manner, by contributing to the creation of a great work of culture. The second idea is that the journey undertaken through a culture is not measured by arrival at some predetermined destination, since it consists of *spiritual progression.* The spiritual journey undertaken through culture is constantly moving on from one original and profound creative spiritual adventure to the next.

One may imagine that it is in the nature of the progression of a spiritual epic, by means of an "organization" such as a culture, that those who take part in it perform different tasks. Still, in this view, there seem to be two basic spiritual roles that cultured people can play in a culture. They contribute either to its observance or to its progression. Those who possess taste and are invested with talent contribute mainly to observance. They seek to cultivate and enlarge cultural way stations into comfortable habitats. They support and sustain their spiritual heritage, but they do not actually contribute to its progression down new cultural trails.

The other role is played by geniuses. They strive to continue the epic journey, directing their creative efforts toward new horizons and new adventures. They impel the spiritual journey forward, contributing in this way to its constant unforeseeable progression. Due to the original creative contribution that they bring to a culture, "If we think of the world's future," we are bound to go wrong. For "we always mean the place it will get to if it keeps going as we see it going now."[36] But, of course, this is not how the spiritual progression of a culture proceeds. Due to the original contributions of geniuses and those who follow in their tracks, it is evident that the world "is not going in a straight line but in a curve & that its direction is constantly changing"[37]—which, I take it, is precisely what is apt to occur in epics.

To perceive a culture in this way, as constantly changing, yet still remaining the same, is to perceive it as a spiritual epic. It is to see that despite the distance already covered, everything in the future is still open. It is to recognize that despite the inherited tradition, there is no way to foretell in which direction the spiritual progression of the culture is bound to proceed. Of course, that is not how most people experience the spiritual progression of their cultures. Even though it may take on the shape of an epic, a culture is a shared form of life, the observers of which experience a host of different activities as constituting a single spiritual enterprise. A culture constantly molds artistic sensibilities in relationship to both its tradition and its progression, so cultured people who are affiliated with it experience it as one common spiritual endeavor. They are then apt to project from where they are situated in it to its future progression. But since it is an epic, the course it takes is not a straight line and such projections are apt to mislead. The conclusion to be drawn from this insight is somewhat ominous:

> If you want to see the epic of a whole culture written you will have to seek it in the works of its greatest figures and hence seek it at a time when the end of this culture can only be *foreseen*, for later there is no one there any more to describe it.[38]

By "later," Wittgenstein means a time when the culture disappears—for instance, when it is transformed into what he refers to as "civilization."

It now emerges that, with regard to the spiritual progression of a culture as an epic, to describe it as an epic, you have to experience it as such, and that means that you need to be affiliated with it. Such an experience is achieved from within the culture. It is the way in which the culture's various creative achievements over the years are experienced by someone who partakes of it and finds them culturally meaningful as instances of the same spiritual tradition. In the case of the high and great musical culture of the West, to which I referred previously, such a description might demonstrate how certain innovative artists and their achievements have provided for new culturally meaningful adventures, while contributing to the same spiritual effort manifested in earlier works. It might demonstrate how their work has been appreciated and elaborated upon by others, who continued it in new directions. To provide such a description requires making use of the musical sensibilities that underpin this cultural enterprise throughout its entire epic progression, up to the point at which it is presented. Such a description would thus express the way an affiliate of the culture experiences all its various tributaries as manifesting the same spiritual effort and still contributing to the production of a great work of art. Such a culture constitutes a shared whole, despite all the changes that have occurred in it.

Four

CIVILIZATION AND ITS SPIRITUAL MANIFESTATIONS

1. Civilization as the "Ashes" of Culture

Even the longest journeys come to an end. From Ludwig Wittgenstein's cultural standpoint, the epic that was once Western high and great culture constituted a spiritual tradition, which, through the efforts made in various arts and ways of life over many years expressed the human spirit in a grand and lofty manner. By its progression through all sorts of new and profound spiritual adventures, while observing a cherished tradition, it eventually acquired the shape of a great cultural epic. It thus enabled different people at different times and places to pool their cultural efforts and make use of their tasteful and creative powers in a common spiritual bond. But all that is now over. From his cultural standpoint, the spiritual epos that was once Western high and great culture no longer exists. Western civilization has arisen in its stead.

As may now be seen, Wittgenstein's gloomy conclusion about "the disappearance of a culture" and the emergence of "civilization" is pronounced against the background of his idealized perspective on what he calls "the high and great culture" of the West. It is important to note that the concept of civilization he uses as a contrast to the high and great culture of the West is not that of a low or popular culture. In Wittgenstein's cultural standpoint, civilization is a spiritual stage of disintegration and mellowing that has overtaken the high and great culture of the West. It does not apply to what is referred to as "low culture." While similar in his rejection of certain trends in modern arts to cultural critics who condemned them as "decadent," his remarks are also made within a conceptual context of discussion that he seeks to clarify.

Recalling the effort that once went into developing cultured taste and observance of tradition in the West, Wittgenstein experiences modern Western civilization as an age devoid of true high culture and he doubts that any new high and great culture will arise out of it. With some feeble hope, he reflects, "Perhaps one day a culture will arise out of this civilization. Then there will be a real history of the discoveries of the 18th, 19th & 20th centuries, which will be of profound interest."[1] But he was not very optimistic regarding such an outcome. On the whole, he felt, "The earlier culture will become a heap of rubble & finally a heap of ashes." Only "spirits will hover over the ashes."[2]

Wittgenstein's lack of sympathy for this civilization arises in connection with what he perceives as its spiritual decline in comparison to what was once the high and great culture of the West. It is in terms of its spiritual manifestations that he sees the emergence of modern Western civilization as coming at the expense of the former high and great culture of the West. The most prominent manifestation of the fall of culture and the rise of civilization in the West seems to him to be the disappearance of a concentrated shared effort to observe a way of life and to contribute to a tradition that aims at and enables human beings to express and experience something lofty and eternal through their culture. It is instructive to note some of the ways in which he clarifies the spirit of this civilization.

2. The Spirit of Science and Technology

From Wittgenstein's cultural standpoint, the goals that modern civilization places before human beings, through, for example, the pursuit of knowledge by the sciences, do not provide a cultural outlet for experiencing and expressing something spiritually lofty and eternal. Modern civilization, with its pursuit of technology and science, is based on cherishing and valuing intellect and the achievements of intellect. Accordingly, it aims to reshape, control, and explain nature by means of science. He views the past high and great culture of the West, on the other hand, as an enterprise based on a spiritual attitude toward life that is untainted by science and the outlook on life it provides. It is the ground for religion, crafts, and art, which still allows nature to be experienced in an inspired and lofty way as something miraculous. To clarify this idea, Wittgenstein focuses on our ability to experience natural events as something marvelous, in contrast to how they are approached and explained through scientific discourse:

> The miracles of nature,
> We might say: art *discloses* the miracles of nature to us. It is based on the *concept* of the miracles of nature. (The blossom, just opening out. What is *marvelous* about it?) We say: "Look, how it's opening out!"[3]

Thus, the past arts in the West were based on a spiritual attitude toward life that enables us to perceive natural events as something miraculous and to be awed by what transpires in nature. Science, on the other hand, dictates an intellectual, theoretical, often mechanical point of view that makes us reach for rational explanations. Consequently, this inspired perspective is completely lost. Wittgenstein notes, "In order to marvel human beings and perhaps peoples have to wake up. Science is a way of sending them off to sleep again."[4] Given the difference in spiritual attitudes that underlie science and our ability to experience the miracles of nature, he remarks, "It is all one to me whether the typical western scientist understands or appreciates my work since in any case he does not understand the spirit in which I write."[5]

It is thus with deep misgivings that Wittgenstein compares the progress at which modern technology and science aim with the inspired attitude of marvel at ordinary natural events, which once lay at the heart of human endeavor. This spiritual attitude was the driving force behind the emergence of religious rituals, myths, and cultural ceremonies, and it was later extended into cultivated expressions of high and great culture in arts. The point is not that science will ultimately fail to afford us a cohesive picture about nature and our place in it. The point is that it is not clear why a picture that hides "the miracles of Nature" from us and renders us incapable of marveling at life should be sought after as an ultimate cultural enterprise, nor why its construction would be considered spiritual progress. So much the worse for us if science is the ultimate word and no high and great culture will arise again, if human beings have irrevocably lost all possibility of regaining the outlook on life and spiritual attitude they once possessed in an age of culture, when they were still able to marvel at life and to be awed by ordinary natural events. It is from this dark perspective on the future of Western culture that Wittgenstein writes the following:

> The truly apocalyptic view of the world is that things do *not* repeat themselves. It is not e.g. absurd to believe that the scientific & technological age is the beginning of the end for humanity, that the idea of Great Progress is a bedazzlement, along with the idea that the truth will ultimately be known; that there is nothing good or desirable about scientific knowledge & that humanity, in seeking it, is falling into a trap. It is by no means clear that this is not how things are.[6]

3. Industrial Modes of Life

Another way in which Wittgenstein clarifies the manner in which "the spirit of this civilization" makes itself manifest is in connection with that to which he refers as "the industry . . . of present day . . . ." The idea is that mass industrial production has brought about a fundamental change in styles of living and attitudes toward life, dictating to human beings in our time a way of life that is dominated by machines and by the products of machines. It has rendered obsolete the tradition in which various manual skills and crafts were once cherished and cultivated. It has also made the things that constitute a way of life for human beings—artifacts, homes, physical settings, jobs, friends, families, communities—more easily acquired, constantly changing, transitory, replaceable, and, thus, also *less meaningful*. In a conversation recorded by O. K. Bouwsma, Wittgenstein described the difference between the respective ways of life afforded to human beings in periods of culture and civilization in the following way:

> there was a time when our lives were furnished rather simply, a house, a place, tools so many, a beast and a circle of people. In this simplicity

> and this stability one grew attached to a limited environment. This gave a life a certain quality—roots. Now, not only are people transient, but also neighborhoods do not remain the same. We live in surroundings to which we are not sentimentally attached. Most of what we use and own can be replaced by something just as good.[7]

In the above clarification, the desire to place one's way of life within the context of something lofty and eternal is an expression of the deeply meaningful way in which a way of life is experienced. It is not merely that, in a time of culture, even simple agrarian ways of life enabled human beings to reach out to something lofty and eternal. Since people experienced the meaning of their lives and what transpired in them from within such simple circumstances and limited environments, they were attached to them and to what they encompassed in a more profound and meaningful fashion. That is to say, they invested their lives with a different spiritual attitude, which inclined them to give their lives meaningful spiritual expressions, by the use of lofty religious rituals and ceremonies.

In contrast to such a simple and deeply meaningful agrarian mode of life, the mode of life that modern urban environments provide makes it difficult to obtain any spiritual sustenance. Echoing Søren Kierkegaard's depiction of the existential despair that arises out of modern modes of life and the abandonment of unhesitant faith in God, Wittgenstein conjoins it to Leo Tolstoy's critique of the bourgeois lifestyle as lacking spiritual meaning and his call for the adoption of a simple peasant mode of life to remedy it. He castigates the modern, urban, technological way of life for producing what he calls "the sickness of a time," which he judges to require a change in a mode of living to be cured:

> The sickness of a time is cured by an alteration in the mode of life of human beings, and it was possible for the sickness of philosophical problems to be cured only through a changed mode of thought and of life, not through a medicine invented by an individual.
>
> Think of the use of the motorcar producing or encouraging certain sicknesses, and mankind being plagued by such sickness until, from some cause or other, as the result of some development or other, it abandons the habit of driving.[8]

As may be seen from the two examples he gives that are apt to produce "the sickness of a time," the motorcar and philosophical problems, Wittgenstein is compounding two ideas under this expression. One concerns a mode of living that produces physical sickness, the other a mode of thinking that produces mental sickness. One is the product of a technological way of life, the other of a metaphysical way of thinking in philosophy. Both, he claims, can only be cured by a radical change in "mode of thought and life."

4. Fascism and Socialism

One of the marks of civilization for Wittgenstein is how it views itself. He notes, "Our civilization is characterized by the word 'progress.' Progress is its form . . ."[9] To see the point of this remark, note the slogan "Historical Progress," which informs certain modern ideologies. In them, human history is represented as having a positive direction of development, through which humanity progresses to beliefs, values, social organizations, arts, and technology more advanced than those of ancient times. This slogan is often conjoined to other catchy ideological slogans such as "Humanism," "Enlightenment," and "Modernity." In Wittgenstein's view, modern civilization sees in its achievements in science, technology, architecture, and social organizations, and values a spiritual advance over past historical achievements. To say in this connection that "Progress is its form" is to say that the idea of human progress underlies the spirit of modernity.

For Wittgenstein, the spiritual attitude of progress is manifested particularly in creative efforts. Typically, creative ventures in this period strive to construct more advanced, complicated, and sophisticated structures. Through them, an effort is made to control and reshape nature. As discussed earlier, Wittgenstein clarifies this spiritual attitude toward creative efforts that underlies what he calls "civilization" by contrasting it with that which underlies what he calls "culture." While the form of the first is progress, the form of the second is spiritual progression that is pursued within the framework of a given cultural tradition. It is achieved by advancing from one inspiring creative adventure to the next, all of which are pursued in a grand and lofty manner. Religion and art in a period of culture manifest a spiritual attempt to express attitudes of awe and wonder at the mysterious nature of the world and the enigmatic meaning of life. In a period of civilization, it is replaced by a spiritual effort to advance forward, to progress through new creative ventures to new constructions. Attitudes of awe and wonder at the mysterious nature of the world and the enigmatic meaning of life are no longer given expression, at least not in the grand and lofty manner they were approached in the past.

For Wittgenstein, then, the spiritual attitude of civilization to life "that is characterized by the word 'progress'" extends not only to certain kinds of ideologies, as opposed to others. He sees culture as being supplanted by civilization in the very emergence of ideological efforts to forge a spiritual bond between human beings over matters that have nothing to do with what was formerly expressed through the high and great culture of the West—whether in arts or in religion. Various ideological movements seek to convert people to their outlook on life by positing inspiring social goals with which they are apt to identify and to which they can then commit themselves. Such are political and social attempts to forge an inspiring spiritual bond between human beings, on the basis of either national or class identities. Hence, his claim that "The spirit of <u>this civilization</u> the expression of which is . . . fascism & socialism." However, these ideological social movements have nothing to do with artistic and religious ways of expressing the human spirit in a great and lofty manner through the high and great culture of the West of the past.

As I read Wittgenstein on these matters, fascism takes on the semblance of a spiritual way of life by pretending to be a grand culture. It, too, operates as a great organization. It, too, mobilizes very basic, powerful forces in human beings as opposed to those of reason and intellect. However, it is also a very violent organization, one devoted to the glorification of (the spirit of) a nationality (rather than of human beings), in which the value of the individual (rather than his or her power) is dependent on his or her contribution to the whole. It even reinforces its pretence to be a grand culture by coercing its participants into observing its ideological goals and way of life. But, of course, nothing spiritually lofty or eternal is being expressed by the nationalist goals of fascism and the oppressive methods by which they are pursued.

Wittgenstein deems socialism to be another similar manifestation of modern civilization. As I read him, socialism is an attempt to forge a social bond between human beings as an alternative to the spiritual bond created formerly within a culture. Socialism seeks to forge a social bond on the basis of class affiliation and shared economic interests. It seeks to "restructure" the social order and to bind people together in a joint social pursuit through public ownership of property and the ideological goal of social and economic equality. But whatever the political and social merits of such a venture, it does not provide a proper spiritual framework for enhancing the ability to marvel at life itself and to perceive the miracles of nature. I take it that for Wittgenstein, the problem with socialism is not in its economic and social goals as such, but in its seeking to offer the pursuit of these social goals as an inspirational spiritual framework for an entire culture. It posits itself as a social alternative to a lofty spiritual attitude toward life that in the past was embodied in human cultures, which it now seeks to replace.

5. Civilization as the Demise of Artistic Ideals

For Wittgenstein, the disappearance of Western high and great culture is closely connected with what he perceives as "the disappearance of the arts" in the Western civilization of his time. He clarifies the concepts of culture and civilization in this connection by noting how the artistic ideals of a culture provide for tradition and nourish new creations and cultured judgments, and what happens to a culture when its past ideals are relinquished or altered. He begins his clarification of this point by noting the role of artistic ideals in aesthetic judgments:

> Why do we say certain changes bring a thing nearer to an ideal, e.g., making a door lower, or the bass in music quieter. It is not that we want

> in different cases to produce the same effect, namely, an agreeable feeling. What made the ideal Greek profile into an ideal, what quality? Actually what made us say it is the ideal is a certain very complicated role it played in the life of people. For example, the greatest sculptors used this form, people were taught it, Aristotle wrote on it. Suppose one said the ideal profile is the one occurring at the height of Greek art. What would this mean? The word "height" is ambiguous. To ask what "ideal" means is the same as asking what "height" and "decadence" mean.[10]

Here, ideal and decadence are concepts used in artistic judgments made within a complicated aesthetic context. They are normative concepts that are not based on the formulation and application of rules. Like the concept of height, which we use in the context of some scale of measurement, or in comparing between things, they are used against a specific cultural background of measuring and judging various achievements. To use them outside this background is like saying that a certain tree is high, without mentioning in comparison to what. Furthermore, the expression "the height of Greek culture," unlike the expression "the height of a person," is a metaphor, signifying perfection and excellence. It suggests that cultures have low and high periods in which artistic achievements attain a lower or higher aesthetic perfection. So the terms "high" and "low" with respect to aesthetic achievements are value-laden. As such, the concept of an artistic ideal used in Wittgenstein's example of Greek sculpture posits a measure for judging the artistic merit of ancient works and those that seek to continue in their tradition. However, as he emphasizes, this is a value-laden measure that does not legislate for entirely different kinds of cultural practices, or for practices that emerge from entirely different cultures:

> You would need to describe the instances of the ideal in a sort of serial grouping. And the word is always used in connection with one particular thing, for there is nothing in common between roast beef, Greek art, and German music. The word "decadence" cannot be explained without specific examples, and will have different meanings in the case of poetry, music, and sculpture. To explain what decadence in music means you would need to discuss music in detail. The various arts have some analogy to each other, and it might be said that the element common to them is the ideal. But this is not the meaning of "the ideal." The ideal is got from a specific game, and can only be explained in some specific connection, e.g., Greek sculpture. There is no way of saying what all have in common, though of course one may be able to say what is common to two sculptures by studying them. In the statement that their beauty is what approaches the ideal, the word "ideal" is not used as is the word "water," which stands for something that can be pointed to. And no aes-

> thetic investigation will supply you with a meaning of the word "ideal" which you did not have before.[11]

Thus, an ideal is not a yet unaccomplished goal that artists strive to achieve. Nor is it simply a past artistic example that manifests a perfected achievement that needs to be emulated, as to be artistically creative is not to copy other artists. It is also not a creative rule that we may try to infer from a number of such achievements, as it is not a form of rule-following behavior. Furthermore, it is useless to try to define the concepts of an aesthetic ideal or of decadence outside their use in the context of some particular cultural practice and tradition. For instance, there may be no relationship between the artistic ideals of Greek sculpture and German music, both of which are incorporated into our culture. In this clarification, the concept of decadence is contrasted with the concept of ideal. Indeed, it means going against the grain of a certain artistic ideal. However, this conceptual distinction needs to be exemplified within particular practices for their meaning to be truly understood and appreciated. Otherwise it would be like learning the concepts of hot and cold without yet learning how to apply them to temperatures, colors, and moods.

In the above remark, an artistic ideal is a cultural achievement in the past of a culture to which its affiliates look back for inspiration. It is judged, experienced, and cherished by them to constitute a perfected artistic feat that is at the basis of their artistic tradition. Georg Henrik von Wright mentions in this connection how, at the time Wittgenstein was working in architecture, he:

> executed a sculpture in the studio of his friend, the sculptor Michael Drobil. It is the head of a young woman. The features have the same finished and restful beauty one finds in Greek sculptors of the classical period and which seems to have been Wittgenstein's ideal.[12]

As may be seen from this example, a cultural ideal is different from the standard meter in Paris that serves as an ideal measure for a meter. About this standard Wittgenstein says, "one can say neither that it is one meter long, nor that it is not one meter long . . ." He imagines also "samples of colour being preserved in Paris like the standard meter."[13] However, an artistic ideal is not such a simple representational standard, and it is described as a perfected achievement. Nonetheless, the achievement we strive for in a work of art is not to copy a past ideal work. It is to create something new that draws its inspiration from a past ideal:

> When one describes changes made in a musical arrangement as being directed to bringing the arrangement of parts nearer to an ideal, the ideal is not before us like a straight line which is set before us when we try to draw it. (When questioned about what we are doing we might cite another tune which we thought not to be as near the ideal.) Some people

> say we have an ideal before our minds in the same way we have a memory image when we recognize a color . . . To see how the ideal comes in, say in making the bass quieter, look at what is being done and at one's being dissatisfied with the music as it is . . . .[14]

As emerges from the last remark, artistic ideals are not like ideal colors or the standard meter. While we may use the achievements of Greek sculpture or German music as an ideal for our aesthetic judgments, artistic ideals are not simply perceived tokens or matters of fact that direct us and which we try to duplicate when we create a work of art. They are past achievements that are used to develop artistic sensibilities and judgments and in relationship to which we should aspire to create and judge new ones. We need first to work our way into acquiring and developing the artistic sensibilities and judgments that manifest them. To attain them is to acquire certain artistic ideals. Once we acquire such ideals, we may judge how some works are closer and others further away from them. To judge the artistic merit of works of art without them is like commenting on them without acquiring the artistic sensibilities and ideals from within which they are created and experienced in a given culture. This is no different from commenting on the meaning of strange cultural practices without finding them personally meaningful to us. In the conception of artistic creativity that underlies this clarification, the goal of self-expression in the arts is divorced neither from affiliation in a given cultural tradition nor from the artistic ideals that are posited in it. Indeed, self-expression in the arts that is divorced from them is not cultured self-expression.

As may now be seen, Wittgenstein is "dissatisfied" with artistic achievements in the modern period not only because they fail to measure up to some artistic ideal that he has. He is dissatisfied with them because they seem to be operating with a different artistic ideal than that which informed the arts in the West in the past. Indeed, they seem to him to be either going against the grain of past Western ideals in the arts, or devoid of any shared artistic ideal. He is culturally dissatisfied with the entire spirit in which arts are practiced and ways of life are pursued in modernity. He experiences the modern period in which he lives as one in which the inspired commitment, which sustained Western high and great culture in the past, and through which artistic traditions and ways of life that were devoted to expressing the spirit of human beings in a grand and lofty manner, are no longer cultivated, pursued or cherished, at least not with the same serious and committed intent and observance. He experiences it as a period in which artistic practices and aesthetic sensibilities have become slack, a period in which cultured human beings in the West have become less discriminating in their aesthetic judgments and their cultured taste has become less refined.

As this happens, the shared spiritual effort and ideals that sustained this culture appear to Wittgenstein to have disintegrated into a host of disjointed creative efforts and nondiscriminating judgments that typify the spirit of what he calls "civilization." He perceives the expressive spiritual efforts in his culture, which formerly were manifested in arts, religious rituals, and styles of living, as having lost their power and glory, manifesting now a spiritual force that is no longer able to nourish "a high and great culture."

6. The Decline of the Arts, and the Cases of Mendelssohn and Mahler

Another way in which Wittgenstein experiences the disappearance of the arts in Western civilization is as a diminution of spiritual power in the creative forces operating in the arts. It is manifested for him as a breakdown of the cohesive forces that formerly were embodied in the observance of a shared tradition and in the attempt to work in a common spirit. The first symptom of the decline of Western high and great culture becomes apparent when the powerful creative forces, which formerly expressed themselves in arts, are tamed and transformed into intellectual forces. When the spiritual tradition of a culture begins to be manipulated by means of intellect, it is a sign that the culture is beginning to decline. That is part of what typifies the modern arts for Wittgenstein. But he discerns an early symptom of this tendency in the works of Felix Mendelssohn.

Wittgenstein judges Mendelssohn, like all assimilated Jews and those born to them, to have employed superb intellectual talents to partake in Western high culture. "The Jew," Wittgenstein remarks, "is a desert region under whose thin layer of rock lies the molten lava of spirit."[15] The idea is that, unlike others, Jews do not affiliate themselves with Western high and great culture by growing up in it and adopting its spiritual tradition in a natural and organic fashion, but by means of a sophisticated intellectual effort to fit themselves into society. The barren force of intellect, which has underlain their economic existence in Europe, also fuels their conscious effort to join a culture that is not organically theirs and become part of it. Thus, their path through Western high and great culture is contrived. Their spirit, even when partaking in Western high culture, is still driven by the force of intellect only. As such, it lacks cultural roots, spiritual integrity, and creative power, and their contribution to the culture lacks authenticity and depth. Hence:

> It might be said (rightly or wrongly) that the Jewish mind is not in a position to produce even so much as a tiny blade of grass or flower but that its way is to make a drawing of the blade of grass or the flower that has grown in the mind of another & then use it to sketch a comprehensive picture.[16]

As a result of the Jews affiliating themselves with Western high and great culture in this way, it begins to undergo crucial changes. It is transformed, becoming more sophisticated, like them, but at the same time also much less powerful and profound. It ceases to be a joint endeavor to express the spirit of human beings in a powerful and lofty manner through the arts, which is pursued on the basis of a shared tradition. Instead, it begins to mirror the attributes of intellect, becoming more universal and more abstract, and thus also less powerful, less deep, and more divorced from Nature.

That, Wittgenstein judges, is the case with Mendelssohn and his music. He perceives such a spiritual transformation to be already evident in Mendelssohn's conscious effort to write music within the tradition of German music. As a composer, Mendelssohn is regularly credited with having done much to enhance and propagate German music. But it is precisely his having striven to do just that, his conscious intellectual pursuit of that goal, which Wittgenstein perceives as distancing his music from its "origins." That is why, according to him, "Mendelssohn's music, when it is flawless, consists of musical arabesques."[17] For the music that best expresses Mendelssohn's (Jewish) spirit is abstract, arising from the spiritual force of intellect. He lacks that which drives the spirit of the true genius in a high and great culture: "strong character."[18] He is devoid of a powerful natural force of his own, which could provide him with integrity and human depth, even while operating from within the shared spirit of his culture.

At a later period, this intellectual feature, which in the case of Mendelssohn is still veiled, becomes blatantly apparent in other artists—predominantly those of Jewish origin. Thus, he perceives the plays of Karl Kraus as mere intellectual abstractions. They are sophisticated but they lack depth. They bring to the stage "stylized human beings,"[19] rather than genuine, singular human beings who possess a distinct nature of their own in the form of a singular character. Being of Jewish origin and, therefore, a writer who operates only out of "intellect," Kraus is judged incapable of producing "a whole human being." He can only create an "intellectual skeleton."[20]

As far as the high and great culture of the West is concerned, the problem is that an artist who creates out of intellect lacks the kind of spiritual force out of which works of genius are fashioned. Artists who operate predominantly through intellect, regardless of their talent, are incapable of contributing to the spiritual progression of their culture in a profound and significant way. The spiritual force of intellect is just not deep, authentic, or strong enough to drive a culture in new and lofty directions on the basis of its past spiritual heritage. What intellect spawns cannot extend and strengthen the spiritual tradition of the culture in which such artists are attempting to participate. As a result, the spiritual progression of the culture is halted and the observance of its tradition lapses. Works of art become more sophisticated, refined, titillating, and abstract, but also less spiritually inspired, uplifting, powerful, and profound. They no longer manifest the ability or even a desire to reach out to something lofty and eternal. The spiritual forces that operate in the culture become lax and the culture begins to stagnate and then to deteriorate, until it finally disappears entirely.

Once a culture disappears, the forces that previously united the observers of its cultural tradition in a shared creative spiritual endeavor "are fragmented and the strength of the individual is wasted through the overcoming of opposing forces & frictional resistances." Artists at such a time are left completely on their own. They lack an appropriate unifying spiritual environment that can sustain them and direct their efforts and in relation to which they might have expressed themselves in a powerful, creative and spiritually meaningful way. They thus tend to fly off in all directions—relinquishing, in the process, all the constraints of past tradition. What is achieved thereby is not "a great work of culture in which the best contribute to the same great end, so much as the unimposing spectacle of a crowd whose best members pursue purely private ends." That is, the result of artistic efforts in modern times is spiritual anarchy: a state of the arts where no attempt is made to consolidate various spiritual efforts into a single cultural whole. That is what typifies the state of the modern arts: "the unimposing spectacle of a crowd" rather than "the coming into being of a great work of culture." It is from this gloomy perspective on the forces operating in modern civilization that Wittgenstein regards modern arts and their lack of true spiritual value. "My own thinking about art and values," he remarks at a very late stage, "is far more disillusioned than would have been *possible* for people 100 years ago . . . there are examples of decline in the forefront of my mind, which were not in the *forefront* for those people then."[21]

The problem regarding the creation of great works of art at a time when a high and great culture no longer exists extends even to those artists who possess great power. As long as a tradition of a high and great culture still existed, such artists could affiliate themselves with it and use their power in the context of that tradition—both to contribute to its spiritual progression and to draw strength from it. With the disappearance of high and great culture in the arts, that is no longer possible. The background against which it was previously possible to express oneself in a powerful and spiritually significant manner is gone. Therefore, even "strong characters" no longer have any outlet for their spirit in the arts. When they try to express themselves in a *powerful* way through the arts, they do so entirely on their own—without benefit of any tradition or shared effort that might sustain them and provide a supportive spiritual context for their creative efforts. In this stagnant state of affairs, their creative efforts no longer contribute to the construction of a "great work of culture," nor do they contribute to the spiritual epic progression pursued through a culture. They thus fail to acquire the kind of spiritual value they might have had at a time of "great culture."

Therefore, at such a time, "genuine & strong characters simply turn away from the field of the arts & toward other things & somehow the value of the individual finds expression. Not, to be sure, in the way it would at a time of Great Culture." That is to say, human beings of potential genius, who in a time of a high and great culture might have contributed to the spiritual progression of their culture toward new adventures, are now no longer able to use their gifts for such purposes. They must turn elsewhere, away from artistic cultural enterprises—perhaps by partaking in some technical, social, industrial, medical or scientific endeavor. But of course, "not, to be sure, in the way it would at a time of Great Culture."

All of which prompts Wittgenstein to consider the case of yet another artist of Jewish origin, Gustav Mahler:

> A picture of a complete apple tree, however accurate, in a certain sense resembles it infinitely less than does the smallest daisy. And in this sense a symphony by Bruckner is infinitely more closely related to a symphony from the heroic period than is one by Mahler. If the latter is a work of art it is one of a *totally* different sort (But this observation itself is actually Spenglerian.)[22]

For Wittgenstein, Mahler's music is a "*totally* different sort" of art, because his music is no longer affiliated with the musical tradition of the high and great culture of the West. Although his music "resembles" music produced in an age of high and great culture, the resemblance is deceptive. It actually belongs to an entirely different kind of spiritual enterprise that embodies civilization in the modern period. To affiliate Mahler's music with the musical tradition of the West is like putting pictures of apple trees in an orchid, believing they too can yield real apples.

Mahler and his music also provide Wittgenstein with a concrete example of the difficult predicament that faces an extremely gifted artist in an age when a high and great culture has given way to civilization. He views Mahler as an artist with great talent, who is still trying to create a great work of art at a time when that is no longer possible; for there is no longer a shared spiritual effort at his disposal of which he can avail himself, and for the progression of which he can work. He is thus forced to rely on his own power *only*—while seeking, nevertheless, to express the human spirit in a lofty and culturally powerful new way. But for all his effort, he only manages thereby to express *himself*. For there is no longer any cultural tradition from within which he can express himself and in relation to which his expression might constitute spiritual progression. His expression may be a strong personal gesture, but it is devoid of the power and glory of a cultural tradition that enables artists to create a deeply meaningful great work of art. Therefore it lacks any spiritual significance.

What, then, is such an artist to do? The problem Wittgenstein is trying to clarify here through the case of Mahler is what he sees as the unfortunate creative predicament facing gifted artists in an age of civilization:

> If it is true, as I believe, that Mahler's music is worthless, the question is what I think he should have done with his talent. For quite obviously it

> took a string of very rare talents to produce this bad music. Should he, say, have written his symphonies & burnt them? Or should he have done himself violence & not have written them? Should he have written them & realized that they were worthless? But how could he have realized that?[23]

Mahler, it seems, cannot even evaluate his symphonies properly, cannot realize that they do not constitute great works of art through music, because evaluating them demands putting them in the context of a tradition of high and great culture and seeing whether and how they contribute to its spiritual progression. But he is no longer working from within the spiritual tradition of the high and great culture of the West in music or, for that matter, any cultural tradition; his compositions demonstrate that. So he cannot even perceive how much his music differs in *kind* from what is part of a high and great culture and, in particular, from what constituted the Western musical tradition of creating a great work of art. But then, what should he have done? Should he have turned away from music entirely—and "done violence to himself"?

Gifted artists living in a period in which culture has given way to civilization who, like Mahler, nevertheless insist on trying to express themselves in a powerful way through the arts, have a genuine spiritual problem. They wish to partake in a great cultural progression by creating a profound work of art, but the absence of an appropriate cultural setting precludes the possibility of their doing so. Since there is no longer a cultural tradition of creation and observance to sustain their efforts, the only value their work has is that it somehow enables them to express themselves, though not in a profound spiritual manner. In that case, artistic endeavor becomes a means for an artist to feel good. It does not provide for something which also has significant spiritual value.

7. Technical Art Forms and Fashions

A further telling way in which Wittgenstein sees the disappearance of the arts (practiced in a period of culture) is through the fading of what he calls "style" and the emergence of art forms, which he stigmatizes as constituting only "fashions" and "technical" improvements:

> A modern film is to an old one as a present-day motor car is to one built 25 years ago. The impression it makes is just as ridiculous and clumsy & the way filmmaking has improved is comparable to the sort of technical improvement we see in cars. It is not to be compared with the improvement… of an artistic style. It must be much the same with modern dance music too. A jazz dance, like a film, must be something that can be improved. What distinguishes all these developments from the formation of a *style* is that spirit plays no part in them.[24]

Wittgenstein does not explain what he means by a "jazz dance."[25] However, the idea expressed in these remarks is clear enough. It builds on the conceptual difference between style and fashion, as well as on the conceptual difference between improvement in arts and improvement in technology, both of which he clarifies as manifesting a spiritual difference. With that goal in mind, he contrasts what he experiences as the culturally spiritless nature of fashions and technological innovations with a style in the arts. To unravel this comparison, we might note that the concept of style often refers to a valued characteristic manner of performing a given practice. Contrast a gifted athlete's fluid running style with the clumsy style of most joggers. Similarly, a cultural style is characterized by a shared valued manner of performing certain practices. In the arts, the formation and development of shared abilities, techniques, judgments, and sensibilities provide for a common artistic style and taste. We refer in this connection to the emergence of different shared styles of painting, such as realism or impressionism, around which "artistic schools" form. In this context, we also make comparisons between artists operating in the same style of painting and how they contribute to its improvement and advancement. We speak of them as "working in the same artistic spirit."

Fashion is different. A fashion—say in dress or in homebuilding—is what lives today and dies tomorrow. It acquires its vitality from its appeal to the aesthetic experience of the moment, by pleasing or titillating us in one way or another. It emerges in connection with newly devised innovations and ways of behavior that attract people and appeal to their desire for novelty. Unlike cultural styles, which are formed and forged by refining aesthetic judgments and sensibilities on the basis of a shared tradition, fashions in the arts do not manifest a cherished tradition or an effort to refine artistic sensibilities and judgments.

In Wittgenstein's terms, to say that fashions lack breeding is to assert a conceptual truth. Fashions are novel ways of doing things that become popular without the need to develop an aesthetic taste or cherish some tradition. They also tend to became outdated after a short time and are destined to be replaced by new ones. Once popular fashions in clothes and even in buildings, which are no longer so, may strike us as outdated and as somewhat ridiculous or crude. We wonder how people could have been taken in by them, how they could have found them appealing. Somewhat similarly, we may find old technologies, such as cars, for example, to be crude and in need of technical improvement in comparison to those of the present. According to Wittgenstein, that is the way we also respond to old films or to a "jazz dance."

In contrast to outdated fashions and discarded technologies, a great style in poetry or painting strikes us as deeply meaningful, even if no one writes or paints in that style anymore. We can appreciate biblical prose and Shakespearean poetry, despite the fact that no one today writes in these styles of expression. The same goes for pieces of furniture and china produced in the high style of past centuries. Works of art which are part of a great and high culture with which we are affiliated, even when they become old and even when the culture has progressed considerably since their time of creation, do not strike us as awkward and in need of artistic improvement.

Biblical prose does not seem to us awkward in comparison with Tolstoy's style. A Bach fugue does not impress us as something clumsy in comparison to a Beethoven sonata. Nor do the paintings of Raphael strike us as needing improvement in comparison to those of David. In true culture, past achievements constitute a culture's spiritual heritage. Their style of expression is cherished, and their artistic significance is cultivated through the observance of the tradition that has formed around them, as manifesting ideal works of art. In that way they are experienced as an integral and cherished artistic part of what takes place in a culture. They are not perceived as either crude or clumsy, or as something which present achievements are an improvement on. But that is not, according to Wittgenstein, the way in which we appreciate old films, nor, in his opinion, is it how a "jazz dance" impresses us.

In my reading of Wittgenstein's remarks in this connection, the concepts of fashion and technical improvement typify the cursory, titillating character of the innovations produced in the West in a period of civilization. In his overview on these matters, any effort to sustain tradition and to work from within a common shared effort to express something deeply meaningful in a grand and lofty manner has been relinquished by Western civilization in the modern period. What emerges from it in the arts are fashions rather than grand and lofty cultural styles.

Under these circumstances, all that remains in the arts for those operating in the spirit of Western civilization is to strive to enhance their own individual self-expression and add new and more complicated and disjointed constructions to what already exists. As Wittgenstein appears to experience modern arts, they are eclectic and titillating only. He sees in them a relinquishing of a spiritual effort to "clarify" by artistic methods of expression "the essence" of human life from an inspired perspective. He disdains these forms of art, as such, on spiritual grounds, perceiving them to be the manifestation of the spirit of civilization in which he does not wish to partake.

8. Clarification of the Concept of Artistic Style

It is useful to distinguish between Wittgenstein's aesthetic judgments of certain arts, such as movies, and his clarification of the concept of improvement in its application to art and technology. We might note in this connection that improvement in many arts as well as the development of artistic style often go hand in hand with technical improvements. Recall in this connection the technical improvement of musical instruments, conducive to the development of classical music in Europe, the improvement in painting due to the introduction of oil paints, in the art of storytelling through the development first of writing and later of printing, and so forth. In many of these examples, the technical improvement is often connected with the emergence of a new artistic style. Nonetheless, we might ask whether such technical improvements contributed to an artistic improvement. In asking this question, we demonstrate that we are able to distinguish between these two different contexts in which the concept of improvement is applied.

Another point is the need to distinguish between the normative standing of Wittgenstein's pronouncements on modern art forms, fashion, and improvement in style and technology, and their conceptual standing. Even if we do not agree with his judgments about modern art, his comments can still strike us as conceptually insightful. That is because they clarify certain aspects of the concepts of artistic and technical practices and their relationships to the concepts of style, fashion and improvement. That is the case even if we do not buy into his critical attitude toward arts in the modern period and the disparaging overview of them that accompanies it. His clarification of the conceptual difference between art, technology, and fashion, as well as the way in which the concept of improvement applies to them in different ways, does not depend on our agreeing with his artistic judgments or sharing his cultural standpoint.

9. Civilization as a Contrived and Artificial Spiritual Attitude toward Life

To the extent that created and observed cultural practices, customs, and ways of life provide us with authentic, deeply meaningful, shared human expressions and experiences, Wittgenstein considers those provided by civilization to be artificial and disjointed. In civilization, the human spirit is transformed into a contrived, sophisticated, and intellectual attitude toward life and what it encloses. Civilization fails to lend us an authentic cultural nature. As such, it drives a wedge between culture and human nature, diminishing our ability to observe past cherished practices and customs, to be sustained by them, and to marvel through them at life. In so doing, it also changes our spiritual aspirations, curtailing our former ability and inclination to reach out to something eternal that is loftier than our contrived and sophisticated ways of subsisting and trying to find pleasure in life.

What emerges from Wittgenstein's remarks on the spirit of civilization is that it is a period in which the powerful and natural forces in human beings, which once found their expression in the creation and observance of cohesive, inspiring cultural practices and customs, are tamed and transformed into intellectual forces. It is a period marked by contrived and disjointed creations in the arts, a period in which the observance of cherished customs and of refined practices lapses, and in which tradition no longer plays a central role in supporting a way of life and in expressing oneself in the arts. It is a period in which past cultural distinctions become blurred—such as, for example, those between different cultures, between different social classes, between the sexes, between the functional and the spiritual, and a period in which a cosmopolitan attitude toward spiritual matters prevails. It is a period in which the customs of different cultures and the styles of different genres are easily mixed as contrived and sophisticated efforts infect the arts and past rituals and customs are abandoned as civil practices and functions replace them. Finally, it is a period in which the power and glory of a culture that aims to express something lofty and eternal no longer appeal to or motivate human beings.

Five

REFLECTING ON WITTGENSTEIN'S REMARKS ON CULTURE AND CIVILIZATION

Thus far, I have sought mainly to disclose and elucidate Ludwig Wittgenstein's remarks on the different human spirits manifesting what he calls "culture" and "civilization." I would now like to discuss their conceptual standing, as well as some personal questions they might raise.

1. Who are Wittgenstein's "Friends"?

In the draft to the foreword to his book, Wittgenstein indicated that he is "writing for friends who are scattered throughout the corners of the globe." When he came to reflect on the ethical implications of his intending the book to be read only by certain people and not by others, he added the following remark:

> If I say that my book is meant for only a small circle of people (if that can be called a circle) I do not mean to say that this circle is in my view the élite of mankind but it is the circle to which I turn (not because they are better or worse than the others but) because they form my cultural circle, as it were my fellow countrymen in contrast to the others who are *foreign* to me.[1]

The locutions used in these passages, "friends who are scattered throughout the corners of the globe" and "others who are foreign to me," are meant to clarify and express his spiritual allegiance and cultural affiliation. They are, however, ambiguous. Are these so-called friends only affiliates of Western high and great culture, or could they also possibly be affiliates of any high and great culture? Are those who are "foreign" to him only those who find meaning in what he perceives to be the spirit embodied in practices that he castigates as "civilization," or might they also be affiliates of foreign cultures?

On the face of it, Wittgenstein should not have the same attitude toward arts that are part of a foreign culture as toward arts being pursued in the West during a time to which he refers as a time of "civilization." For, first of all, his attitude toward what is transpiring during civilization is molded by the fact that he experiences it as manifesting a spiritual attitude that has replaced the spirit of Western high and great culture that once prevailed and in which he still wants to partake. He does not perceive civilization as a cultural effort that is continuing alongside Western high and great culture, but as a pseudo-cultural effort that has overcome and replaced it. Wittgenstein experiences civilization not only as a false inheritor of the high and great culture of the West, but also as both the symptom and cause of its disappearance.

Second, unlike civilization, a foreign culture is a genuine cultural enterprise, but one with which he himself is not affiliated. Indeed, Wittgenstein sees the influence of creations that derive from a foreign culture, such as African art, on various artists, as a symptom of the decline of Western high and great culture and the rise of Western civilization. Adjoining Oswald Spengler's contention that we do not really understand artistic creations that are not of our own culture, he remarks that Westerners who appreciate African art appreciate it differently from those who are affiliates of that culture.[2]

The insertion of foreign elements into the high and great culture of the West appears to him disingenuous, as they do not stem from the refined cultured taste that embodies the spirit of this culture. In contrast to artistic creations of a foreign culture, the innovations that make up Western civilization do not strike him as belonging to the kind of spiritual effort that provides for any culture, either Western or African. They strike him as telling examples of the "disintegration" of the spiritual effort that provided in the past for the high and great culture of the West.

2. Self-Clarification versus Metaphysical Explanation

Thus far, I have avoided addressing two nagging questions that arise in reading Wittgenstein's remarks on the spirits of culture and civilization. First, to what extent does he use the distinction between culture and civilization as a metaphysical distinction? Second, is Wittgenstein correct in his remarks with regard to the disappearance of Western high and great culture? To help formulate my response to these questions, I would like to place it in the context of his suggestive claim that the progression of Western high and great culture is in the nature of an epic.

Given that what sustains any culture at any given time in history are the creative practices and cultural sensibilities of its affiliates, the same holds also for its continued progression as a spiritual epic. In either case, an outsider's perspective of it must rely on the cultural attitudes, judgments, and sensibilities of those who are affiliated with the culture. Otherwise it will miss what is culturally meaningful to them in the practices and innovations that emerge from within it. It is this aspect of a culture that—from Wittgenstein's perspective—can only be experienced and described by displaying various instances of cultural appreciation, judgment, and taste. It cannot be explained by means of the alleged constituents of "taste," "judgment" and "appreciation" that sustain a culture. To want to explain what is culturally meaningful in a given cultural enterprise in this way is to want to explain what renders it culturally meaningful to those who are affiliated with it, albeit without using the explanation as a means for affiliating anyone with that culture. Thus, "to explain a culture" in this way to others is not to acculturate them into it by refining their cultured taste. It is "to explain a culture" in a way that does not affect cultural appreciation and judgments. It is to want to make the meaning of a culture understandable through intellect alone, leaving the person to whom it is thus explained an unresponsive "foreigner": someone to whom that culture is not personally meaningful.

To the extent that observance of cultural practices manifests shared sensibilities, judgments, and taste, it also manifests shared ways of appreciating the meaningfulness of a given cultural enterprise. As such, it is an internal feature of a culture. It is a cultural privilege bestowed on affiliates once they have been properly acculturated. To the extent that such judgments demand cultural affiliation, they themselves can be made, evaluated, and appreciated in a culturally meaningful way only by those who are themselves affiliates of the culture in which they are made. But then, the same applies to Wittgenstein's remarks on the difference between the practices of a given culture and those that manifest the civilization that follows it. They, too, are internal judgments to the culture in which they are made. For they compare the practices and achievements of a culture in which their author stands with the practices and achievements that have inherited them, in which he does not partake, as they provide for the civilization that has replaced it.

Indeed, to experience certain practices and innovations as the expressions of civilization and not as the expressions of a former culture is to perceive them as having transgressed the bounds of one's culture. Thus, the distinction that Wittgenstein draws between culture and civilization is cardinal to his cultural standpoint. It manifests the way in which he experiences the social, ideological, industrial urban environment of his time and how he relates to artistic works providing what he regards as both outstanding and tasteful examples of Western high and great culture, as well as to those exemplifying its deterioration. It expresses his cultured taste and sensibilities. Someone who does not share in them, who does not perceive a spiritual difference between "high and great" artistic creations and those he experiences as exemplifying cultural deterioration and thus providing for the emergence of Western "civilization," is an affiliate of a somewhat different spiritual enterprise.

It follows from this last comment that Wittgenstein uses the distinction between culture and civilization in a different way than Spengler does. For Spengler, the distinction between culture and civilization transcended any particular culture and the cultural sensibilities and judgments that sustain it and enable its affiliates to experience its practices and customs as deeply meaningful to them. The distinction could be explained to someone who was foreign to a specific context in which it was applicable, just as it was applicable in the same way to all cultures. Wittgenstein, by contrast, uses the distinction to express and clarify his own attitudes and sensibilities toward the cultural innovations and artistic trends of his time. The remarks he offers in this connection are both personal clarifications and context-laden. They are internal to his different ways of responding to cultural innovations in the West belonging to the past, as opposed to those that belong to his present time. They are aimed at clarifying the different ways in which he experiences them, confirming that many modern innovations embody a "spirit [that] is alien & uncongenial to the author."

3. A "Theory of Deterioration"?

During Wittgenstein's discussions on aesthetics, Rush Rhees, who was among those who attended them, asked some questions about what he called Wittgenstein's "theory" of deterioration. Wittgenstein replied by denying he had any such theory:

> Do you think I have a theory? Do you think I'm saying what deterioration is? What I do is describe different things called deterioration. I might approve deterioration—"All very well your fine musical culture; I'm very glad children don't learn harmony now" . . . My example of deterioration is an example of something I know, perhaps something I dislike . . .[3]

As may be seen from this exchange, Wittgenstein would like to deny that his clarifications constitute either a metaphysical theory, like Spengler's, or what he calls "a value judgment." He offers an example:

> Our dress is in a way simpler than dress in the 18th century and more a dress adapted to certain violent activities, such as bicycling, walking, etc. Suppose we notice a similar change in Architecture and in hairdressing, etc. Suppose I talked of the deterioration of the style of living. If someone asks: "What do you mean by deterioration?" I describe, give examples. You use "deterioration" on the one hand to describe a particular kind of development, on the other hand to express disapproval. I may join it up with the things I like; you with the things you dislike. But the word may be used without any affective element . . . like using a technical term . . . .[4]

We ought to distinguish two different issues. One is whether "deterioration" expresses disproval and is always used in an "affective" manner. Two is whether, in its use, a person is offering "a theory" of deterioration or is merely expressing through it a personal attitude. I take it that in denying that he has a theory, Wittgenstein wants to say that he is expressing through this concept his experience of the change in style. What he does not say at this point is that the example of deterioration of a style instantiates Spengler's distinction between culture and civilization. Indeed, he uses this example to clarify his experience of the change in spiritual attitudes and sensibilities expressed in styles of dress and living in Western society during the modern period.

Thus invested with personally edifying examples, the distinction between culture and civilization is transformed into what in another context of discussion he calls a "perspicuous representation":

> The concept of perspicuous representation is of fundamental importance for us. It denotes the form of our representation, the way we see things. (A kind of "Worldview" as it is apparently typical of our time. Spengler.) . . .[5]

Thus, Spengler's distinction between a period of culture and a period of civilization is an historical worldview. It provides a grand theory (conception, overview, scheme, ideology, or dichotomy) of the spiritual underpinnings of human societies. Wittgenstein transforms it into a set of perspicuous representations of the way "we see things" by clarifying his own judgments of various human innovations and ways of life in the West during the modern period according to this distinction. They function as "connecting links" to this way of seeing things and appreciating the meaning of the distinction.

Wittgenstein can, therefore, claim that he is not putting forward a theory, which in his understanding is a scientific or metaphysical explanation of the underpinnings of any human society. He is only offering a set of perspicuous representations of the way he experiences the spiritual meaning of various innovations and practices in the West during his time as a deterioration of a previously shared spiritual effort to express something lofty and high in art and ways of life. In doing so, he is able to "see the connections" between various cases of deterioration of this spiritual effort.

Thus, just as grammatical remarks provide perspicuous representations of our understanding of the meaning of words, so aesthetic judgments provide perspicuous representations of how we appreciate the spiritual effort underlying different human innovations and practices in our environment. This is particularly so when they are formulated in connection with the different spiritual attitudes underlying culture and civilization in the West during the modern period. For, in Wittgenstein's view, in this period, human beings may partake of the same language and belong to the same society while assuming either of these two different spiritual attitudes.

Since Wittgenstein's remarks on the examples that embody the spiritual distinction between culture and civilization serve to clarify his aesthetic attitude, artistic sensibilities, and cultural standpoint, they are also instances of self-clarification. They clarify the way he himself experiences and appreciates the spiritual effort embodied in different works of art that provide for the high and great culture of the West. Those who share his artistic sensibilities and are in agreement with his aesthetic judgments, share his spiritual attitude and cultural standpoint. They are his spiritual "friends." Those who do not are spiritually "foreign" to him. The former will understand him without needing to explain and justify their agreement with his judgments and attitude. The latter will not, finding his aesthetic judgments and attitude to be prejudiced and without proper justification.

4. The Idea of Culture as an Epic

Wittgenstein uses the rich and powerful metaphor of an epic to describe the progression of Western high and great culture. Accordingly, there is a spiritual difference between affiliates of Western high and great culture at different historical periods of this spiritual journey. Something that strikes modern affiliates of this culture as a worthy and meaningful innovation within this cultural tradition might have seemed bizarre to their ancestors had they encountered it. To the extent that other cultures also share this feature, this predicament applies to their affiliates as well.

To say that cultural progression is an epic is to say that it is an indeterminate shared spiritual adventure, which is pursued through several generations. On my reading of this insight, it should encourage us to attain a more detached philosophical perspective on our own cultural commitments. It should remind us that most of what is dear to us about our own culture and makes us into the particular cultured human beings we are, is probably destined to be supplanted. Our ingrained aesthetic attitudes and sensibilities may turn out to be outdated; our moral values may in time be transvalued; our entrenched ideals of human life may wear out their usefulness and become obsolete. For beyond the limits of our present cultural horizon, there are new discoveries and inventions to be made, new creative adventures to be forged, new human bonds to be solidified, and alternative lifestyles from which to choose. So, despite the inherited tradition and the distance already covered with respect to culture, everything is still open.

Thus, the idea that the spiritual progression of a culture is in the nature of an epic provides an insightful outlook on the cultural affairs of human beings. Not only may it be of relevance to how Wittgenstein experiences Western high and great culture, but it pertains to the experiences of other human beings in connection with other cultures as well. At the same time, it provides an ambiguous ending to Wittgenstein's reflections on the spiritual manifestations of culture and civilization and his attempt to clarify his cultural judgments from this perspective, one that may be of relevance to others and their experience as well.

For what ultimately shapes a cultural epos into a single whole and sustains it, whether in the arts, religion, or even as a social enterprise, is that certain human beings feel themselves to be observing and creating within the same spiritual tradition of old, despite all the twists and turns it may have taken. Although some cultured human beings like Wittgenstein may feel that Western high and great culture has disappeared, having been transformed into the contrived, fragmented, uninspiring creative efforts of civilization, others may feel that it has merely advanced to new creative adventures, undertaken in a worthy and even similar cultural spirit as before.

It follows from the above insight that nothing inherent in the practices and customs of a given culture precludes the possibility of its progressing to new cultural innovations: works of art and customs that, although lying beyond the cultural sensibilities and scope of past generations, are experienced by present generations as a worthy cultural contribution, continuing in the same spiritual tradition. We either appreciate new artistic expressions as culturally meaningful innovations contributing to the spiritual progression of our culture, or we fail to do so. The most that can be said is that some cultures exhibit (and perhaps even allow for) more creative progression than others.

But if the spiritual progression of a culture is indeed an epic, then some change must occur in it. Even its tradition may change as new interpretations of past achievements are made accessible, or as the focus on previous details shifts, or as certain archaic elements are discarded as "inessential." The outcome of such progression is that some affiliates of a given culture are liable to find themselves incapable of keeping up with its spiritual pace because they fail to experience, in the emergence of new creations and the relinquishing of certain old ones, the same spiritual effort embodied in their culture of old.

When the creative innovations that emerge in a culture within the life span of a person are not very striking, this problem does not arise. However, when they arrive at a rapid pace, as they seem to in the modern era, some of us may find ourselves confronted with spiritual adventures at a pace we cannot keep up with. The spiritual progression of our culture, if that is what it still is, may then leave us stranded behind, no longer able to continue the journey. Of course, we will not experience the event in that way, but as a change of direction, a disregard for tradition, the disintegration of a shared spiritual endeavor into fragmented endeavors, a titillating, contrived, or complicated effort that has forsaken the attempt to express through our culture something lofty and eternal. We may experience through these innovations that the culture we cherish is being transformed into a host of shallow and disjointed creative enterprises for which we have no regard, and in which we are unable to partake. We may then feel that we are the last preservers of a spiritual tradition, which few any longer observe. Finally, we shall experience the disappearance of our culture.

5. The Fate of Philoctetes

There is an ancient Greek story about the predicament of those of us who, like Wittgenstein, fail to join what others around them experience as the spiritual progression of their culture. As the story is told, during the course of the epic journey of the Greek armies to Troy, Philoctetes, bitten in his foot by snake, found it difficult to continue. He moaned and complained of his suffering and anguish, making a general nuisance of himself. Finally, his companions had enough and abandoned him on one of the islands. The journey continued without him.

The fate of Philoctetes provides a telling parable for what eventually happens in the course of a cultural epic to those incapable of keeping up with it. They are left behind. The spiritual journey goes on without them. Of course, that is not how they themselves are apt to see the situation. They may feel that the journey has veered off course. They may see no direction to it at all, or that it has been fragmented into individual efforts only. They are apt to experience the situation in that way because, as Wittgenstein reminds us, they "think of the world's future" as "the place it will get to if it keeps going as [they] see it going now and it doesn't occur to [them] that it is not going in a straight line but in a curve & that its direction is constantly changing."[6]

Or, they may even think of this possibility, but still not be able to accommodate themselves to the path it is taking. Perhaps, like Wittgenstein, they may eventually come to think of themselves and of those fellow human beings who share their cultural sensibilities and spiritual attitude as a few remaining "friends who are scattered throughout the corners of the globe," former members of a spiritual tradition who are isolated and abandoned on their cultural islands in a sea of civilization; a "small circle of people" as he remarks, who form "my cultural circle . . . fellow countrymen in contrast to the others who are *foreign* to me."[7]

So finally, how can we tell whether the spiritual progression of our culture is still continuing (and it is us who are being left behind), or whether the culture has disappeared (and we are the only ones left to notice it)? The question resonates familiarly, echoing philosophical reflections produced in what we took to be an entirely different setting of inquiry for Wittgenstein: *How can we determine whether we have failed to follow an old rule in a new and unfamiliar way, or whether it is the rule that has changed? How can we determine whether we have failed to perceive a family resemblance between old and new artistic achievements, or whether all resemblance between them has ceased to exist?*

The answer to this tantalizing philosophical riddle, which underlies many of Wittgenstein's remarks, not only about arts and ways of living, but also on language, mathematics, and mind, is that it does not really matter! For, ultimately, the question whether the culture with which we are affiliated has disappeared or only progressed to new spiritual adventures beyond our comprehension and sensibility is not one that will be resolved for us by means of a straightforward *objective* answer. Nor does it call for such an answer. For those of us who are able to recognize and experience in current practices and innovations the progression of a shared cultural effort that began a long time ago and is still continuing, the culture with which we are affiliated will appear to be a viable human enterprise—it will still be infused with the spirit of old. For those who, in new innovations and practices, are unable to perceive and experience the progression of a cultural effort with which we are affiliated and which is pursued in the same spirit as of old, this effort will appear to have strayed off course and its spiritual goals to have been abandoned. If so, our culture may then appear to us to have disappeared. Indeed, for us it *will* have disappeared, leaving us feeling that we are the last preservers of its spirit, stranded and abandoned on our shrinking cultural island in an expanding sea of civilization.

The moral of this last insight is that philosophy cannot help us resolve the matter one way or another. That is to say, the spiritual progression of our culture, just like its disappearance, cannot be determined for us according to some predetermined objective spiritual standard to which we might cling. For each of us, it depends on the way in which we relate to what human beings create, observe and cherish by experiencing it as the continuation, progression, deterioration or disappearance of a cultural tradition in which we share.

Third Study

THE COMMON SPIRIT OF HUMAN BEINGS

In 1930/1931 Wittgenstein read James George Frazer's account and explanation of myth, magic, and religion in *The Golden Bough* and wrote a series of comments about it.[1] Later, in 1948, he again wrote several comments on this text. He used Frazer's discourse to clarify his own thinking on the spiritual nature of human beings, expressing his deep personal concern with this subject. Accordingly, after describing key elements in Frazer's explanation of myth, magic, and religion, I discuss Wittgenstein's criticism of it and the conceptual account of such practices he offers instead. Within that context, I elaborate on two subjects. The first is the philosophical insight Wittgenstein advances regarding the symbolic nature of myth, magic and religion and the spiritual attitudes towards life expressed in them. The second is Wittgenstein's insight into the common spiritual nature of modern human beings and those of ancient cultures, which enables us to grasp the expressive meaning of myth, magic, and religion without an explanation. Within this framework, I also discuss some philosophical responses to his comments. Finally, I consider the relevance of Wittgenstein's insights on this subject to his pessimistic outlook on the spirit that manifests modern culture.

One

FRAZER'S EXPLANATION OF MYTH, MAGIC, AND RELIGION

James George Frazer presents his monumental account and explanation of Myth, Magic, and Religion as a scholarly "voyage of discovery." Its point of embarkation is Virgil's description of the priest-king of the grove of Diana awaiting his own murder under sacred oaks. He begins his explanation with a highly charged description of J. M. W. Turner's picture of this event: "The scene is suffused with the golden glow of imagination . . . a dream-like vision of the little woodland lake of Nemi- 'Dianna's mirror,' as it was called by the ancients." On the northern shore of this lake by the Alban hills near Rome, he tells, was the sacred grove and sanctuary of Dianna of the Wood, sometimes known also as the lake and grove of Aricia. In it grew a certain tree, round which prowled a man with a drawn sword, expecting at every instant to be set upon by an enemy: "He was a priest and a murderer; and a man for whom he looked was eventually to murder him and hold the priesthood in his stead. Such was the rule of the sanctuary," Frazer tells.[1]

After relating the gruesome tradition to several myths and rituals of magic from which the priest emerges as king, Frazer asks two questions: "Why had Diana's priest at Nemi, the king of the Wood, to slay his predecessor?" and "Why before doing so had he to pluck the branch of a certain tree which the . . . ancients identified with Virgil's Golden Bough?"[2] To answer these questions, he invites his readers to sail along with him on a very long scholarly voyage to ancient cultures in "strange foreign lands with strange foreign peoples," where strange and horrifying myths were told and strange and horrifying rituals of magic and religion were practiced. His description of myth, magic, and religious practices throughout the world, which he arranges according to kinds by their similarities and purposes, is astonishing, overwhelming and very impressive.

Frazer explains the similarity between ancient myths and rituals in different cultures by postulating a historical relationship of influence. Eventually, he also answers the question he posed about the priest-king of Nemi by noting that ancient kings were often priests who were revered as being, in some way, gods. Such kings, he explains, were expected to provide rain and sunshine in due season, to make the crops grow. Strange as it may seem to us, he claims:

> a savage hardly conceives the distinction commonly drawn by more advanced peoples between the natural and the supernatural. . . . In a world

> so conceived he sees no limit to his power of influencing the course of nature to his own advantage.[3]

Frazer then goes on to explain the elaborate ritual of the priest-king of the grove of Diana awaiting his own murder as a rite of spring, the succession of the priest-kings being designed to secure the succession of the crops. He explains many other rituals and ceremonies in a similar manner, describing them as the use of magic to bring about desired ends, and he explains magic as simple-minded science.

One might wonder why people in ancient cultures availed themselves of magic, since it is not efficacious. Frazer's answer is that to them, it always seemed to work:

> A ceremony intended to make the wind blow or the rain fall, or to work the death of an enemy, will always be followed, sooner or later by the occurrence it is meant to bring to pass. . . . Similarly, rites observed in morning to help the sun rise, and in the spring to wake the dreaming earth from her winter sleep, will invariably appear to be crowned with success. . . . Hence the practical savage, with his conservative instincts, might well turn a deaf ear to the subtleties of the theoretical doubter…[4]

Frazer traces the principles of magic to two ideas: first, that like produces like, or that an effect resembles its cause; second, that things which have once been in contact with each other continue to act on each other at a distance after the physical contact has been severed. He calls the first the Law of Similarity and the second, the Law of Contact, or Contagion.[5] He also claims that when the principles of thought in magic replace legitimate explanations, they yield a science. Illegitimate explanations yield magic, "the bastard sister of science." He suggests that the thinking behind religion is similar, but applied in a theoretical and not just a practical context, providing "a belief in powers higher than man and an attempt to propitiate them."[6]

Religion, Frazer explains, assumes that we can persuade the mighty beings who control the course of nature to deflect it for our benefit. This view of nature is opposed to the principles of magic as well as of science, both of which assume that the processes of nature cannot be turned from their course by pleading, threats or intimidation. Perhaps this is because unlike gods, they are not taken to constitute beings that are able to understand human speech acts. Thus, the distinction between the two conflicting views of the universe turns on whether the forces governing the world are conscious and personal or unconscious and impersonal.[7]

Frazer adds that this explanation accounts for the strong hostility expressed in many religions toward magic, as it denies the existence of supreme beings that control nature. In response to possible counterexamples, he notes that magic also deals with spirits, which are personal agents of the kind that religion also assumes to exist. However, he explains, "it treats them exactly in the same fashion as it treats inanimate agents; that is, it constrains or coerces them, instead of conciliating or propitiating them as religion would do." Thus, magic assumes that all personal beings, whether human or divine, can be manipulated by appropriate ceremonies and spells that can make things happen.[8]

Two

WITTGENSTEIN'S CRITICISM OF FRAZER'S CONCEPTUAL EXPLANATION

1. The Truth about Myth, Magic, and Religion

Ludwig Wittgenstein's reading of James George Frazer is critical from the onset. "One must start with error and convert it into truth," he writes in his opening comment. This approach is reminiscent of his later criticism, in the first section of *Philosophical Investigations*, of what he there calls Augustine of Hippo's "picture of the essence of human language," which he stigmatized as being based on "a primitive idea of the way language functions." He justifies his focusing from the start on the "error" in Frazer's explanation of the essence of these practices, with the remark that without revealing "the source of the error . . . hearing the truth won't do any good. The truth cannot force its way in when something else is occupying its place."[1] Wittgenstein does not state at this point what that "truth" is, what "error" has been committed by Frazer, and what lies at its source that makes it difficult for "the truth to force its way in"—let alone why that is important to him.

For why indeed does Wittgenstein care about such an academic subject as the way in which ancient human beings reacted to life and world through Myth, Magic, and Religion? The answer, I suggest, is that it is not just an academic subject to him. For in explaining these practices, Frazer is explaining both the nature of Myth, Magic, and Religion and the nature of human beings who find meaning in them. On reading Frazer's account of these practices, Wittgenstein responds to them as spiritual practices, expressing deep human concerns that underlie his own life, despite being a modern person.

Thus, "the truth" he would like to help "force its way in" and which it would do no good to merely state, as I am doing now, is double-edged. It concerns the spiritual nature of Myth, Magic, and Religion and the common underlying spiritual nature of human beings in ancient and modern cultures, a spirit expressed through them, manifesting our shared humanity. It is Wittgenstein's impression that Frazer distorts the expressive spiritual nature of such practices and disregards the common human experiences, existential concerns, and expressive dispositions manifested in them. As a result, he becomes a disgruntled voyager on Frazer's ship.

However, my aim here is not to evaluate the validity of Wittgenstein's criticism of Frazer's account of Myth, Magic, and Religion. It is to use his criticism to study his comments on the common spiritual nature of human beings as it is manifested in Myth, Magic, and Religion, and the philosophical method he uses to bring this out.

Curiously, Frazer, too, saw a similarity between ancient and modern human beings through these practices. According to him, ancients and moderns both approach life by reasoning about its underlying causes, trying to manipulate and influence them. The difference between them is that in the modern era, such reasoning is conducted properly through scientific theories that are implemented in medicine and technology. In ancient times, it was improperly conducted through Myth, Magic, and Religion, which, in Frazer's explanation, "turn a deaf ear to the subtleties of the theoretical doubter." Explaining such practices as faulty ways of reasoning, Frazer thinks he has an answer to why people tell myths, practice magic, and adopt religious beliefs: it is because they reason in a faulty manner. He perceives Myth, Magic, and Religion as primitive ways of reasoning about the causes of events, which sometimes has been carried over into modernity by certain superstitious segments of the population. Thus, according to Wittgenstein, the error that does not enable the truth about the common spiritual nature of human beings in ancient and modern times "to force its way in," is Frazer's. It lies in his faulty explanation regarding the essence of Myth, Magic, and Religion as instrumental and theoretical ways of reasoning about the primary causes underlying life and the world.[2]

This explanatory stance manifests Frazer's acceptance of the Positivist view of the supposedly historical progress achieved in modern cultures, which, in that view, has taken humanity from its former belief in Myth, Magic, and Religion to reliance on scientific explanations. In it, Myth, Magic, and Religion are the first historical stage in human progress toward knowledge, philosophy the second, and science the third. Thus, in effect, Wittgenstein criticizes Frazer for having followed Positivism by seeking to explain the essence of Myth, Magic, and Religion as errors in theoretical and instrumental ways of thinking, suggesting along the way that it was Frazer who erred in his thinking. They are not examples of theoretical and instrumental ways of thinking at all:

> Frazer says that it is very hard to discover the error in magic—and that is why it lasted so long—because, for example, an incantation that is supposed to bring rain certainly seems efficacious sooner or later. But then it is surely remarkable that people don't realize earlier that sooner or later it's going to rain anyhow.[3]

In light of this criticism, Frazer would seem to have regarded people in ancient cultures as simply less intelligent than modern people: "It is very remarkable that in the final analysis all these practices are presented as, so to speak, pieces of stupidity. But it will never be plausible to say that mankind does all that out of sheer stupidity."[4] For Wittgenstein, ancient human beings who invented and observed these practices were not very different from modern ones in their intelligence, as evidenced by their invention of the techniques of hunting, farming, building, clothing, and preparing food.[5] Hence, the creation and observance of these practices is not explained by human inability to reason properly. Accordingly, Wittgenstein concludes that error and progress are the marks of science and technology, not magic:

> The distinction between magic and science can be expressed by saying that in science there is progress, but in magic there isn't. Magic has no tendency within itself to develop.[6]

In the above insight, it is typical of an instrumental practice based on intellect and reasoning, like science and technology, to progress toward more advanced discoveries and innovations. But magic, like religion and myth, is not of this kind. We do not stop using magic, telling myths, or praying according to a given religion because these practices have not progressed to new explanations, discoveries, and innovations. We have no such expectations of them.

To see the point of Wittgenstein's criticism of Frazer's instrumental explanation of the conceptual nature of Myth, Magic, and Religion, imagine visiting aliens who seek to understand the purpose of the human practice of dancing. They might note that they understand the purpose of walking, as it gets us from one place to another. But they are baffled about the purpose of dancing, as it does not seem to get us anywhere. If they were to theorize that we dance because of a mistaken idea that it can get us from one place to another, they would be committing a category mistake of the sort that Wittgenstein describes as the "error" in Frazer's explanation.

2. The Conceptual Nature of Myth, Magic, and Religion

To explain the essence of Myth, Magic, and Religion is to explain their conceptual nature. Like all cultural phenomena, their conceptual nature is manifested in their use by human beings, what they experience and grasp through them, and the role they play within a cultural stream of life. To describe these features and to place them in relation to basic human propensities, inclinations, and spontaneous ways of behavior, as well as to compare them with other phenomena and practices that manifest different human propensities and have a different role in the stream of human life, is to clarify their conceptual nature.

In Wittgenstein's comments, Myth, Magic, and Religion are inherently expressive and symbolic. They emerge in the form cultural rituals, enacted metaphors and symbolic narratives that use figurative modes of speech. Being expressive, they differ from predominantly instrumental practices, such as agriculture, cooking, or building shelter, which are not predominantly expressive. Being symbolic, they differ from predominantly non-symbolic expressive practices, such as playing music, engaging in sports, or complaining about headaches, which need not manifest anything symbolic. To say this is not to deny that they may have other purposes as well, just as to say that cooking is an instrumental practice is not to deny that it may also have aesthetic and social purposes as well. While this description does not exhaust their conceptual nature, it describes a central conceptual feature that typifies them. To help place Myth, Magic, and Religion within a conceptual category of expressive and symbolic cultural phenomena, we may note that they are akin to such ritualistic practices as shaking hands, dressing-up for a holiday dinner, or standing at attention during memorial services, which are symbolic social cultural expressions of friendliness, celebration and reverence.

One way in which we characterize the practice of telling myths, performing magic, and engaging in religious prayer, is as expressive and symbolic practices that cater to the human spirit. In ordinary use of language, the word "spirited" is often used to describe the expressive and lively nature of people and their animated behavior as contrasted with listless or lethargic behavior. While our spirit may be moved by all sorts of practices in which we engage, such as art, sport, work, or social rituals, telling a myth, performing magic, and engaging in religious prayer are paradigmatic spiritual practices.

Three related conceptual features characterize them as spiritual: first, their expression and promotion of an attitude of awe and wonder over the mysterious, often enigmatic nature of life and world and the unfathomable deep meaning of events taking place therein; second, the manner in which they both express and promote, through symbolic actions, poetic uses of language and powerful images, inspiring worldviews of supernatural powers and beings, underlying and controlling life and world; and third is their expression of deep, existential concerns that accompany the life of human beings in all cultures. Typically, such concerns emerge in the form of dreads, anxieties, cares, worries, fears, hopes, wishes, hates, loves, attachments, remorse, guilt, sadness, grief, wonder, faith, and more.

By providing, through their rituals, symbolic narratives and figurative uses of language, an expressive conceptual system from within which existential concerns are expressed and addressed, Myth, Magic, and Religion transform them into inspiring spiritual attitudes toward life and what it encompasses. In their enacted, expressive, symbolic form, they tend to promote and enhance pivotal conceptual distinctions about the sacred and profane, good and evil, as underlying life and world and as constituting something powerful that may be addressed or placated. Along with these come also edifying lessons, world-pictures, and shared perspectives on the enigmatic nature of life and its meaning. As such, these practices reveal a spiritual disposition for creating and observing expressive symbolic practices that is part of the underlying existential nature of human beings in all cultures, even if it may have attained its most powerful expression in ancient cultures.

3. Spiritual versus Instrumental

To describe Myth, Magic, and Religion as spiritual practices is to offer a somewhat banal categorization of their conceptual nature. I do so because this categorical description of their conceptual nature underlies Wittgenstein's criticism of Frazer's explanation of them as instrumental practices. The upshot of this banal but philosophically useful conceptual reminder is that in Wittgenstein's insight, Myth, Magic, and Religion are neither cultural practices manifesting an intellectual disposition for reasoning, nor cultural practices manifesting an expressive spiritual disposition that was exclusive to the ancients. When we buy into Frazer's explanation of the conceptual nature of Myth, Magic, and Religion as faulty, primitive, scientific-like ways of reasoning, our understanding of the expressive spiritual nature, needs, and inclinations of human beings falters. The failure blinds us to an important aspect of human spiritual nature and cultural life, underlying both the lives of the ancients and our own.

To gain philosophical insight into the conceptual nature of these practices as manifesting the common underlying spiritual nature of human beings in both ancient and modern cultures requires placing them first in their proper conceptual category. In Wittgenstein's critique, this is Frazer's error. He reduces these expressive symbolic practices to the category of fallacious ways of reasoning.[7] He thus renders those who find spiritual meaning in Myth, Magic, and Religion into stupid human beings, alienating us thereby both from them and from our own expressive human nature and spiritual needs.

Wittgenstein claims that it will not help to state outright what this category is. He does not say why. Perhaps it is because Frazer's error stems from a widespread philosophical view about Myth, Magic, and Religion, which informs the modern age, precluding us from seeing the truth about them and hindering us from acknowledging our own spiritual needs and inclinations. Perhaps it is because he believes that to "make the spirit explicit,"[8] as he calls it elsewhere, is to try to explain what can only be expressed, resulting in murky assertions that promote metaphysical nonsense. However, to classify Myth, Magic, and Religion as spiritual practices is, although culturally commonplace, philosophically helpful. It does not explain what constitutes a spiritual practice, nor does it limit such a practice merely to Myth, Magic, and Religion. It only draws attention to the difference between them and merely instrumental practices, reminding us along the way that the three are inherently expressive of a human spirit. It is this essential feature about them that Frazer confounds when he explains them as primitive science.

The irony is that despite being in error, Frazer's account of Myth, Magic, and Religion contains a kernel of truth: those who find meaning in them "might well turn a deaf ear to the subtleties of the theoretical doubter." However, for Wittgenstein, that is not because they are guilty of faulty ways of reasoning, but because being expressive and spiritual, they do not manifest ways of reasoning at all:

> Frazer's account of magical and religious views of mankind are unsatisfactory: it makes these views look like *errors*. Was Augustine in error, then, when he called upon God on every page of the *Confessions*?[9]

Frazer faulted the use of Myth, Magic, and Religion as not allowing the possibility of their being in error. In Wittgenstein's criticism, this shows that they are not used as practices that manifest ways of reasoning. Therefore, to explain Myth, Magic, and Religion as "errors in reasoning" is to be mistaken about their conceptual category by intellectualizing them. As a result, they are regarded as (mistaken) theories about life and world that are entertained without proper methods of reasoning that may yield confirmation or falsification—a kind of primitive and faulty science.

To draw attention to the fact that they do not constitute an intellectual discourse and, therefore, should not be regarded as (faulty) ways of reasoning that promote (mistaken) theories, Wittgenstein notes the role of religious discourse in the life of its users—for example, the use Augustine made of it to call on God to guide him. When Augustine beseeched God, he was expressing his deep existential concerns and spiritual need, which he transformed into an inspiring religious ritual of prayer. Through it, he voiced both his spiritual need and his faith in God. He was not putting forward a theory that he found always to be confirmed.

A corollary to this insight is that the telling of myths, the employment of magic, and the recital of religious prayers are all spiritual rituals. As such, they are of a similar category: ways of both expressing and confronting deep existential concerns by transforming them through expressive cultural rituals and moving stories into inspiring spiritual attitudes toward life. Therefore, they are not errors in thinking, any more than singing and dancing are errors in thinking or calling upon people to open their hearts to the suffering of others is a biological error in thinking. Wittgenstein emphasizes this conceptual point by noting how, in all cultures, human beings relate to practices that are based on errors in reasoning:

> It can indeed happen, and often does today, that a person will give up a practice after he has recognized an error on which it was based. But this happens only where calling someone's attention to his error is enough to turn him from his way of behaving. But this is not with religious practices of people and *therefore* there is *no* question of an error.[10]

In this insight, instrumental practices are grounded in rational ways of thinking. As such, people will often change a given instrumental practice when an error is pointed out to them that it is insufficient to bring about the desired end. For Wittgenstein, that is not the case with religious practices, as they are inherently expressive and symbolic. Ironically, this was also Frazer's point when he noted that, for users of these practices, "there is no question of an error" regarding them. Wittgenstein turns this telling feature into a conceptual truth about the nature of such practices without accepting Frazer's derogatory evaluation of them as errors in reasoning. For they are expressive spiritual rituals and narratives, just as shaking hands and asserting a cordial refrain in greeting someone, or raising a glass of wine in a social situation and pronouncing a blessing are expressive social gestures and rituals.

It is important not to confuse this conceptual point with a claim that there are no changes in spiritual practices. Not only do spiritual practices change over the years, but also, the change is sometimes accompanied by a change in beliefs and dogmas that accompany them. To evaluate Wittgenstein's remark, we need to consider whether such changes arise by "calling someone's attention to his error" in instrumental ways of reasoning.

4. The Expressive Meaning of Symbolic Actions and Speech

To repeat, according to Wittgenstein, telling a myth, performing magic, and engaging in a religious ritual manifest a human disposition for symbolic behavior and poetic figurative ways of speech. These practices are used by human beings to express, enhance, and confront existential concerns and attitudes of awe and wonder at the enigmatic meaning of life and the mysterious nature of the world. They cater to these concerns and attitudes in two ways: by providing a culturally rich and powerful expression for them and by promoting, thereby, an inspired attitude toward life and what it encloses. This spiritual disposition is as natural to human beings as the physical disposition to scratch where it itches. Spiritual rituals and figurative ways of speech that accompany and support them, it might be said, are ways of scratching our existential concerns through inspiring symbolic actions that bring spiritual satisfaction to our souls. Therefore, things said in rituals of praying, blessing, celebrating birth, mourning, atonement for sins, preventing evil, or casting magical spells, just like the practice of telling awe-inspiring myths, have expressive, symbolic, non-theoretical, inspirational, spiritual meaning.

To better appreciate Wittgenstein's attempt to sever the conceptual link between what is said in such practices and what is explained through a theory, note how things said in our own cultural rituals seem strange if taken as theoretical principles in which we believe and on which these rituals are based. In graveside eulogies, we sometimes address the dead, declaring to them how dear they were to us and how much we will miss them. We may speak of them as "resting" or as "sleeping in peace," "having departed from this earth and gone to heaven," and so forth. This is despite the fact that we are modern human beings who are acquainted with science and technological ways of reasoning. Someone unfamiliar with the inspired, metaphoric, figurative use of language on such occasions might think we really believe that the dead can hear us speak, that death is a form of sleep, or that the dead travel to a different geographical location from where they lived or where their bodies are buried. Indeed, when challenged about the matter, we may say all kinds of things, depending on the kind of metaphors that have developed in our culture in connection with rituals of mourning and expressions of grief.

Nonetheless, we know quite well that addressing the dead is not like conversing with a neighbor. We also know that death is not really sleep. We do not lower our voices in graveyards so the dead will not hear us or to keep them from waking. We do so out of reverence. We also know that dead people do not really travel to a new place of dwelling, as their bodies remain where they were buried. Such ways of talking are inspired, symbolic, metaphoric extensions of the ritual of burial and mourning. They should not be confused with ways of talking to living people in practical situations, just as a ritual of burial should not be confused with purely instrumental practices of disposing rubbish.

Indeed, a characteristic feature of rituals is their enacted symbolic meaning. They are akin to expressions that convey their meaning through the use of analogy or simile. To confuse them and the language used in their context with practical actions and discourse would be like misunderstanding the metaphor "dirty hands" in moral discourse as describing hands that are physically dirty. Or to suppose that when we speak of love filling a person's heart or of a difficult problem tearing a person's brain apart, we are putting forward an anatomical theory.

The conceptual insight that Myth, Magic, and Religion are expressive symbolic spiritual practices seems to bear a certain resemblance to the Logical Positivists' view of the emotive meaning of ethical assertions, which were said to lack "cognitive content." A problem with this analogy is that Myth, Magic, and Religion do not appear to be merely ways of expressing and confronting existential concerns by promoting inspiring spiritual attitudes toward life. They also promote certain views and beliefs about life and world in those who find meaning in them. This conceptual feature distinguishes them also from what some years later John Langshaw Austin called "performative utterances," such as greeting by saying "Hello," averring by saying "I swear," apologizing by saying "I am sorry."[11] Performative utterances are linguistic actions that are akin to social rituals, which are not always based on acquiring certain beliefs about the nature of life and world. Thus, it might be claimed that in some cultures people do believe that the dead can hear their requests and prayers.

My first comment in this connection is that to speak of the dead hearing our prayers is conceptually different from speaking about a politician hearing our request to intercede with a municipal problem. The first is a religious ritual. The second is not. Therefore, the meaning of requests formulated in prayers is different from those made in everyday social circumstance, just as prayers are different speech acts from those used in human interaction. We do not formulate them in the same way, and we do not judge their result in the same way. Nonetheless, it often happens that people who engage in these forms of behavior also maintain various religious beliefs that support them and out of which they seem to arise. The comment Wittgenstein offers regarding beliefs accompanying spiritual practices is suggestive, but sparse. He notes that when Frazer:

> explains to us that the king must be killed in his prime, because the savage believes that otherwise his soul would not be kept fresh, all one can say is: where that practice and these views occur together, the practice does not spring from the view, but they are both just there.[12]

A way of fleshing out the above suggestion is to note that beliefs asserted in connection with Myth, Magic, and Religion are often an extension of the expressive nature of these practices in a symbolic use of language. In saying that "the king must be killed in his prime, . . . otherwise his soul would not be kept fresh," observers of the ritual are not giving a reasoned theoretical or practical explanation on which it is based, as they would in explaining why meat needs to be eaten soon after an animal is killed. Such an assertion is a linguistic expression of the symbolic nature of the ritual itself: a further expression of it.[13] It elaborates on and enhances it, by means of the very symbols that embody this ritual, using an instrumental practice as a simile. Another way of expressing this point is to say that the belief is no more a reason for the practice than the practice is the reason for holding the belief. Therefore, Frazer's "very idea of wanting to explain the reason for such a practice—for example, the killing of the priest king—on the basis of what its observers say seems wrong . . . ." For what is said in that connection by observers of the practice is not a theoretical explanation on which it is based. Rather, it is a figurative, symbolic, inspired assertion that grows out of, accompanies, compliments, expresses and enriches it.

Consider the Christian ritual of taking one's hat off during prayer or in church, as compared with the Jewish ritual of covering one's head during prayer or in a synagogue. Both religions have all sorts of explanations as to why reverence of God is expressed thusly. Someone who took these explanations as competing theories about the nature of holy reverence would be making a conceptual mistake about the expressive spiritual meaning of such religious assertion. Following Wittgenstein's insight on these matters, such assertions are to be regarded as internal to the practices. They are verbal expression of them, rather than theoretical explanations.

Another related way in which Wittgenstein clarifies the conceptual nature of spiritual practices is by placing actions rather than propounded doctrines at their heart. He describes this point in connection with religion:

> I can well imagine a religion in which there are no doctrinal propositions, in which there is thus no talking. Obviously the essence of religion cannot have anything to do with the fact that there is talking, or rather: when people talk, then this itself is part of a religious act and not a theory. Thus it also does not matter at all if the words used are true or false or nonsense.[14]

"Doctrinal propositions" are religious dogmas, often formulated as theological worldviews and abstract religious principles. Religious practices are often accompanied by such formulated doctrines that seek to lend them metaphysical articulation and support. However, Wittgenstein is imagining here the possibility of religious practices that express and enhance a religious attitude toward life, which is not supported by metaphysical explanations, worldviews, or religious doctrines. They are only ritualistic. The words that accompany them, if at all, have only an expressive symbolic role, just as saying "How do you do?" when being introduced to someone is a ritual of cordiality, not a request for medical or business information.

It follows that we ought to distinguish between language used in rituals or a so called "religious speech act" and language used in asserting religious claims. Consider the monotheistic assertion that God is one, emanating out of Judaism. In point of fact, this assertion is part of the prayer of Shma Israel. Being a prayer, it is a spiritual expression of faith in God that watches over Israel. To assert it within a ritual of prayer is not to propound a religious doctrine within a theological debate, even if it does have the same linguistic form as a propounded religious doctrine. This is so, just as complaining of a headache is not to offer a medical diagnosis. Thus, so-called doctrinal propositions that are incorporated in the expressive symbolic nature of religious rituals and symbolic narratives do not operate as a theological doctrine, having the form and function of a metaphysical worldview.

In this insight, the role of religious practices is the experience, expression, and promotion of a personally meaningful spiritual attitude toward life and what it encloses. Hence, there is no compelling reason to base it on theoretical doctrinal propositions. We do not require a theoretical base for finding meaning in various social gestures, such as waving to friends on their departure or shaking hands with them when meeting. Once we are acculturated to them, we do so without needing a theoretical support for the inclination to engage in such practices. Similarly, in my reading of Wittgenstein's remarks, there is no reason to propound theoretical doctrines that would support our inclination to engage in spiritual practices that cater to our existential concerns, by promoting an inspired religious attitude toward life and what it encloses. A religious attitude toward life may be expressed in ways of life and symbolic actions without basing it on any theological doctrine. That is, not unless we are unable to do so for various cultural and personal reasons.

A problem with the attempt to rid religion of all theoretical principles is that many religious practices are not like social rituals or aesthetic attitudes to life and world, which may underlie our lives without propounding theoretical principles. First, they are historically connected to propounded doctrines, emerging in the form of religious principles and worldviews. Second, the concept of a religious attitude toward life is not the same as the concept of an aesthetic attitude toward life. To remove all worldviews from religious practices would turn them into expressive gestures of a spiritual attitude toward life that can scarcely be articulated, perhaps only through poetry and metaphors. In Wittgenstein's insight, it is an attitude toward life that invests our lives with spiritual meaning; albeit without our being able to describe of what this meaning consists, save for the fact that we are no longer concerned about life and death as we were before it. Religious rituals are symbolic practices, the aim of which is to express and promote a religious attitude toward life. They are like enacted metaphors that provide insight through their inspiring ways of expression, which cannot be paraphrased.

This is not to deny that religious practices are often accompanied by "doctrinal propositions." As I read Wittgenstein on this matter, he wants to distinguish between things said in the practice of a ritual from theological principles that are not part of it but are asserted to explain and support it. He wants to "imagine a religion in which there are no doctrinal propositions, in which there is thus no talking." In this conception of the matter, prayers and blessings are not "talking." Theological doctrines are. Myths belong in the first category, alongside prayers and blessings. This is even when they are narrated to "explain" certain rituals. They are expressive and symbolic narratives that enrich these rituals for those who find meaning in them.

5. Symbols, Expressions, and Signs

To remark that Myth, Magic, and Religion are symbolic is to note that their form of expression is both figurative and inspirational. Hence, the language used in them, whether in the performance of rituals or the assertion of beliefs that are internal to them and their modes of expression, is also expressive, symbolic, figurative, and inspirational. This is in contrast to the attempts to base these practices and narratives on some rational explanation and theory. To appreciate this conceptual point, note first that Wittgenstein is focusing here on the expressive and symbolic aspect of these practices and narratives. This is not to deny that they may have other aspects as well. To clarify their expressive, inspirational, and symbolic conceptual nature, it helps to focus first on the expressive aspect of symbols. Elsewhere, Wittgenstein does so in connection with natural expressions of friendliness that are rendered into symbols of friendliness:

> A friendly mouth, friendly eyes, the wagging of a dog's tail are primary symbols of friendliness: they are parts of the phenomena that are called friendliness. If we want to imagine further appearances as expressions of friendliness, we read these symbols into them.[15]

So, there are typical facial and bodily expressions of an attitude of friendliness in both human beings and dogs. Our ability to recognize them as such enables us to distinguish other facial or bodily expressions of an attitude of friendliness, such as a smile, wink, or pat on the back. In this way, a paradigmatic picture of a crying face might symbolize sadness, just as a paradigmatic picture of a smiling face might symbolize joy. Here symbols emerge out of typical facial and bodily expressions of various emotions and social attitudes, and are then used to both represent and express them. Like expressive gestures and actions that manifest their meaning, such figurative symbols also manifest their meaning.

Therefore, to say that myth, magic, and religious rituals are symbolic practices is to say that they provide enacted figurative symbols that both express existential concerns and promote inspiring attitudes toward life and what it encloses. To appreciate this conceptual point, it may help to contrast the expressive use of symbols with the non-expressive, practical use of signs. Both symbols and signs have meaning, but of a different kind. Consider, for example, the difference between a traffic light and a national flag. The first is a (non-linguistic) sign that serves a functional purpose in directing traffic, denoting when to stop and when to go. The second is a (non-linguistic) symbol that serves a ceremonial purpose in expressing, demonstrating, inspiring and enhancing feelings of national identity and patriotism.

It is conceptually important to note in this connection that the distinction between symbol and sign emerges from the actions and the context in which they are embedded, not from the objects used therein. A national flag may serve not only for ceremonial purposes but as a sign for designating the seats of emissaries from different countries in the United Nations, or to show that a citizen of that country is participating in a sporting event. Public washrooms may use words to mark those that are for men and those that are for women or pictures of the figures of a man and a woman. In the latter case, the picture-sign is also an iconic symbol of sexual identity, having a practical non-expressive, non-inspirational, normative social role. The picture of a person on a driving license serves as an identifying sign of that person. The picture of a head of state hanging in governmental offices serves as a symbol of governmental authority bestowed on what takes place therein. When the inscribed name of a hated enemy is burned or the name of one's love is etched in gold and hung on a chain, it is used as a symbol. When a name is written on the address of a postcard it is used as a sign. Thus, part of what determines whether something is used as a symbol or a sign is whether it is used in an expressive or in an instrumental way. Wittgenstein notes this point in connection with how we regard our name:

> Why shouldn't it be possible for a person to regard his name as sacred? It is certainly, on the one hand, the most important instrument which is given him, on the other, like a piece of jewelry hung around his neck at birth.[16]

Our name is the linguistic expression we use to identify ourselves to others. It is also the linguistic point of orientation from which our self-identity emerges. To forget one's name is like losing one's bearings at home. When someone makes a mockery of our name or mispronounces it, we may feel that what symbolizes us in a very intimate way has been mutilated. When we are forced by circumstances to exchange it for another or for a number, we may feel that something embodying our very essence has been taken away from us.

While symbols are expressive, not all expressions are symbolic. A kiss may be an expression of love and affection for another person without symbolizing anything. Represented in a statue of two people kissing, it is rendered into a symbol of love and affection. Thus, while symbols are inherently figurative and expressive, not all expressions are symbolic. However, both symbols and expressions are figurative, embodying their meaning. In this respect, they differ from arbitrary signs, such as traffic lights or the letters of the alphabet, whose meaning is fixed by convention. They also differ from natural signs, such as high fever that indicates sickness or smoke that indicates fire for those who know their meaning, neither of which expresses anything.

What sometimes confuses the distinction between symbol and sign is the attempt to apply it to the behavior of animals. We say about the wagging of a dog's tail that it is an expression of friendliness, as well as that the dog is exhibiting a sign of friendliness, and even a sign of *its* friendliness. In Wittgenstein's own examples: "A friendly mouth, friendly eyes, the wagging of a dog's tail are primary symbols of friendliness." However, we do not say that in wagging its tail a dog is exhibiting a symbol of friendliness or a symbol of its friendliness. We say that it showing a sign of friendliness. Nor do we say of a person who looks at us with friendly eyes or is smiling in a friendly way that he or she is exhibiting symbols of friendliness. Thus, "friendly mouth," "friendly eyes," or the "wagging of a dog's tail" are primary *signs* or expressions of friendliness, not symbols. However, these signs may be transformed into symbols. When a person makes a conscious effort to "put on a friendly face" or when an artist paints such features on the face of a saint, they are both trying to show signs of friendliness and to symbolize their friendliness. One way in which an expressive sign of friendliness, such as patting someone on the back, smiling at someone, or holding someone's hand may be transformed into a symbol of friendliness is through a cultural social ritual of shaking hands. To be rendered into cultural symbols, they have to be incorporated into a shared expressive practice of symbolization.

It is helpful to note that, just as a given word may be used in a metaphoric and literal context, the same word can be used in an instrumental and symbolic context. Words such as lion, dog, cat, and pig are linguistic signs used in instrumental linguistic practices to refer to certain kinds of animals. However, within a given culture, these animals may come to symbolize certain features of behavior or traits of character, transcending the features used to refer to them by different names. In Western culture, lions are a symbol of majesty, tigers of ferociousness, dogs of loyalty, cats of self-centeredness, and pigs of gluttony. It is thus possible to distinguish between the symbolic traits of lions and the non-symbolic features of lions, just as it is possible to distinguish between the symbolic meaning of the word "lion" and its ordinary instrumental meaning.

To further elucidate the difference between the expressive use of symbols and the instrumental use of signs, it may be helpful to note that, in the above examples of animals that symbolize various traits, it is not merely the names of the animals that are endowed with symbolic meaning, but the animals themselves. Thus, the symbolic meaning of lions is expressed when their image is used in royal emblems, or when the lion is called the "king of beasts." Similarly, symbolic meaning is evoked when someone is called a "fat pig" or another person's "running dog." Indeed, a symbol may not be a physical entity at all. It may be a mythical figure symbolizing heroic struggle against adversity, such as Prometheus in the Greek myth. It may be a glorified, tragic, historical event in the life of a people, such as the fall of Masada to the Jewish people. It may be a religious figure embodying love, compassion, self-sacrifice, and salvation, as is Jesus to Christians. Someone who knows the linguistic meaning of the words used to name such animals, persons, places, or events may not be aware of the symbolic meaning that they have for a given culture. Such a person may then be said not to share in the symbolic meaning of the language, as well as not to partake of its cultural spirit.[17]

Wittgenstein clarifies the expressive use of spiritual symbols when commenting on the conceptual nature of certain ancient religious rituals that aim to elevate spiritual concerns. He characterizes them as akin to enacted metaphors. Rush Rhees describes Wittgenstein's thinking on this matter in connection with what he wrote on the scapegoat ritual described in the Bible.[18] The ritual is one of purifying people of their sins. It was conducted on the Day of Atonement by the head priest putting his hands on the goat's head and confessing the inequities, sins and transgression of the people of Israel, placing them thereby on to the head of the goat, and then sending it into the desert. After which the priest took off his clothes, washed himself, and then put them on again.[19]

To seek justice by punishment or reparations for a committed offence is a practical, moral, or legal way of dealing with transgressions. To encumber a goat with human inequities, sins, and transgressions and to send it into the desert is to unburden the human soul by means of an inspiring ritual that enacts metaphors and analogies based on ordinary events. Within this context, the priest's washing himself after laying the sins of the people on the goat is also part of the ritual: an act of purification performed after coming into contact with sin. The entire ceremony is an inspired way of representing, expressing, confronting, and elevating existential concerns ensuing from perceived moral and religious transgressions through a symbolic action, the meaning of which does not readily emerge from a description of the empirical facts that embody it.

6. The Foundation for a Religious Symbol

The remark that Myth, Magic, and Religion are spiritual practices based on the inspiring and expressive use of symbols is my way of rephrasing Wittgenstein's clarification of their expressive symbolic conceptual nature. Wittgenstein describes two natural dispositions on the part of human beings as "the foundation" for symbolic practices. The first is our natural inclination to react in an expressive way to what concerns us:

> When I am furious about something, I sometimes beat the ground or a tree with my walking stick. But I certainly do not believe that the ground is to blame or that my beating can help anything. "I am venting my anger". And all rites are of this kind. Such actions may be called Instinct-actions . . . .[20]

The point of this comment is not to reduce rituals to what Wittgenstein calls "instinct-actions." It is to combat the idea that rituals arise out of reasoning about cause and effect. They arise from natural inclinations on our part to express what concerns us. Later, in discussing the question, "How do words *refer* to sensations?" Wittgenstein resorts to a similar genealogical account. He notes first, "This question is the same as: how does a human being learn the meaning of the names of sensations?—of the word 'pain' for example." He then offers the following account:

> Here is one possibility: words are connected with the primitive, the natural, expressions of the sensation and used in their place. A child has hurt himself and he cries; and then adults talk to him and teach him exclamations and, later, sentences. They teach the child new pain-behaviour.
>
> "So you are saying that the word 'pain' really means crying?"—On the contrary: the verbal expression of pain replaces crying and does not describe it.[21]

Just as sensation words are connected to primitive, natural, expressions of sensations and used in their place, rituals are connected with primitive, natural expressions for existential concerns and are used in their place. Of course to do so, rituals have to be created and adopted by a cultural community. This is where the second natural spiritual disposition of human beings comes into play. Human beings have a natural inclination to create and observe rituals that provide symbolic expression for their existential concerns. We not only beat the ground when we are angry, we also create shared symbolic practices expressing anger, friendship, reverence, love, grief, and so on. Both these ways of behavior arise out of the common nature of human beings and are the genealogical foundation for the creation and observance of shared symbolic practices.

A problem with this genealogical account of the conceptual foundation of rituals is that cultural rituals do not correspond in a one-to-one fashion with so-called basic instinct-actions. Moreover, in many cases, we want to say that rituals promote and produce in their observers certain experiences and attitudes toward life, rather than cater to existing ones. I take it that Wittgenstein's point here is more of a general insight: namely, that a ritual does not arise out of reflection and reasoning, but out of a natural inclination for expressive behavior and symbolization. As such, it does not arise out of erroneous beliefs.

The insight emerging from these reminders of the natural inclination of human beings to express themselves in instinctive behavior and to create symbolic practices for their deep concerns overturns Frazer's claim that Myth, Magic, and Religion are practices based on theoretical and instrumental ways of reasoning. In Wittgenstein's critique, practices based on theoretical and instrumental ways of reasoning are neither expressive nor symbolic. They do not emerge out of instinctive expressive actions and they do not enact metaphors, similes, and analogies. Rather, they manifest ways of reasoning that lead to the advancement of explanation and theory, which he calls "opinion." They do not lead to the creation and observance of rituals and inspiring symbols that express existential concerns: "No opinion serves as the foundation for a religious symbol. And only an opinion can involve an error."[22]

The same holds for all cultural symbols and rituals, which express, enhance, and promote spiritual attitudes toward life. Raising a flag on a national holiday or standing at attention to commemorate the dead are not actions that manifest opinions derived by reasoning. They are rituals and symbolic gestures, expressing attitudes of reverence, honor, and appreciation. They are more like enacted metaphors and similes of an attitude of honoring and valuing certain things or people, than the advancement of opinions about their merit and value.[23] Wishing someone success on the coming examination or lifting two crossed fingers in a gesture of good luck, just like cursing someone or spitting on the picture of a hated enemy, are expressive symbolic gestures rather than actions derived by reasoning about cause and effect. Thus, just as rituals and gestures have their own inspired, symbolic, expressive logic, beliefs in Myth, Magic, and Religion have the same inspired, symbolic, expressive logic. They are not based on reasoning, particularly not with regard to practical matters, and none of them are the expression of opinions. Accordingly, Wittgenstein points to the inclination of human beings to express their concerns through symbolic enactments, which are not based on their reasoned opinions about them: "I believe that the characteristic feature of primitive man is that he does not act from *opinions* (contrary to Frazer)."[24]

The remark should be read in the context of the present discussion. Of course, people in ancient cultures also had opinions about various things and sometimes acted upon them, just as we do. However, this is not the way in which symbolic spiritual practices that take the form of rituals are created. Later, he pronounces a similar insight in connection with language:

> The origin & the primitive form of the language game is a reaction; <u>only</u> from this can the more complicated forms grow.
>
> Language—I want to say—is a refinement, "in the beginning was the deed."[25]

Thus, "primitive man" and "the primitive form of the language game" provide two similar philosophical viewpoints on the creative origin of cultural practices, which are not based on reflection and opinion. Since what Wittgenstein calls a "language game" includes such linguistic practices as asking question, requesting, and describing, all of which are practically useful, the origin of cultural practices has little to do with whether it is for practical or expressive purposes. To give credence to Wittgenstein's comment about behavior that is not based on opinion, it might be said now that symbolic practices are usually not pursued by forming opinions about their instrumental usefulness, even after acquiring their use. When we take part in them, we have different expectations and a different approach from how we approach and use instrumental practices that are aimed at practical matters. In the latter, our continued use of them is often supported by forming an opinion about their usefulness for achieving practical aims, just as giving up their use is often the result of forming the opinion that they are not as useful for such purposes as we thought. It thus might be said that, when spiritual practices are judged to be instrumentally useful for changing certain states of affairs in the world, rather than for changing the spiritual state of their observers, this is an indication that they are based on what we call "superstition." For of course, all spiritual practices may be instrumental in promoting a certain attitude toward life in those who perform them. Consider the spiritual and ethical benefit experienced by fasting on holy days and praying for atonement.

7. Attitudes and Opinions

To further clarify typical human responses to the flow of life through actions that are not based on opinions, Wittgenstein elsewhere uses the concept of attitude, *Einstellung*, to bring it out: "—Our attitude toward what is alive and to what is dead, is not the same. All our reactions are different—. . ."[26] This is in contrast to a philosophical attempt to justify the proposition that there are other living creatures besides us. Such an attempt seeks to explain our natural reactions to living creatures, as the outcome of a justified opinion that we form. He also contrasts attitude toward opinion in connection with the meaningful way in which we grasp other people and react to them: "My attitude toward him is an attitude toward a soul. I am not of the *opinion* that he has a soul."[27] Still later he adds the following:

> Instead of "attitude toward the soul" one could also say "attitude toward a human."
>
> But what is the difference between an attitude and an opinion?
> I would like to say: the attitude comes *before* the opinion.
>
> (*Isn't* belief in God an attitude?)[28]

The conceptual distinction drawn by Wittgenstein between attitudes and opinions reveals two different ways in which we relate to things and understand their meaning. Opinions arise out of thinking about things. They are the product of reasoning and are similar to conjectures, hypotheses, and ideas that are entertained in the mind through propositions. People often differ in their opinions about things. Opinions may be contested and are debatable. We may be asked to justify an opinion we have, to provide better and more convincing reasons for it. We expect opinions to be rational and to be based on good reasons. An opinion can be imparted or refuted by rhetorical means: through explanation and persuasion.

Attitudes are different. They are not instances of thinking and reasoning, are not comprised of ideas, and are not entertained in the mind through propositions. When we are worried about our children's health, we have an attitude of concern toward them, which is replaced by an attitude of relief when we find that what concerned us has passed. To be only of the opinion that they are not healthy is not yet to be concerned about them, but a point of view that may be held by any uninvolved observer. Attitudes are related to ways of seeing and experiencing various aspects of things, to desires, feelings, concerns, likes, and dislikes. They are ways in which we grasp the meaning of things that make up our lives in a very personal, basic, immediate, and noninferential fashion. Our opinions belong to our intellectual makeup: to what we think is the case. Our attitudes embody our apprehensions, attachments, cares, desires, hopes, aversions, and dreads: to how the case affects us. This is not to say that attitudes lack content. Attitudes are ways of experiencing and apprehending the nature and significance of things to us. As such, they are rich in content and may be manifested in beliefs, supported by opinions, and accompanied by feelings and thoughts.

In rational human beings, attitudes and opinions are often related to one another, each affecting the other. Opinions may support attitudes, and attitudes may be expressed in opinions. When my attitude of admiration for someone diminishes, my previous high opinion of that person diminishes also and vice versa.

An attitude toward another person as possessing a soul and to living things as creatures and not just inanimate objects is manifested in our reactions to them, perception of them, approach to them, and in the experience they arouse in us—all of this in isolation from any scientific theoretical opinion we may adopt regarding them. Such differing attitudes toward various kinds of things, people, living creatures, and objects, underlie our unmediated common human ways of relating to them. In this way, Wittgenstein uses the conceptual distinction between attitude and opinion as a "grammatical reminder" to deflate philosophical attempts to justify what has been called "belief in other minds." Such beliefs are opinions. But we do not relate to the existence of other people through opinions.

A problem with using the concepts of attitude and opinion to clarify the conceptual nature of spiritual practices is that we have all sorts of attitudes. Just as our concern about our children's health manifests an attitude of love for them, our reactions to ordinary utensils reveal a practical, instrumental attitude toward objects. Spiritual attitudes toward life and what it encloses are different. One of their distinguishing features is to shift our focus and ways of approaching life from practical considerations to expressing our existential concerns and attaining inspiration.

On the basis of the distinction between attitude and opinion, it might now be said that Myth, Magic, and Religion emerge out of common human concerns, experiences, and attitudes toward life and what it encloses, not opinions. This means that beliefs expressed in connection with the three are not the declaration of opinions. To that extent, it may be said that in denying that Myth, Magic, and Religion arise out of opinions, Wittgenstein is drawing a conceptual distinction between belief as an existential attitude of faith and belief as a hypothesis or opinion that something is the case. To believe that it will rain tomorrow is to have an opinion about the matter: what Bertrand Russell called a "propositional attitude." To have faith in someone is to trust that person, just as to be concerned about the future is to worry about it. Trust and concern are existential attitudes, not opinions entertained in the mind through propositions.

To have faith in magic or religion is to have faith in what they symbolize. Faith in them is manifested in their ability to transform existential concerns into inspiring spiritual attitudes toward life. Hence, Wittgenstein is suggesting that faith in Myth, Magic, and Religion does not emerge from opinions about life and world that emerge by reasoning and are entertained in the mind through propositions we take to be true. A corollary to the insight that the three do not emerge out of opinions is that beliefs expressed in their connection are also not opinions, but inspired assertions, expressing spiritual attitudes toward life that arise in their connection.

8. Faith in the Efficacy of Myth, Magic, and Religion

The conceptual remark that Myth, Magic, and Religion are spiritual practices entails a conclusion that faith in them is different from faith in the efficacy of instrumental practices. Wittgenstein notes this point in the following comment:

> I read among many similar examples, of a rain-king in Africa to whom the people pray *when the rainy period comes*. But surely that means that they do not really believe that he can make it rain, otherwise they would do it in the dry periods . . .[29]

Therefore, this practice, as well as the practice of praying to other gods, is not properly explained by regarding them as faulty opinions derived from bad reasoning. They are expressive practices that are akin to expressive gestures, manifesting hopes, wishes, gratitude, fears, and worries:

> Burning in effigy. Kissing the picture of one's beloved. That is *obviously not* based on the belief that it will have some specific effect on the object, which the picture represents. It aims at satisfaction and achieves it. Or rather: it *aims* at nothing at all; we just behave this way and then we feel satisfied.[30]

In this insight into the conceptual nature of such rituals and gestures, the satisfaction achieved through performing them does not derive from a belief that the action affects the object represented in it. It derives from the expressive nature of the action itself. Otherwise, one would have to wait to find out how it affected the object of the picture. Similarly, the satisfaction derived from wishing someone good luck on the final exam is in the expression of the wish itself, not in its effect.

Note the pronoun Wittgenstein uses in describing these practices: "we." Indeed, he often criticizes Frazer by relating the strange practices Frazer describes to familiar expressive ways of behavior of modern human beings, neither of which are based on a belief in their causal effect. He also criticizes Frazer by noting that those who used magic were quite rational about their everyday affairs: "The same savage, who stabs the picture of his enemy apparently in order to kill him, really builds his hut out of wood and carves his arrows skillfully and not in effigy."[31]

Therefore, when magic is performed, something else is happening that has its own logic. That is the inspired, expressive, figurative logic that underlies spiritual practices, such as the telling of awe-inspiring myths, the casting of mysterious magic spells, and the performance of sacred religious practices.

It is important to note in this connection just how these rituals differ from other kinds. Consider, by way of example, social rituals of honoring war heroes or greeting guests cordially. Such rituals have both an instrumental and ethical function. In the first example, they both promote the value of valor in war and induce people to risk their lives in times of war. In the second case, they promote the value of hospitality and facilitate social interactions. If such rituals were found to be counterproductive to their instrumental aims of promoting valor in war and facilitating social interactions, they would probably be abandoned. From Wittgenstein's insight up to this point, it emerges that Myth, Magic, and Religion are different. Unlike social rituals, they are practices that are immune to error, as their purpose is mainly spiritual.

What ought to strike us at this point is the somewhat banal reminder that human beings conduct their lives not only out of rational, instrumental ways of reasoning, but also by enacting their existential concerns and attitudes toward life in inspiring, symbolic, figurative ways. When these expressions are shared, they bestow cultural shape on the enacted dreads, passions, desires, wishes and hopes. In doing so, human beings acknowledge both the contingencies of life and aspects of life that are meaningful to them. Wittgenstein notes this point in connection with the inclination of human beings in all cultures to create and observe rituals and ceremonies:

> The characteristic feature of the awakening mind of man is precisely the fact that a phenomenon comes to have meaning for him. One could almost say that man is a ceremonial animal. That is, no doubt, partly wrong and partly nonsensical, but there is also something right about it.
>
> That is, one could begin a book on anthropology by saying: when one examines the life and behavior of mankind throughout the world, one sees that, except for what might be called animal activities, such as ingestion etc., etc., etc., men also perform actions which bear a characteristic peculiar to themselves, and these could be called ritualistic actions.
>
> But then it is nonsense for one to go on to say that the characteristic feature of these actions is the fact that they arise from faulty views about the physics of things. (Frazer does this when he says that magic is essentially false physics or, as the case may be false medicine, technology, etc.).[32]

My reading of this comment is that it views Myth, Magic, and Religion as inspired symbolic expressions of existential concerns, promoting and enriching shared spiritual attitudes toward life. They manifest our common human nature, which gives rise to such concerns, as well as our natural human tendency to channel these concerns into expressive rituals that transform them into inspiring spiritual attitudes toward life. By explaining Myth, Magic, and Religion and the rituals in which they are expressed as emanating from faulty ways of reasoning, Frazer strips such cultural practices of their spiritual meaning, reducing them to a theoretical and instrumental meaning, which lacks either inspiration or spiritual meaning. In doing so, he leaves humanity devoid of any inclination for symbolic spiritual expression.

Three

WITTGENSTEIN'S CRITICISM OF FRAZER'S HISTORICAL EXPLANATION

1. Acknowledging What We Understand

Ludwig Wittgenstein's criticism of James George Frazer's explanation of the essence of Myth, Magic, and Religion as practices based on reasoning has been bolstered over the years by the advance of symbolic theories in anthropology.[1] From the standpoint of such theories, both Frazer's explanations and Wittgenstein's critical comments may seem outdated. However, the central point on which Wittgenstein's comments hang remains pertinent and worth elaborating, as it concerns what he regards as the common underlying spiritual nature of human beings in all cultures. In Wittgenstein's' approach this enables us to understand the expressive meaning of unfamiliar spiritual practices without explanation. On the basis of this approach Wittgenstein criticizes not only of Frazer's conceptual explanation, which reduces Myth, Magic, and Religion to practices based on reasoning, but also Frazer's very attempt to explain them. "The very idea of wanting to explain a practice—for example, the killing of the priest king—seems wrong to me."[2] That is because "every explanation is after all a hypothesis."[3]

At first sight, the last claim seems wrong. When we explain to someone how to shift gears in an old car or how to get from the Philosophy Department to the Students' Hall, we are not intent on putting forward a hypothesis. Nor are we attempting to put forward a hypothesis when we explain the meaning of the word "cat" to a child by pointing to the neighbor's cat and saying "this is a cat." We are also not putting forward a hypothesis when we explain the meaning of a given poem. We are interpreting it. Wittgenstein may be justified in that he is responding to Frazer's effort to interpret the meaning of practices exemplifying Myth, Magic, and Religion, which he pursued through his generic explanation of the ritual killing of the priest-king of the grove of Diana.

In his explanation, Frazer traced its origin to many strange and often horrifying rituals, myths, and beliefs prevalent in several cultures in the ancient world. In Wittgenstein's criticism, to explain the origin of this ritual in this way is to put forward a generic hypothesis. Such a hypothesis contrasts with our initial response to its description, which manifests our immediate understanding of its expressive meaning. This understanding is based on grasping it as a ritual and on the dread and horror that arise in us when we are confronted with it. More particularly, we grasp it as a shocking ritual that enacts a cycle of murders of kings by their usurpers, expressing in a gruesome fashion the dread of murder and its inherent relationship to royal stature. The explanation of its historical origin is both conjectural and besides the point to our expressive reaction to its expressive meaning.

As may be seen, the objection Wittgenstein raises to Frazer's historical explanation is different from that which he raises to his conceptual explanation. The objection here is that historical explanations of the origins of a particular ritual are irrelevant to grasping and clarifying its current expressive meaning. In contrast to such explanations, Wittgenstein would rather lean on the immediate and unlearned response we have to such a ritual as a way of grasping its expressive meaning, which he then tries to clarify. In this approach, philosophical discourse about the expressive meaning of strange cultural practices should begin by placing such practices in relation to our own ways of experiencing and responding to them. We then draw upon the immediate way in which they affect us. To respond to a ritual in this way is to grasp the meaning or point that is expressed in it. It is to grasp the way in which it manifests existential concerns that we share with those who enacted it.

Therefore, the assumption of a common human existential nature does not figure as a premise from which we deduce the correct explanation of the ritual. Rather, when we respond to the ritual as something that speaks to us in a powerful and meaningful way, we are expressing a common human existential nature we share with its observers. In other words, our shared existential human nature is internal to our understanding the ritual as expressing the dread of murder through a gruesome drama, enacting a cycle of murders underlying a king's life. Put differently, it might be said that not only the ritual is expressive, but so is our understanding of it.[4]

Since our understanding of the ritual expresses the existential human nature we share with the ancients who created and observed it, the meaning of the ritual no longer strikes us as requiring a hypothetical reductive or historical explanation that will render it intelligible to us. As in the case of Frazer's conceptual explanation, the objection to his historical explanation is based on Frazer's distancing himself from the way in which these spiritual practices affect him. By contrast, Wittgenstein wants to acknowledge the way in which he is affected. The assumption underlying this procedure is that the way in which he is affected by them is the same way in which most human beings in both ancient and modern times are affected by them—before they begin trying to explain their meaning by theoretical hypotheses.

Thus, philosophical discourse about the spiritual meaning of strange cultural practices that embody myths, magic, and religious rituals, ought to begin by acknowledging their powerful effect on us. As such, it is expressive, descriptive, non-inferential and non-historical. That is, its aim is to clarify our experience and grasp of the meaning of these practices. In the particular case at hand, we need a description that helps us acknowledge the meaning of the practice as expressing dread of murder and promoting human attitudes of concern about life and death, which are dramatized in connection with the life of kings. By doing so, it may help us acknowledge and clarify our own fears, and through them, our existential concerns and attitudes toward life, death, and murder. Wittgenstein expresses this insight in the following way:

> I believe that the attempt to explain is already therefore wrong because one must only correctly piece together what one *knows* without adding anything, and the satisfaction being sought through the explanation follows of itself.[5]

When Frazer describes this ritual as a cycle of murders of priestly kings by their usurpers, he is piecing together what he knows about it. When he explains its historic origin he is offering an irrelevant hypothesis that does not help us understand the expressive meaning of this ritual. It may well be that Frazer took this track because he found this ritual as something horrible. But his explanation of its historic origins does not clarify his experience of it:

> And the explanation isn't what satisfies us here at all. When Frazer begins by telling the story of the king of the Wood of Nemi, he does this in a tone which shows that he feels, and wants us to feel, that something strange and dreadful is happening. But the question "why does this happen?" is properly answered by saying: Because it is dreadful. That is, precisely that which makes this incident strike us as dreadful, magnificent, horrible, tragic, etc., as anything but trivial and insignificant, is also *that* which has called this incident to life.[6]

As I read Wittgenstein's comment here, Frazer turns to explain this ritual because he experiences it as manifesting something dreadful. However, he responds to the dread he experiences through it by explaining how civilized people could have invented such a dreadful ritual. In Wittgenstein's critique, from the way in which Frazer describes it, he assumes that the experience of dread that arises in him was shared also by those who enacted the ritual, and that is exactly why it was enacted. Hence, he approaches this ritual first by recognizing it as a ritual and second by responding to its expressive spiritual meaning. Therefore, to shed conceptual light on the expressive meaning of this ritual to those who invented and observed it, what is required is to acknowledge our ability to recognize it as a spiritual ritual and our ability to experience the dread it expresses. Having done so, we can turn to Frazer's puzzlement as to why civilized human beings would want to enact their dread of murder in such a manner.

To bring insight to what puzzles us about enacting dread of murder in a ritual, recall the way in which a horror film fascinates us—we are both repelled and captivated by it. In the same way, human beings create such myths and enact such rituals out of their fascination with and apprehension of dread and horror. We are both fascinated and repelled by what is creepy, disgusting, evil, sinister, and threatening. This tendency on our part does not detract from our ability to prefer beauty, goodness, pleasantness, and decency over them. It highlights them, making us more aware of their significance to us. In a somewhat similar manner, we express the value and significance of rescue, deliverance, recovery, liberation, and salvation by reminding ourselves of what it is like to be trapped, imprisoned, sick, enslaved, and miserable. On this approach, if we wish to understand strange human spiritual practices, we first need to acknowledge their effect on us, noting the way in which they give powerful expression to human concerns that are not strange to us. In doing so, we remind ourselves of the existential concerns and attitudes toward life that we are apt to share with the human beings that express them in these ways. Subsequently, we may note also the way in which we ourselves are drawn to either express or observe expressions of such deep human concerns.

2. Experiencing Dread at a Ritual of Murder

Years later, when discussing our ability to appreciate works of art created in a foreign culture, Wittgenstein took a different approach. When asked if a European could "appreciate Negro art" he was more hesitant. He claimed that it is not clear on the basis of what we are to say that a European appreciates "Negro art":

> If you say he appreciates it, I don't yet know what this means. He may fill his room with objects of Negro Art. Does he just say: "Ah!"? Or does he do what the best-Negro musicians do? Or does he agree or disagree with so and so about it? You may call this appreciation.

However, he also claims that these are different appreciations altogether.

> You do something different with them. Suppose Negroes dress in their own way and I say I appreciate a good Negro tunic—does this mean I would have one made, or that I would say (as at the tailor's): "No . . . this is too long", or does it mean I say: "How charming!"?[7]

It is not clear from the above discussion whether Wittgenstein changed his former view or whether he distinguishes between appreciation of art in a foreign culture and grasping the expressive meaning of its myth, magic and religious practices. On the latter assumption, to grasp its expressive meaning does not entail appreciation of it as a culturally valued spiritual practice. To appreciate an expressive practice is to make meaningful room for it within our own life: to observe it. To grasp its expressive meaning is to be struck by it. In this account, we grasp its meaning because the practice expresses shared existential concerns that characterize the common spiritual nature of human beings.

How similar to the ancients need we be to grasp the expressive spiritual meaning of their rituals? Consider this question in connection with what is enacted in the murder of the priest-king at Nemi: how much do we need to be apprehensive about life and anxious about death to experience dread of it? Wittgenstein does not say. It would seem that, at the least, we need to share certain concepts, existential concerns, and attitudes toward life, out of which the ancients created and observed this ritual. In particular, we need to share the concept of murder and the dread of murder. A person to whom murder is not a violent and forbidden act, and for whom death by murder is not a frightening possibility, would have a problem in responding to the expressive meaning of this ritual, as enacting something dreadful. Such a person may not appreciate the horror of living under the constant threat of being murdered. An understanding of other concepts on which this ritual is built can then enrich and further our understanding of its expressive meaning. By acquiring the concept of priest or king and learning to esteem and honor persons fulfilling these roles in a culture, we can understand why someone would aspire to this role. A person who wonders why anyone would aspire to the role of a king, what honor and glory could possibly be attached to it, or how social honors and glory could be motivating factors in human behavior, is more limited in his or her ability to respond to the expressive meaning of this ritual: particularly to the way it conjoins dread of murder to such an esteemed role.

Of course, we are apt to understand much more than that when we are confronted by such a ritual. We understand that it expresses deep human concerns, that it is not an entertaining comedy or an enacted mystery about who murdered the king, and approach it from our conceptual understanding of the nature of spiritual rituals and myths. Therefore, Wittgenstein approaches Frazer's account of strange myths, magic, and religious rituals by noting, first, that, like Frazer, he understands that they are instances of Myth, Magic, and Religion and, second, how they affect him. In his ability to understand their conceptual nature and respond to them accordingly, he is no different from someone who comes upon a new culture but is nonetheless able to distinguish between practical innovations and spiritual rituals. As such, he is able to distinguish between gruesome initiation rites and gruesome tortures used to extract secret information or to inflict punishment. He is able to do that on the basis of these shared concepts, which emerge out of a common spiritual human nature, manifesting common human existential concerns, attitudes, dispositions, and conceptual understandings. They provide an enriching background against which the ritual is enacted and through which we respond to its expressive meaning without need of any explanation.

To say that we and the ancients have common existential concerns and shared concepts of Myth, Magic, and Religion is not to say that we share the same culture, or that our attitudes toward the three are the same as theirs. We do not need to have faith in them to acquire these concepts, just as we do not have to own a horse and a car to tell horses apart from cars and to respond to them differently. That is because we are (modern) human beings, not extraterrestrials of a different nature, who are unfamiliar with such concepts. Since we possess both them and the underlying human concerns they express, we are able to respond to their expressive meaning. At most, we are sometimes astounded by their manifestation in ancient cultures and philosophically puzzled when we try to define their essence, or explain how we are able to understand their expressive meaning.

Since Frazer begins his discourse by noting that his explanatory voyage concerns ancient myths, ancient rituals of magic, and ancient religious ceremonies, he is able to identify them as such, even when they take the form of strange and unfamiliar practices. The concepts of Myth, Magic, and Religion are not new to him, even if their instantiations in ancient cultures are unfamiliar. Thus, just as we do not need an explanation of the conceptual nature of familiar expressive practices observed in ancient cultures, such as celebrating, blessing, praising, greeting, cursing and grieving, we do not need an explanation of the conceptual nature of Myth, Magic, and Religion to understand the expressive spiritual role they played in the lives of human beings in ancient cultures. At most, we might need help with a specific puzzling case. For example, we may be puzzled by a particular ritual or myth in a strange culture, but not by the very existence of such rituals, which give symbolic spiritual expression to people's deepest concerns—not unless we are philosophers who view human life through an intellectual glass darkly, a glass that renders it either rational or foolish. Such conceptual misunderstanding stems from distancing ourselves from our own existential nature and its cultural forms of symbolic expression, resulting in a desire to explain them as "primitive ways of reasoning."

3. Acknowledging the Common Spiritual Nature of Human Beings

Frazer's declared reason for his scholarly voyage to the ancient world was to trace the recurrence of the same kind of rituals and myths in different cultures, which he explained by historical influence. For Wittgenstein, there is no need for such an explanation to understand why rituals in different cultures may manifest a common spirit. We are not surprised to find that, in many different cultures, human beings tell stories, express feelings, use metaphors, bless, curse, and so forth. Similarly, we should not be surprised that in many cultures human beings give symbolic expression to common existential concerns through myth, magic, and religious practices. Therefore, we should not be surprised that these expressions manifest what he calls a "common spirit."

Instead of joining Frazer on his explanatory voyage into strange cultures, Wittgenstein engages in philosophical anthropology, illustrating how easy it is to invent spiritually expressive symbolic gestures and rituals:

> One sees how misleading Frazer's explanations are—I believe—by noting that one could very easily invent primitive practices oneself, and it would be pure luck if they were not actually found somewhere… Recall that after [Franz] Schubert's death his brother cut some of Schubert's scores into small pieces and gave such pieces, consisting of a few bars, to his favorite pupils. This act, as a sign of piety, is *just* as understandable to use as the different one of keeping the scores untouched, accessible to no one. And if Schubert's brother had burned the scores, that would be understandable as a sign of piety . . .
>
> Indeed, if Frazer's explanations did not in the final analysis appeal to a tendency in ourselves, they would not really be explanations.[8]

As I read the above comment, the invention of inspiring rituals to express piety and reverence is part of our common expressive human spiritual nature. Without recognizing this human tendency, the idea of historical influence would not explain why such rituals are adopted. A corollary to this insight is that there are typical human concerns and basic ways of expressing them that are conducive to the creation and observance of rituals. In Wittgenstein's view, the fact that human beings have a common expressive nature is sufficient for clarifying the conceptual nature of strange expressive practices. Once we note that we are inclined to pre-cultural expressive behavior, such as beating the ground with a stick when we are angry, there is no need to hypothesize about historical influence on cultures to explain their similarity. All sorts of similar practices may emerge out of common basic human expressive inclinations:

> an historical explanation, say, that I or my ancestors previously believed that beating the ground does help is shadow-boxing, for it is a superfluous assumption that explains *nothing* . . .
>
> Once such a phenomenon is brought into connection with an instinct which I myself possess, this is precisely the explanation wished for; that is, the explanation which resolves this particular difficulty. And further investigation about the history of my instinct moves on another track.[9]

The argument here is too scathing. Frazer was arguing for historical influence on cultural practices, not on what Wittgenstein describes as "instinct," which is an expressive pre-cultural way of acting. There are many different ways of performing a ritual of greeting someone, which in the West is done by shaking hands. Someone may be interested in how this particular way of performing a ritual of greeting came to be adopted. I take it that in Wittgenstein's approach, this is an historical question that does not touch on what puzzles us about the very inclination of human beings to create and observe rituals of greeting. In the context of this philosophical puzzlement Frazer's explanation of the historical relationship between various rituals in different cultures is an unnecessary hypothesis to explain why rituals emerging from different cultures are often expressive of the same human concerns.

In my reading of Wittgenstein's comments in connection with this philosophical puzzlement, we need to acknowledge our common expressive human spiritual nature instead of looking for historical explanations of why certain ritual is observed. This nature is manifested in the inclination of human beings in all cultures to create, adopt, and observe symbolic expressions for events and experiences deeply meaningful to them. What gets Frazer's historical explanation off the ground is his and our prior understanding of the conceptual nature of such practices, as constituting symbolic expressions of human concerns. What makes rituals that are observed in different cultures symbolic expressions of the same human spirit is not the behavior itself, but the fact that they are expressions of the same human concerns and attitudes toward life. Burning Schubert's scores would express the same spirit of piety as cutting them and giving small pieces to his friends, just as burying the bodies of dead people, burning or embalming them express the same spirit of reverence toward them:

> All these *different* practices show that it is not a question of the derivation of one from the other, but of a common spirit. And one could invent (devise) all these ceremonies oneself. And precisely that spirit from which one invented them would be their common spirit.[10]

According to the above comment, gestures that express the significant memory of someone may take all sorts of forms. Nonetheless, they manifest a common human spirit, which is the desire to provide an expressive, inspired, symbolic enactment of the memory of that person. In manifesting such a spirit they differ, for example, from rituals of magic that seek to offset evil. Both rituals of magic and those of preserving the memory of someone differ in spirit from rituals of prayer for rain or good harvest. Frazer sought to explain the similarity of certain rituals by tracing their historical connections. Wittgenstein's criticism is that he did so because he failed to acknowledge that they derive from the common expressive spiritual human nature, manifesting the shared existential concerns of human beings.

4. Description of a Sinister Spirit

Rush Rhees claimed that Wittgenstein's point about a common spirit underlying certain rituals in different cultures is exemplified most clearly in his comments on Frazer's descriptions of the Celtic Beltane fire-festival (May fire), performed by children in eighteenth-century Scotland, which he calls "The Fire-Festivals in Europe." The ceremony included passing portions of a cake between the participants. The unlucky person in the ceremony who ended with the burnt cake was declared the Beltane witch. That person was then made to leap over the fire. Frazer comments that undoubtedly human beings were once sacrificed on these occasions. The present celebrations, he claimed, are a substitute for the original. Wittgenstein was impressed with the fact that we are able to regard them, despite their many differences, as rituals of human sacrifice. He claimed that this appreciation of their symbolic nature is not dependent on whether, in the past, human beings were actually sacrificed. Their sinister spirit is manifested irrespective of it, and it gives depth to our understanding of them.[11]

Frazer explained these rituals by considering what ancient people expected to gain from them. For Wittgenstein, that does not explain the disquieting impression with which we are left when we note that they are rituals of human sacrifice. We feel implicated by that impression, as though it expresses something in us. The celebration of the Beltane festival by Scottish children 150 years ago, making a festival out of burning a living man, strikes us as deep and sinister.[12] Rhees asks at this point why we feel there is something deep and sinister in the ritual sacrifice of a human being, noting Wittgenstein's remark that it derives "from an experience in ourselves."

In my reading of this remark, the horror of human sacrifice, of rituals in which lots are drawn to decide who will be sacrificed, or of suffering under torture, is a dread that we can easily experience and relate to. It emerges from deep human existential concerns, which such rituals express and which we share with those who invented them. The fire festivals are inspired enactments of such dread, enabling those who partake in them to express their dread of being chosen by lot to be burned. It also expresses their sinister human nature, which is expressed by participating in a ritual of choosing someone to be burned by lot and by celebrating both the horror of burning someone and the fact that they were not chosen for this ordeal. It is this experience that arises in us when we are confronted with these celebrations that reveals their sinister inner spiritual nature:

> I believe it is clearly the inner nature of the modern practice itself that seems sinister to us. . . . When I speak of the inner nature of the practice, I mean all those circumstances under which it is carried out and which are not included in a report of such a festival, since they consist not so much in specific actions which characterize the festival as in what might be called the spirit of the festival; such things as would be included in one's description, for example, of the kind of people who take part in it, their behavior at other times, that is, their character; the kinds of games which they otherwise play. And one would then see that their sinister quality lies in the character of these people themselves.[13]

The inner nature of a given ritual, like the inner nature of people, is the spirit in which it is practiced. This spirit manifests the existential concerns, values, and character of the human beings who are drawn to make use of it to confront them. The inner nature of the ritual of celebrating birthdays of family members is our desire to rejoice over their very existence, expressing thereby our love for them. The inner nature of the ritual of shaking hands when meeting people is the desire to greet them in a friendly manner. Note that just as different rituals may manifest different spirits, a given cultural practice can be pursued by different people with different spirits, manifesting thereby different attitudes, aims, values, and characters. Thus, a game of soccer may be pursued with a playful spirit that aims at having fun through a competitive physical activity. It may also be pursed with an aggressive combative spirit, the aim of which is to triumph over others by winning. The way in which we pursue the game may manifest both our own spirit and the spirit of the game.

Some human practices are inherently sinister and cruel, embodying a sinister spirit by their very nature. Such is the practice of choosing someone by lot to be tortured to death, which manifests the sinister and cruel nature of those who engage in it. This is not to deny that cruelty may be part of the nature of all human beings. However, in the practice of torturing the innocent, this aspect of human nature is cultivated and promoted. Sometimes the sinister spirit of a given cultural practice comes out in a chilling way. As Frank Cioffi has pointed out in his discussion of Wittgenstein's comments on Frazer, the sinister aspect of this practice comes out most pertinently from the fact that casting lots as to who shall be burned was done by the use of a cake. In other circumstances, a cake symbolizes a happy celebration and friendship. He notes that this is the same impression we have of a kiss used as sign of betrayal.[14] In a similar way, we may find something sinister about the character of people who enjoyed watching gladiators fight in the arena to their death, as though it were a kind of sport. This is because we grasp it as corrupting the spirit of sport and with it also the souls of those who are inspired through it to make a sport of cruelty and to find pleasure in savagery.

In Wittgenstein's response to the ritual that Frazer describes, its sinister aspect is extended to the character of the people who invented and took part in it. It constitutes their inner nature, which is the spirit from within which they created and practiced it. This is regardless of whether it is just a mock pretence of burning a person or one that is left over from a real ritual of burning that was once practiced. In either case, the inner, spiritual, nature or character of such practices is the inner, spiritual, nature or character of the people who observe them.

According to Jacques Bouveresse's discussion of this point, "Frazer does not take account of the fact that that the profound and gloomy nature of these ceremonies is a function of the experience they evoke in us, which allows us to impute this character to them."[15] It is not merely the fact that human beings suffer when they are burned that is so horrible for us. It comes about from the sinister character of the people who find inspiration in choosing someone to be burned by drawing lots in a ritual that mimics ceremonies of celebration and by enjoying watching others suffer by burning. In this reading of Wittgenstein's comments, our grasp of the sinister aspect of the ritual is related to its inherent expressive features, which we grasp without any historical explanation about its origin. Nor does it matter whether it is an enactment of a ritual in which people were once really burned or just play making of burning people.

But why does the sinister character of this ritual implicate us and the rest of humanity? As I understand Wittgenstein's point here, we are implicated by it in the same way that we are implicated by watching a horror movie with both repulsion and fascination. To be repelled by the sinister aspect of a practice is to acknowledge the effect of its sinister spirit upon us. We are reminded that it derives from existential concerns and attitudes toward life that we share with those who enacted it: namely, dread at being chosen to be burned and relief at someone else being chosen for this ordeal. By responding with understanding to the sinister aspect of this ritual, we acknowledge that we share with those who observed it the same deep human existential concerns and dispositions, which provide for our common human spiritual nature. This is so, despite the fact that we may differ from them in the cultural spirit on which our lives are based, so that we may find this ritual too abhorrent and its spirit too sinister for expressing our own existential concerns and spiritual dispositions.

5. The Spirit of Myth, Magic, and Religion in Everyday Language

Wittgenstein notes that our understanding of the expressive meaning of Myth, Magic, and Religion is demonstrated by our use of the same kind of spiritually expressive language that grows out of them. In his later reflections, he offers several reminders of this fact:

> The use of the word "fate." Our attitude to the future & the past. To what extent do we hold ourselves responsible for the future? How much do we speculate about the future? How do we think about past & future? If something unwelcome happens:—do we ask "Who's to blame?" Do we say, "Someone must be to blame for it?"—or do we say "It was God's will", "It was fate?"
> In the way in which asking a question, insisting on an answer, or not asking it, expresses a different attitude, a different way of living, so too, in this sense, is an utterance like "It is God's will: or "We are not masters of our fate." What this sentence does, or at least something similar, a commandment too could do. Including one that you give to yourself. And conversely a commandment, e.g. "Do not grumble!" can be uttered like the affirmation of a truth.[16]

Note that regardless whether we are religious, we are capable of understanding words used to express a mythical, magical, or religious attitude toward life in these examples. Our ability to understand them demonstrates that despite being modern, we are still affiliated in the linguistic culture that created the use of these words for spiritual expression. Wittgenstein reminds us of the spiritual experiences that are expressed through them, particularly the experience that manifests a religious attitude toward life:

> When someone who believes in God looks around him and asks, "Where did everything that I see come from?" "Where did everything come from?" he is *not* asking for a (causal) explanation; and the point of his question is that it is the expression of such a request. Thus, he is expressing an attitude toward all explanations. But how is this shown in his life? It is the attitude that takes a particular matter seriously, but then at a particular point doesn't take it seriously after all, and declares that something else is even more serious.
>
> In this way a person can say it is very serious that so-and-so died before he could finish a certain work; and in another sense it doesn't matter at all. Here we use the words "in a profounder sense."[17]

The "profounder sense" is the deeper, more important, and more meaningful sense. It emerges from an attitude toward life in which its value and meaning are not affected by such contingencies. It is a spiritual attitude toward life such as is expressed in religious rituals. Hence, a religious attitude toward life bestows a profounder meaning on life than that which is revealed through scientific explanations and practical everyday considerations. Therefore, to speak of a spiritual way of grasping life is to speak of an inspired way of understanding and expressing its profounder meaning.

By contrast, a spiritually "meaning blind" person is someone who does not understand the language of spiritual inspiration. Such a person may attempt to translate it into the language of theoretical and practical ways of reasoning. That is what Frazer has done in his explanation of Myth, Magic, and Religion, although he demonstrates by his very use of language and his ability to the three for what they are that he is not blind to their spiritual meaning:

> Frazer: "That these observances are dictated by fear of the ghost of the slain seems certain…" But why does Frazer use the word "ghost?" He thus understands this superstition very well, since he explains it to us with a superstitious word he is familiar with.[18]

Thus, in his use of language Frazer demonstrates that he shares with the ancients the same concepts through which they approached life in a spiritually meaningful manner: that he is not spiritually meaning blind. At the same time, he tries to distance himself from them by explaining these concepts in a scientific manner, as errors in reasoning. Wittgenstein ridicules this approach, suggesting that when telling of someone dying because of fear from the retribution of a ghost, "Frazer would be capable of believing that the savage dies because of an error." He therefore castigates Frazer for his philosophical point of view on spiritual matters:

> Frazer is much more savage than most of his savages, for they are not as far removed from understanding of a spiritual matter as a twentieth-century Englishman. *His* explanations of primitive practices are much cruder than the meaning of these practices themselves.[19]

In my reading of these comments, their philosophical point does not emerge simply by recognizing a category mistake committed by Frazer, when he reduced spiritual meaning to instrumental meaning. It emerges by noting that the concepts that served the ancients to express themselves in an inspired way are not strange to us. Our use of them demonstrates that we are able to draw upon their powerful, inspiring expressive meaning just as the ancients did. It shows that we possess the same linguistic expressions that served them, that we have the same existential concerns and spiritual nature from which they experienced life and out of which they invented myths, magic, and religious rituals to both express and confront their deepest human concerns. Therefore, to regard their inspired symbolic expressions of those concerns as primitive ways of reasoning, is to fail to acknowledge our own underlying spiritual nature and the concepts that serve us to both express it and attain an inspiring spiritual attitude toward life. It is to fail to acknowledge our shared humanity with the ancients, which renders explanation of the expressive meaning of these practices redundant.

The philosophical insight that emerges thereby about our language is that it is deeply rooted in both our human spiritual nature and our cultural past. In our language, we employ concepts that we share with our so-called primitive ancestors, which are expressive of existential concerns, impulses, and attitudes toward life that manifest a common human spiritual nature. That is the case despite the fact that we are modern human beings who are versed in science and who may not be inclined, as the ancients were, to make use of Myth, Magic, and Religion to express our existential concerns and to put our trusting spiritual faith in them.

Four

WITTGENSTEIN'S METHODS OF ATTAINING INSIGHT ABOUT SPIRITUAL RITUALS

Ludwig Wittgenstein's comments in this text on Myth, Magic, and Religion are mostly a reaction to James George Frazer's account and explanation of these practices in ancient cultures. However, they also exemplify certain methods he used for gaining philosophical insight into such practices without seeking to "explain" them in historical or reductive discourse. It is edifying to note three particular ways in which he goes about this project.

1. Clarification

A key concept Wittgenstein uses to bring insight into what puzzles us about these practices is what he calls "clarification." Elsewhere, he describes his philosophical discourse in general as "my work of clarification."[1] He notes, "the task of philosophy is . . . to clarify the use of existing language."[2] He also suggests, "philosophical problems are misunderstandings that must be removed by clarification of the rules according to which we are inclined to use words."[3] At times, he contrasts philosophical clarification with metaphysical efforts that take the form of foundational explanations. He remarks in this connection that mathematics does not need what he calls "a foundation," just as ordinary propositions about physical objects and sense impressions do not need an analysis. They need "clarification of their grammar."[4]

Clarifications are not explanations of the meaning of words and the sense of propositions that are aimed at the uninitiated. They are also not hypothetical empirical claims that aim to reduce our concepts to some other concepts or an analysis of their basic constituents. They are remarks that bring philosophical insight to those of us who are philosophically puzzled about the meaning of our cultural practices, linguistic or otherwise, and our ability to understand them.

As may now be seen, several of Wittgenstein's remarks about Myth, Magic, and Religion are philosophical clarifications of these concepts and of the examples that Frazer gives of their instantiation. Since he clarifies them in several different ways, it is edifying to note some of the ways in which he does so. One way is by placing them in their proper category. The procedure is similar to his placing psychological concepts in their proper categories: for example, by noting that "Intention is neither an emotion, a mood, nor yet a sensation or image. It is not a state of consciousness. It does not have genuine duration."[5] Similarly, he places the concepts of Myth, Magic, and Religion in the category of expressive spiritual rituals and narratives, which provide symbolic expressions of human existential concerns and attitudes toward life. To further this conceptual point, he contrasts their expressive spiritual use with the use of technical or instrumental measures aimed at achieving certain practical ends, which are based on reasoning and theoretical explanations.

A second way is by contrasting symbolic uses of language with practical uses, offering insightful examples of the different grammar of words used in these two different kinds of practices. For example, "'You can't hear God speak to someone else, you can hear him only if you are being addressed'—That is a grammatical remark."[6] The remark clarifies the spiritual meaning of the locution "to hear God speak," as contrasted with the social meaning of the locution "to hear the president speak." It reminds us that it makes no sense to try to eavesdrop on what God says to someone else, but it might make sense to eavesdrop on what one person says to another. Thus, this remark clarifies the expressive spiritual conceptual nature of religious discourse, by juxtaposing it with an instrumental social discourse. Here we might note that, unlike instrumental practices, expressive spiritual practices are indeed immune to error. At the same time, Wittgenstein is careful not to render all spiritual practices the same, as Frazer was inclined to do when he reduced them to bad instrumental ways of thinking: "Religious faith & superstition are quite different. The one springs from fear & is a sort of false science. The other is a trusting."[7]

A third way in which Wittgenstein clarifies the conceptual nature of these practices is by expressing the powerful effect on him of a given practice in a poetic manner. In doing so, he provides an insightful metaphor or simile for what he experiences in connection with its expressive spiritual meaning. Unlike a newly discovered truth, arrived at through a reductive or historical explanation, an expression that emanates from an insightful, poetic description of our experience of a given spiritual practice is spiritually edifying. It is a species of realization brought about by a telling illustrative expression, not by the acquisition of new information or the confirmation of an explanatory hypothesis. It is akin to drawing a striking portrait of someone or telling an illustrative story about that person, which conveys insight about the character of that person. In the case of the murder of the priest-king of Nemi, Wittgenstein describes how he understands its expressive meaning in the following way: "If a narrator places the priest-king of Nemi and 'the majesty of death' side by side, he realizes that they are the same. The life of the priest-king shows what is meant by that phrase."[8]

In this insight, both the ancient ritual and the poetic phrase "the majesty of death" emerge out of the same human spiritual nature and have a similar expressive spiritual meaning. Wittgenstein refers to them as "ceremony" and "symbol," claiming that they can be substituted for each other, neither explaining the other:

> Someone who is affected by the majesty of death can give expression to this through such a life.—This, of course, is also no explanation, but merely substitutes one symbol for another. Or: one ceremony for another.[9]

As we are still able to understand the meaning of this expressive phrase, we are also able to understand a ritual that enacts it. We only need to be reminded of the ritual's symbolization of the familiar phrase. This is a task that Wittgenstein takes upon himself as the "narrator" of the ritual's expressive meaning, by describing in an insightful metaphor how he grasps its expressive meaning through this phrase. Presumably, his ability to act as the narrator of the ritual's expressive meaning manifests both his grasp of the concepts of life, death, murder, and majesty and his ability to experience the dread of murder. In that he is no different from most of us. We are creatures that are concerned about death, both our own and that of those who are dear to us; we dread its approach. We are also liable to make use of it by murdering one another. Against this human background, the concept of death acquires special significance for us. We speak of a "terrible death," "frightening death,""shameful death," "cowardly death," "vengeful death," "heroic death," "beautiful death," and so on.[10] Wittgenstein's clarification of the expressive, symbolic meaning of the ritual of the priest-king of Nemi bestows majesty on death by joining murderer and victim in a spiritually expressive act that is at once the murder of one king and the crowning of a new king.

Some have seen a problem with Wittgenstein's clarification of the meaning of the ritual, since it relates to a ritual that emerges out of a culture that is not his.[11] However, in expressing his impression of its expressed meaning, Wittgenstein is also expressing what he takes to have been the expressed meaning that its observers experienced through it. In doing so he is not hypothesizing about what they meant to express thereby. He is expressing his experience of it, which is an expression of how he is struck by it. At the same time, since the ritual is a meaningful human action, his expression of its meaning is also an expression of how he grasps what it meant to those who created and observed it. As such, it might seem that Wittgenstein is indulging here in armchair anthropology. Now, in a way, this may be both true and false. To the extent that armchair anthropology is hypothesizing about the meaning of expressive practices of human beings in other cultures that we are unable to understand, he is not doing that. To the extent that it is expressing our immediate understanding of expressive practices in other cultures, then he is. The point of such an expressive venture is not that we have no need to study other cultures to understand them. The point is that when we study other cultures, we approach them against the background of how we grasp the behavior of human beings there as exemplifying the common behavior of human beings. Elsewhere, Wittgenstein notes this point in connection with common linguistic practices of human beings across cultural divides:

> Suppose you came as an explorer into an unknown country with a language quite strange to you. In what circumstances would you say that the people there gave orders, understood them, obeyed them, rebelled against them, and so on?
>
> The common behaviour of mankind is the system of reference by means of which we interpret an unknown language.[12]

"The common behavior of mankind" manifests the common nature of human beings: a human nature that, among other things, gives rise to concepts of death, murder, and king, as well as the desire to lend them inspiring spiritual expressions. This is the unformulated, shared linguistic and cultural background against which Wittgenstein approaches this ritual and from within which he experiences its meaning. It is within the context of this experience that his poetic grasp of the spiritual meaning of the ritual is expressed.

A fourth way in which Wittgenstein clarifies the nature of these practices is by offering insightful reminders that relate them to our own, natural, non-rational ways of behavior and inclinations. He uses this method of clarification in relation to what appear to be the puzzling, non-rational forms of behavior that ancient rituals display. To strip away what he finds puzzling about them, he recalls his own natural, non-rational ways of behavior and inclinations that are akin to them: for example, his inclination when he is furious about something to beat the ground or a tree with his walking stick. Other examples of the symbolic relationship between expressive behavior and what is meaningful to us are the following:

> Goethe's signature intimates something Goethian to me. To that extent it is like a face, for I might say the same of his face . . .
>
> Or do I *identify* the signature with the person in that, e.g. I love to look at the signature of a beloved human being, or I frame the signature of someone I admire and put it on my desk? (Magic that is done with pictures, hair etc.)[13]

In the above example, we relate to the signature of someone we admire as to a picture of that person. The inclination to preserve it is a symbolic expression of how that person is meaningful to us. Compare this expressive inclination on our part with the business-related practice of preserving signatures and pictures of people on bank cards, which is merely instrumental. In contrast, to collect pictures of esteemed people or cherished memorabilia from our past is to respond to them in a symbolic and expressive manner. This kind of clarification of the expressive symbolic meaning of puzzling, cultural practices, by relating them to our own natural ways of acting and experiencing the meaning of things is what Frank Cioffi, in his discussion of Wittgenstein's comments on Frazer, calls "self-clarification."[14] It relates strange and puzzling cultural practices to our own natural expressive responses.

A fifth way in which Wittgenstein clarifies the conceptual nature of Myth, Magic, and Religion is by relating them to meaningful experiences and attitudes toward life that are expressed in them with which he can easily identify. An example in point is his clarification at one time of the concept of the absolute ethical good, which he equated with the religious meaning of life expressed in Western monotheism. Wittgenstein presented this clarification in a public lecture he called "Ethics," which he delivered soon after his return to Cambridge in 1929. In it, he mentioned three experiences that promote a desire to talk about the religious meaning of life or God. The first is a mystical experience of wonder at life or the world:

> I believe the best way of describing it is to say that when I have it *I wonder at the existence of the world.* And I am then inclined to use such phrases as "how extraordinary that anything should exist" or "how extraordinary that the world should exist." I will mention another experience straight away . . . the experience of feeling absolutely safe. I mean the state of mind in which one is inclined to say, "I am safe, nothing can injure me whatever happens" . . . A third experience of the same kind is that of feeling guilty and again this was described by the phrase that God disapproves of our conduct. Thus in ethical and religious language we seem constantly to be using similes. And if I can describe a fact by means of a simile I must also be able to drop the simile and to describe the facts without it. Now in our case as soon as we try to drop the simile and simply to state the facts, which stand behind it, we find that there are no such facts. And so, what at first appeared to be a simile now seems to be mere nonsense.[15]

Describing the above experiences clarifies for Wittgenstein the concept of the religious meaning of life arising out of Western monotheism, which posits faith in God as an absolute solution to existential concerns, existential wonder and the spiritual value of life, which he refers to as "ethical." Within this context of clarification, he also claims that religious assertions based on such experiences are only expressive figures of speech, what he calls "similes." They are not descriptions of facts that may confirm or falsify these assertions. He does not object to the use of similes. Poetry, for example, widely employs similes to express experiences in a rich and powerful fashion. Such statements as "ferocious as a tiger," "cool as a cucumber," "bursting with anger," or "filled with love," make use of similes and metaphors that can be replaced by descriptions of features of character and emotions that do not mention them, even if some of their expressive power is lost in the transaction. He remarks, however:

> the desire to say something about the ultimate meaning of life, the absolute good, the absolute valuable, is not of this sort. It cannot be replaced

> in a similar way by non-metaphoric descriptions of the value or meaning of life and world for us.[16]

In my reading of these remarks on the ethical meaning of life, they clarify that religious claims made in this connection express a desire to say something factual about God in literal, non-metaphoric, non-symbolic discourse. However, inspired, expressive, metaphoric, and symbolic ways of talking about the spiritual meaning of life or God cannot be replaced by literal speech through propositions describing facts that make up the world. That is because they only function to express a certain spiritual attitude toward life and the world.[17] Thus, rituals often consist of the enactment of such spiritually moving similes.

A sixth way in which Wittgenstein clarifies the nature of these practices emerges in connection with remarks he made later when commenting on his lecture on ethics:

> At the end of my lecture on ethics I spoke in the first person: I think that this is something very essential. Here there is nothing to be stated anymore; all I can do is to step forth as an individual and speak in the first person.[18]

As I read this remark, instead of trying to confirm or refute religious discourse, we need to clarify our personal attitude toward it, noting the way in which it is, or is not, expressive of how we engage and experience life in a meaningful manner. Therefore, in addressing the question of its meaning, we need to speak in the first person regarding its inspirational meaning for us. To do so is to acknowledge our spiritual attitude of faith, or lack of faith, in what a mythical, magical, or religious discourse expresses. Therefore, the difference between believers in Myth, Magic, and Religion and nonbelievers is manifested in the personal meaning these practices have for them. Those who have spiritual faith in what these practices express grasp them as having a genuine inspirational claim on their lives, manifesting their experience of the mythical, magical, or religious meaning of life. Those who do not have faith in what they express may understand the meaning of a mythical, magical, or religious discourse and the inspirational role it plays in the lives of its believers, albeit without having a mythical, magical, or religious attitude toward life, and without finding this discourse spiritually meaningful or valuable to them.

For unlike the shared use by human beings of psychological concepts in all languages to express our feelings and ascribe feelings to others, a culture's use of mythical stories, magical ceremonies, and religious rituals may divide us into those who find inspirational meaning in them and those who do not. Therefore, when clarifying their conceptual, spiritual nature, we must also clarify the way in which they are or are not spiritually meaningful to us personally.[19] That is no different from the need to clarify our appreciation or lack of appreciation of a given work of art by noting in what way, if any, it touches our souls and is artistically meaningful to us personally.

The difference between clarifying (the meaning of) a concept and clarifying the way in which something or someone is personally meaningful to us is what Wittgenstein describes as the difference between a meaning that can be described and a meaning that cannot, but only expressed. Spiritual rituals and artistic activities are ways of expressing inspiring experiences and attitudes toward life. When we try to describe what is spiritually meaningful and inspiring to us about them in propositions, we are reduced to banalities or to metaphysical explanations that fail to make sense. Karl Kruse expressed this point by noting that the profound spiritual aspects of human life can be expressed in art and religious ritual, but not explained by philosophy. Wittgenstein carries this insight further by noting that, in dealing with spiritual matters, we must pass from conceptual clarifications to clarifications of our personal attitudes of faith or lack of faith in what these concepts and practices express.

A seventh way in which Wittgenstein clarifies the nature of these practices is by drawing analogies between them and spiritual practices that are prevalent in his culture, as illustrated by the following example:

> The religious actions, or the religious life, of the priestly-king are no different in kind from my genuinely religious action of today, for example, a confession of sins. This, too, admits of being "*explained*" and not explained.[20]

In the above insight, to explain the meaning of the ritual of the "priestly-kings" is to theorize about its meaning to those who created and observed it. To clarify its meaning is to illuminate its meaning in the context of spiritual concerns and ritualistic behavior that are familiar to us from our own culture. The comparison leads Wittgenstein to compare it with a ritual that was personally meaningful to him: a confession of sin. The concept of sin pertains to ethical failure on our part about which we feel deep remorse, leading us to confess as part of our repentance and wish to transform our ethical nature.

Someone who wonders why people find spiritual meaning in confessing a sin may be inattentive to the conceptual distinction between sin and crime. The first is a spiritual concept; the second is a legal one. The first is acknowledged in a personally powerful and spiritually authentic manner by experiencing guilt after committing a sin and by feeling remorse and a desire to confess as a way of "cleansing" the soul. The second is acknowledged by distinguishing between lawful and unlawful actions and by choosing whether to abide by the law. When we feel remorse at something we have done, regardless whether it is lawful, we are relating to it as to a sin. In religious discourse, the concept of sin is often enriched by describing it as an act that God abhors and forbids. However, our use of this concept does not depend on acquiring religious faith. It is often the other way round: a religious attitude may evolve from it.

In Wittgenstein's insight, the same human spiritual nature that leads us to want to confess a committed sin led the ancients to create the ritual of the priest-king at Nemi. Both manifest the common spiritual nature of human beings. Neither requires a hypothetical explanation to be understood as a spiritual expression of deep existential concerns. Accordingly, the expressive spiritual meaning of puzzling ancient rituals may be clarified by drawing analogies between them and spiritually expressive practices that are meaningful to us, such as a confession of sin. When we do that, they direct our attention to common ethical and existential concerns and common human inclinations to lend them expression in spiritual rituals. Both these concerns and the inclination to express them provide for our shared humanity.

An eighth way in which Wittgenstein clarifies the nature of these practices is by describing them as growing out of the natural inclination of human beings to make use of gestures: "In the ancient rites we have the use of an extremely developed gesture-language."[21]

The language of gestures is the language of expressive and symbolic behavior. Such are ordinary social gestures, as waving to a friend in a crowd, kissing someone on the cheek, or shaking hands, as well as flying a national flag or standing at attention when that is done. In this insight, the language of expressive spiritual gestures is still preserved in our ordinary concepts. Wittgenstein notes this by paying closer attention to our use of language through which various ancient spiritual attitudes toward life and what it encloses are still expressed:

> I should like to say: nothing shows our kinship to those savages better than the fact that Frazer has on hand a word as familiar to himself and us as "ghost" or "shade" in order to describe the views of these people . . . .
>
> An entire mycology is stored within our language.[22]

> And when I read Frazer, I continually would like to say: We still have all these processes, these changes of meaning, before us in our verbal language . . . .[23]

Thus, we might consider a flag "sacred" and refrain from using a worn-out one as a dishrag. If somebody were to do so, we might see that as "defiling," "dishonoring," or "desecrating" it. Someone who is incapable of understanding how any material object can induce such an attitude might find both the symbolic gesture-language and our spiritually inspired descriptions of these actions as an expression of mythical beliefs in the sacred spiritual essence of flags unintelligible. Such a person may even accuse us of bad reasoning and of holding irrational beliefs. However, these attitudes, gestures, and uses of language are not the result of theoretical and practical ways of reasoning, nor are they instances of superstitions, no more than are our cultural traditions of burying the bodies of dead people rather than disposing of them as refuse.

As may now be seen, it is not simply that Wittgenstein is interested in clarifying the meaning of symbolic forms of behavior, while scientifically oriented scholars such as Frazer are interested in their explanation. Rather, he is interested in clarifying the meaning of human behavior because he wants to arrive at a deeper understanding and description of the common expressive spiritual nature of human beings in culture.

2. Representation

A key concept Wittgenstein employs to bring philosophical insight to the conceptual nature of Myth, Magic, and Religion as symbolic spiritual practices and forms of discourse is what he calls "representation." He uses it in two primary ways. In the first, he likens these practices to ways of representing the meaning of things from an inspired point of view by the use of symbols. As such, they are not aimed at explaining the nature of things any more than a graduation ceremony is an explanation of what it means to finish school. They are more like striking expressive pictures of meaningful aspects of life that have an inspirational function. In later remarks he offers the following example:

> Religion teaches that the soul can exist when the body has disintegrated. Now do I understand this teaching?—Of course I understand it—I can imagine plenty of things in connection with it. And haven't pictures of these things been painted? And why should such a picture be only an imperfect rendering of the spoken doctrine? Why should it not do the *same* service as the words? And it is the service which is the point.[24]

So, we use both imagination and pictures to express our understanding of pivotal concepts to which are referred in spiritual practices. In this case, religious teaching of the existence of the soul after death serves as an extension of prayer for the welfare of the soul after death. Both provide symbolic pictures of the concept of soul. Concepts pictured in these ways are akin to poetic metaphors that inspire us. A religious picture of the soul is not a theoretical model that offers a scientific explanation of the soul. Unlike passport pictures, such pictures are inspired, figurative symbols. Their religious meaning emerges from the expressive religious service they perform. They are akin to rituals that enact spiritual metaphors and similes. To mistake the use of such pictures for scientific explanations of psychological features of life is the same as mistaking a religious ritual for an instrumental practice based on reasoning.

The second way in which Wittgenstein uses the concept of representation is to distinguish between scientific explanations and conceptual descriptions. The first add to our knowledge by revealing the hidden causes of events. The second add to our understanding by formulating insightful accounts or illustrations of what we already know and with which we are familiar: sometimes in the form of an edifying "synopsis" of various practices that fall under a given concept. Thus, he says of Freud's discourse on humor in jokes, that it offers a "wonderful representation" of the humorous point of a joke.[25] Freud set out to explain the psychic mechanisms behind jokes. Whatever one may think of that venture, in the pursuit of it, Freud tells all sorts of jokes, which he divides into various kinds, thereby illustrating various funny ways of reasoning manifested in jokes.

Similarly, Wittgenstein might have said that Frazer provides a "wonderful representation" of ancient myths, magical ceremonies, and religious rituals, manifesting deep existential concerns and promoting inspiring spiritual attitudes toward life and its contingencies. He could have then added that the project was undermined by Frazer's attempt to explain the generic source of the ritual at Nemi by conjecturing in an unsupported manner about the historical influences for its invention on the basis of perceived similarities between it and various other rituals. It would have been clear then that the important point for him is to represent these different rituals in a perspicuous manner as manifesting a common spirit, regardless of their historical influences on one another. The historical explanation is not necessary for the purpose of assembling the data that demonstrates this point. Wittgenstein notes this in the following remark:

> The historical explanation, the explanation as a hypothesis of development, is only *one* way of assembling the data-of their synopsis. It is just as possible to see the data in their relation to one another and to embrace them in a general picture without putting it in the form of an hypothesis about temporal development.[26]

As should now be apparent, like Frazer, Wittgenstein is also striving to provide a key to Myth, Magic, and Religion, albeit not a hidden scholarly one. It is a conceptual key that clarifies their categorical nature as expressive symbolic enactments of existential concerns that promote certain spiritual attitudes toward life and what it encloses. This key is to be used by providing a representational synopsis of their instantiation in both similar and different ways in various cultures that displays their common spiritual nature. As such, it is not a secret key that unlocks the hidden message of Myth, Magic, and Religion in strange cultures, but one we have always possessed and which we need only to both acknowledge and represent correctly in an insightful synopsis. By doing so we gain access into its use:

> "And so the chorus points to a secrete law" one feels like saying to Frazer's collection of facts. I *can* represent this law . . . by means of the arrangement of its factual content alone, in a "perspicuous" representation.
>
> The concept of perspicuous representation is of fundamental importance for us. It denotes the form of our representation, the way we see things. (A kind of "Worldview" as it is apparently typical of our time. Spengler.)
>
> This perspicuous representation brings about the understanding, which consists precisely in the fact that we "see the connections." Hence the importance of finding *connecting links*.[27]

As Brian R. Clack has shown in his discussion of this remark, Wittgenstein is combining in it two ideas, derived from three sources of influence on his thinking.[28] The first idea is derived from the physicists Henrich Hertz and Ludwig Boltzmann, who were early influences on his thinking. Both stressed the need to confront puzzling metaphysical questions in science, such as "What is energy?" by describing the way we apply the puzzling concept in different circumstances, rather than by trying to explain its essence. In doing so, we disclose connections between different uses of the concept, which are not based on a common essence. In a similar way, an insightful "synopsis" of various spiritual rituals allows us to "see the connections" between various ways of expressing existential concerns.

The second idea is derived from Oswald Spengler, who wrote on the spiritual underpinnings of cultures as manifested in prominent historical communities, and whose pessimistic volume on the spiritual decline of the West as a culture appeared at the end of the First World War.[29] In it, Spengler presented an historical worldview, featuring two main tenets. The first was that the various innovations of a culture in art, science, and technology bear a certain family resemblance, as they all embody the same idea. The second was that historical cultures develop like plants: sprouting, blossoming, and decaying. Spengler then compared different innovations and practices of a culture in different fields and at different historical periods. The description was supposed to disclose connections. Similarly, a description of them within the same field at different historical periods was also supposed to show certain connections: the former are more creative, immediate, and spiritually powerful; the latter are more contrived, rational, and spiritually less powerful.

As I read Wittgenstein in this connection, to gain conceptual insight into what puzzles us about Myth, Magic, and Religion, we can proceed in two ways. One is to describe different instances of them, representing their conceptual nature by depicting the multiple ways in which they are expressed in an insightful synopsis. This is akin to how the grammar of the meaning of a given word is demonstrated by showing its varied uses in the stream of life.

In the case of spiritual practices, it is accomplished by arranging various rituals or myths so that their similarities and differences may be perceived in an edifying manner. This procedure is similar to the way in which Freud represented the humor in jokes by listing all kinds of jokes and arranging them according to certain similarities and differences—albeit without trying to explain their psychological mechanism as Freud did. The philosophical insight that is supposed to emerge from this arrangement is akin to that which emerges from seeing pictures of various trees arranged according to kinds, size, and shape, and seeing morphological similarities and difference between them. Through such an arrangement, the botanical nature of trees is represented in a perspicuous manner rather than defined and explained. It enables us to appreciate the wonder and significance of trees in all their immense variations. Thus, Wittgenstein allies his attempt to bring philosophical insight into the meaning of Myth, Magic, and Religion with a descriptive, non-explanatory discourse that can bring out their cultural significance in a spiritually edifying manner, not with an explanatory one.

3. The Picturesque Meaning of "Spirit"

One way in which existential concerns are represented in Myth, Magic, and Religion is by means of inspiring stories and poetic uses of language. A telling example of this is the way in which the very concept of spirit is employed therein. Having once played a central role in myth, magic, and religious discourse about nonmaterial beings and gods, and having once been the focus of theological and philosophical metaphysical explanations, the concept of spirit has now fallen out of philosophical grace. It no longer seems necessary to most philosophers to dwell on it, even when expounding on the inspiring aspects of human expressions and ways of life. As already emerges from Wittgenstein's use of this concept in his discourse, he wants to redeem it, albeit without engaging in metaphysical explanations about the constituents of the human spirit. The difficulty of following him in this matter is that his reflections on the concept of spirit are, therefore, rarely formulated in an explicit manner. It is worthwhile, however, to trace and elucidate them.

Earlier, under the influence of Arthur Schopenhauer's view of spirit as the will animating the world and its creatures, Wittgenstein had written the following: "One conception: As I can infer my spirit (character, will) from my physiognomy, so I can infer the spirit (will) of each thing from its physiognomy."[30] Here, the spirit of different kinds of creature, including human beings, is manifested in their physical demeanor or life-form. Later, he rephrases this insight in connection with the concept of soul. "The human being is the best picture of the human soul," he writes."[31] An expressive living natural figurative picture, it may be added. In these clarifications of the concepts of a human soul and spirit, both are inherently related to the human life-form. It may now be said that in the way in which a human being is a natural living expressive figurative picture of the human soul, our use of the very terms "soul" and "spirit" is the use of poetic locutions that provide inspiring expressive pictures of human beings.

What confuses some readers of Wittgenstein at this point is that at the same time, he also castigates metaphysical explanations that reduce our grasp of things to some so-called spiritual or mental activity:

> because we cannot specify any *one* bodily action which we call pointing to the shape (as opposed, for example, to the colour), we say that a *spiritual* [mental, intellectual] activity corresponds to these words.
>
> Where our language suggests a body and there is none: there, we should like to say, is a *spirit*.[32]

This injunction against metaphysical explanations that usurp the concept of spirit, turning it into a unique, incorporeal substance that performs mental activities, does not extend to our ordinary expressive use of it when describing the way in which people engage life in some particular animated manner. We speak in this connection of "the spirit" in which people approach their lives and what they embody, referring thereby to their will, desire, and attitude toward their life. We also extend it to the way in which a certain expressive practice is pursued, referring to its "inner nature," "character," or "spirit."

The above use of the concept of spirit is often accompanied by inspiring locutions that promote poetic pictures in which the concept of spirit is transformed into a substantive. We speak in this connection of the spirit of a person and what characterizes it in particular. This poetic way of referring to the spirit of a person renders it into an incorporeal being that resides within people and provides them with animated life. We say in this use of the concept that someone has a happy or sad spirit, a lively or depressed spirit, and so forth. The tendency to reify the concept of spirit is typical of mythical and religious discourse. Both transform characteristic features of things and beings into symbolic reified substantive entities. Of course, the spirits of people are manifested in the expressive attitudes they have to life and what it encloses. To refer to them through myths, magic, and religious discourse as to entities that exist on their own is to refer to them in a symbolic discourse. To describe this human tendency, as I am doing now, is to clarify the reified concept of spirit as an inspiring metaphor.

In contrast to the above clarification, to explain the concept of spirit as a non-material, supernatural kind of entity that underlies human life is to transform an expressive symbolic discourse into an explanatory theory that is metaphysics. It is edifying to reflect in this connection on the way in which mental features of life are reified in modern scientific and philosophical discourse. A typical example is the emergent use of the concept of "mind" in modern philosophy, which aims at replacing the previous mythical concepts of soul and spirit. In non-philosophical discourse, the concept of mind is used to refer to mental features of living beings, which involve what Gilbert Ryle called "heed concepts."[33] In ordinary speech, we also use various substantive poetic locutions to refer to such mental dispositions, describing them thereby as emanating out of a special mental organ called "the mind." We say of someone who is very good in reasoning that he or she has a sharp mind, of someone who acts crazily that he is losing his mind, of a problem that frustrates us that it is driving us out of our mind, of people who are overtaken with love that they cannot get the person they love out of their mind, and so forth. Of course, these locutions are mostly metaphoric. However, in metaphysical explanations, such enlightening picturesque descriptions of animated life are taken literally. In them, the mind is transformed into an organ or a system residing within people, which possesses mental states and performs mental processes.

Wittgenstein reflects on the standing of the concepts of mind, spirit, and soul in ordinary non-philosophical human discourse in the following remark:

> Then is it misleading to speak of man's soul, or of his spirit? So little misleading, that it is quite intelligible if I say "My soul is tired, not just my mind."[34]

In my reading of this remark, the distinction between the concepts of mind and soul is brought out by relating them to our expressive discourse. The first is used to express a burdensome attitude toward one's life typified by lack of vigor in pursuing life and what it holds in promise. The second is used to express a feeling of intellectual sluggishness, such as may be felt at the end of the day after writing too much. At the same time, the remark reminds us that the very concepts of soul and mind are expressive poetic metaphors and symbolic uses of language that have been incorporated into ordinary discourse. Note in this connection that there is nothing wrong in reifying these concepts in this manner. No so-called category mistake is committed thereby, just as no category mistake is committed when we speak of "time running out" toward the end of a game. They are poetic symbolic uses of language that promote expressive insightful pictures that enrich our perspectives and inspire us.

To note the expressive, poetic, symbolic usage of these concepts in the stream of human life is to remind ourselves not to mistake them for metaphysical or scientific explanations that would transform them into a non-expressive, non-poetic, non-symbolic mode of discourse. There is nothing wrong with picturing the human soul or spirit in reified terms, just as there is nothing wrong in symbolizing the concept of time by the image of a clock or everyday life by the expressive locution "the stream of life." That is as long as we remember that this poetic mode of speech is just part of the natural inclination of human beings to express themselves in picturesque ways. It is natural for human beings to picture their spirits and souls as incorporeal beings residing within them, as it is natural for human beings to conjure fantasies and images. We are creatures that have expressive artistic inclinations, and we tend to make insightful symbolic pictures of reality and our ways of conceiving of it in the language we use. However, this is not the case when philosophers use the concept of mind to theorize about the underlying mechanism of human dispositions and psychological propensities.

In my reading of Wittgenstein's reminders on our use of the concepts of mind, spirit, and soul, these concepts have a meaningful, edifying, expressive function in the stream of human life. To use them outside their expressive function, so as to theorize and explain the underpinning of human life, is to engage in metaphysics that seeks to transform expressive artistic linguistic innovations into a rational explanation of the constituents of human reality. Therefore, to use the picturesque concept of spirit in ordinary expressive discourse is not to buy into a metaphysical explanation that seeks to build on it. They are different enterprises; just as to play a musical instrument is not to explain the nature of music.

As may now be seen, just as it is possible to distinguish the expressive use of the concept of spirit from its metaphysical exploitation, it is possible to distinguish between two kinds of pictures that arise in these connections. One is a poetic, symbolic picture that enriches our perspective and expresses our attitude toward life. The other is a misleading picture that is at the basis of metaphysical explanations about the essence of mind and spirit. The two pictures differ from one another in the way in which explanations and artistic creations differ from one another.

Five

PHILOSOPHICAL REFLECTIONS ON WITTGENSTEIN'S COMMENTS

1. The Ways of Human Inspiration and Reasoning

As can now be seen, in his comments on James George Frazer's discourse on Myth, Magic, and Religion, Ludwig Wittgenstein is advancing a conceptual distinction between two different kinds of cultural practices and ways of discourse. He also advances a conceptual distinction between two different kinds of human disposition that are manifested in them. There are practical practices, exemplified in cooking, building, and tilling the land, and there are expressive practices, among which are also symbolic spiritual practices exemplified by Myth, Magic, and Religion. The former are the product of reasoning, and they are supported by explanations, opinions, conjectures, hypotheses, and theories. The latter are the product of existential concerns, ethical aspirations, and attitudes of awe and wonder at life, and they are supported by colorful expressions, insightful pictures, edifying stories, inspiring rituals, enriching metaphors, enlightening similes, and powerful symbols. The former are useful for developing both instrumental techniques and a scientific discourse aimed at explaining the causal mechanisms underlying natural phenomena. The latter are useful for developing an expressive cultural discourse, as exemplified in Myth, Magic, and Religion, which are aimed at promoting and enhancing a spiritual attitude toward life and what it encompasses.

As I read Wittgenstein on this matter, we are cultural beings who possess both a rational mind and a passionate, concerned, awed, inspired, expressive soul and spirit. The former is exemplified in a practical and intellectual approach to life: by our ability to invent various means to attain desired ends and to reason and explain things in a cogent and rational manner. The latter is exemplified in our ability to experience and express the meaning of things to us in an inspired and powerful manner. It is the latter ability that finds expression in arts, rituals, and ceremonies, some of which also take the form of myth, magic, and religious practices.

Although in his comments on Frazer, Wittgenstein tends to distinguish between ways of reasoning and ways of expressing inspired attitudes toward life, human beings may be inspired by myriad things. These include scientific explanations, medical discoveries, the invention of instruments, philosophy, sports, arts, fighting, politics, family life, aiding others, building things, cooking, tilling the land, making money, teaching, writing, reading, and so forth—all the diverse activities that may embody human life. Nonetheless, we can distinguish between practices the role of which is inspirational, aimed at emphasizing the significance (or meaning) of things in the stream of life, and practices with a practical role. The search for a cogent scientific theory that explains a particular natural mystery may inspire a scientist and those who subsequently make use of the theory. However, its scientific merit is evaluated not through its inspirational effect, but in its explanatory success. In a different way, someone may dance or paint as a way of earning a living, but the artistic value of what that person does is supposed to be measured by its inspirational effect on us, not by its financial reward.

The distinction between instrumental and inspirational practices, like the distinction between expressive and theoretical discourse, is an edifying reminder of different features of cultural practices. However, two qualifications should be added at this point. The first is that the distinction is too restricting if it is used as a theory that divides cultural practices into two distinct kinds. Many human practices and discourses exemplify both features. Consider in this connection conceptions of morality, justice, and the good life that emerge in different cultures. They provide both inspiring values and ethical outlooks on life and practical social norms. The same may be said also of Myth, Magic, and Religion. They are spiritual practices that provide powerful expressions for existential concerns and inspiring outlooks on life. They also contribute to the formation of a shared human cultural identity that is socially beneficial.

The second qualification that needs to be added to Wittgenstein's comments is that to say that spiritual practices are aimed at expressing existential concerns in an inspiring fashion is not to say that they always inspire us. Inspiration, like the meaning of things that are dear to us, does not reside in them, but in us. To find spiritual inspiration in a myth, ritual, or certain religious practice is to acknowledge its spiritual meaning by experiencing it as personally meaningful.[1] However, what some of us find spiritually meaningful may not be experienced as such by others. Yet, one of the features providing for the very existence of culture is our ability to be inspired by the same shared expressions, practices, and symbols, in language, arts, and human affairs.

2. Spiritual Deficiency as "Meaning-blindness"

To better appreciate the role of expressive spiritual practices in pursuing and engaging life, it is instructive to imagine cultural beings that are able to reason and follow rules, but lack the need, ability, or inclination to develop inspired expressions of the way in which they experience and engage life. Lacking strong passions, deep attachments, and existential concerns, in the form of dreads, hopes, wishes, and the ability to marvel at life and wonder about its meaning, they would not develop inspiring expressions of mythical, magical, and religious attitudes toward life. Lacking the inquisitive, questioning minds that make us wonder about natural mysteries, they would not pursue empirical research and invent theoretical explanations to solve these mysteries Wittgenstein considers this possibility in two invented philosophical contexts of reflection. One is in connection with people who are insensitive, as they are brought up not to express any feeling:

> Imagine that the people of a tribe were brought up from early youth to give no expression of feeling *of any kind.* They find it childish, something to be got rid of. Let the training be severe. "Pain" is not spoken of; especially not in the form of a conjecture "Perhaps he has got . . . ." If anyone complains, he is ridiculed or punished. There is no such thing as the suspicion of shamming. Complaining is so to speak already shamming.[2]

The other is in connection with what he calls "aspect-blindness" or "meaning-blindness." In one example, he considers someone who cannot see a sign as pointing in the direction of an object or place that it designates:

> Anyone who cannot understand and learn to use the words "to see the sign as an arrow" – that's whom I call "meaning-blind." It will make no sense to tell him "You must try to see it as an arrow" and one won't be able to help him in *that* way.[3]

Seeing the sign as an arrow that points in a certain direction is to see a certain aspect of the sign. The concept of an aspect, he suggests, is akin to the concept of an image.[4] Someone who cannot see it is like someone who cannot see colors. In an analogy he draws to clarify this idea, he notes that "Aspect-blindness will be *akin* to the lack of a 'musical ear.'"[5]

A satirical fantasy of emotionally insensitive and artistically meaning-blind cultural beings that predates Wittgenstein's reflections on this subject is drawn by Jonathan Swift in the fourth and last book of *Gulliver's Travels, Voyage to the Country of the Houyhnhnms.*[6] The noble and benign creatures that rule the country are Swift's satirical description of Plato's virtuous philosophers in the shape of rational horses. They lack arts and spiritual rituals, possessing only useful technical and social practices. They do not use language to tell stories or to express themselves in metaphors and poetry, as they cannot conceive of using language to "say what is not." By their unwavering allegiance to rational truth in everything, they are divested of art, Myth, Magic, and Religion.

In my reading of Swift's satire, Gulliver is the misguided naïve philosopher who is taken in by the Houyhnhnms' rational, virtuous nature, which underlies their way of life. As a result, he begins to despise his own kind for not living according to the high standards of rationality and virtuous habits they exhibit. It might be said that in Wittgenstein's criticism, Frazer approaches the Myth, Magic, and Religion of ancient cultures with the same disdain that Gulliver develops for his own kind. In Frazer's case, he diminishes the spiritual aspect of human nature, which leads humans to express their existential concerns, passions, and wonder about life through the use of these symbolic practices, by consigning them to the category of faulty ways of reasoning. Lacking Swift's satirical ability, Wittgenstein only castigates Frazer for his attempt to reduce the symbolic spiritual aspects of cultural life to either rationally well grounded or rationally ill grounded "opinions." Elsewhere, he wonders what human beings who could not understand the expressive discourse of myths, magic, and religion would be like:

> What must the man be called, who cannot understand the concept "God," cannot see how a reasonable man may use this word seriously? Are we to say he suffers from some *blindness*?[7]

Lest we miss the point behind the last question, he earlier refers to this form of blindness as "meaning-blindness."[8] He compares such meaning-blind people to mental defectives. They are not able to understand the meaning of the word "intend" when it refers to a future action in as yet unperceived surroundings. Nor are they able to use a word that has two different meanings, within different linguistic contexts: for example the word "till," which may refer to an object or to a period of time, or the word "is," which may be used for predication, as in "the rose is red," or for identity statements, as in "2 + 2 is 4." He also imagines human beings who are unable to perceive certain aspects of things and to understand assertions regarding them: such as that a particular triangle is standing on its base, or is lying down. They also do not grasp certain psychological aspects of human life, failing to perceive the difference between a smiling face and a sad face or other people as living creatures.

The instructive idea of meaning-blindness can illuminate other abilities we have, such as the ability to enjoy music, to find humor in a funny joke, to recognize a resemblance between two things, and more. It can illuminate also our everyday use of metaphors and similes to express and describe things from an inspired point of view. (An example in point would be the very word "inspire" that I have been using here in regard to the "spiritual" nature of Myth, Magic, and Religion, as it literally means blowing wind or spirit into something.) Consider human beings who are unable to make use of metaphors and similes or of symbolic discourse. They would then likely mistake Myth, Magic, and Religion for bad science.

Thus, the idea of meaning-blindness illuminates the spiritual meaning of an inspired discourse that expresses our existential concerns and attitudes toward life. It brings out the way in which such a discourse expresses what we love, hate, dread, desire, hope, and wish for, as well as the meaningful way in which we experience both ordinary and extraordinary events in our lives. It is instructive to note that we not only experience life and what it encompasses in meaningful ways, but we also tend to express the meaningful ways we experience it in metaphors, similes, and works of art. We do so through the use of language and rituals that inspire us, such as those exemplified in myth, magic, and religious practices.

To see the point of the above reminders, imagine cultural beings that differ from us in that they neither experience life in such meaningful ways nor want to express it in inspiring ways. They could be described as meaning-blind to these aspects of life. Since they do not experience such aspects of life in personally meaningful ways, they would also not form any particular personal attitude toward them nor be inclined to express it in an inspired, culturally shared fashion.

As they do not experience disgust, loathing, and revulsion, they are not likely to develop cultural taboos and religious prohibitions pertaining to certain kinds of food and behavior. At most, if they are intelligent, they may sanction or forbid them on the basis of practical ways of reasoning. As they lack deep existential concerns, dreads, passions, desires, attachments, expectations, hopes, and wishes, they are not likely to experience in a deeply meaningful way relief, recovery, escape, deliverance, or salvation, nor frustration, disappointment, distress, despair, depression, or hopelessness.

As they do not view their past with shame, remorse, or satisfaction, they would not invent rituals of repentance or gratitude. As they do not grieve over the death of others, they would not invent rituals of lamentation. As they do not rejoice over marriages or the birth of their children, they would not develop cultural rituals to celebrate these events. As they are not concerned about hunger and famine, they would not celebrate harvest or invent prayers of thanksgiving for their meals. As they do not marvel at the very existence of life, they would not express their wonder in moving rituals and inspiring narratives. Such beings would not invent myths, magic, and religious practices nor find any spiritual meaning in observing them.

My last remark points to the conceptual difference between a person who does not believe in God and a person who is meaning-blind to the concept of God. The former has deep existential concerns and spiritual dispositions, although they do not lead to religious belief. Such a person is like someone who has musical abilities, but has not developed them to the extent of appreciating classical music. The latter has no existential concerns and spiritual dispositions. Such a person is unable to believe in God in the same way that a person devoid of a musical ear is unable to enjoy music, or the way a color-blind person is unable to see colors. At most, such a person may form a belief that God exists. Such a belief is a sort of religious opinion, which may be acquired and supported by rational reasoning. It takes the conceptual form of a hypothesis. It is very different from an existential attitude of faith in God, which is experienced as bestowing spiritual meaning on one's life in a very personal, non-inferential, and immediate way.

It does not follow that a person who is not meaning-blind to religious discourse will automatically thereby attain religious faith. We are able to understand the spiritual meaning of Myth, Magic, and Religion to people in our own and in other cultures without making use of them ourselves. We are able to do so because we are human beings and not only rational philosophers or Houyhnhnms. As such, we are beset by existential concerns and are apt to develop inspiring or deflating attitudes toward our lives. Therefore, the concept of a spiritual attitude toward life is meaningful to us. That is so even if we do not possess the spiritual attitudes toward life that are expressed in certain religious rituals. We are able to understand them since we possess the same underlying human nature in connection with which particular expressive religious spiritual attitudes toward life emerge. That is no different from understanding the pleasure some human beings find in eating snails and frogs, even if they turn us off. This is because pleasure in eating is not a strange phenomenon to us.

As may now be seen, the idea of meaning-blindness is a methodological procedure Wittgenstein uses to gain philosophical insight into the significance of both ordinary aspects of things and ordinary human abilities manifested in our use of concepts. It enables us to appreciate the difference between the use of concepts based on acquiring opinions about various aspects of life, and the use of concepts based on existential concerns and inspiring attitudes toward various aspects of life; between understanding the theoretical meaning of things and experiencing their meaningfulness to us in a personal way. It brings conceptual insight to the significant way in which we experience the meaning of things, enabling us to appreciate this ability of ours by envisioning it as missing from our lives.

That is no different from learning to appreciate good health by noting its significance when we become sick. It helps us take note of significant features of human existence that, in the flow of life and in our philosophical reflections, we are apt to pass over as not worth mentioning. Swift used this methodological measure to help us appreciate the limitations of basing human life on rational thought and the importance to us of feelings and emotions, through which we give artistic and spiritual expression to our lives. Wittgenstein uses it to help us appreciate the conceptual nature of symbolic spiritual practices and the common spiritual nature of ancient and modern human beings from which they arise, reminding us in this way of our shared humanity.

3. Instrumental Practices and Symbolic Rituals

To distinguish between expressive and instrumental practices is to note that they are activities that are pursued for different purposes. An example that Wittgenstein suggests is how human beings both decorate their swords and sharpen them. As appears from his criticism of Frazer's view, Myth, Magic, and Religion are linked predominantly to decorating swords, not to sharpening them.

Several commentators attribute to Wittgenstein the claim that magic is only expressive, not instrumental, and so also religious practices.[9] A. J. Ayer has argued in this connection that while some rituals may be purely expressive and symbolic, not all of them are so.[10] He suggests that the example Wittgenstein gives of the ritual (described by Frazer) of adoption formerly prevalent in Bulgaria, where a woman would take a child she intended to adopt and push and pull it between her legs, is symbolic. Another example that Wittgenstein gives, of inflicting damage on an enemy's picture, is not. It is intended to kill that person.

My first comment is that the example used by Ayer to show that the purpose of a ritual may be to inflict harm on an enemy is not as clear-cut as it is made to appear. When, in the heat of a demonstration against a hated enemy nation, the mob burns, rips, and stabs pictures of that nation's leaders, they are not intending thereby to bring harm to them, not in any practical sense. We would not accuse them on the basis of such behavior as trying to kill those leaders; not even of doing things that they believe may inflict harm on them.

At most, it is a symbolic enactment of a wish to harm them, just as spitting on the flag of an enemy nation is the enactment of a wish to disgrace it. Human beings in all cultures are able to distinguish between expressions of hate and intentions to harm, between enactment of wishes and practical actions, and there is no reason to confuse them. What may sometimes confuse us about this matter is an unfamiliar practice in an unfamiliar culture. As Frank Cioffi has noted, if human beings who practiced magic interpreted our expressive practice of kissing the pictures of our loved ones as instrumental magic, they would be making a mistake about their meaning. It is similar to one that philosophers make when they interpret all magic as merely expressive behavior.[11]

Second, as these examples demonstrate, not all expressions of emotions and enactments of wishes are a form of magic. A person who uses magic is trying to cause something to happen through symbolic actions and rituals. This often involves a belief in the efficacy of symbolic action or ritual, as having a causal effect on the course of things, in a way that merely expressive symbolic gestures of hate and love do not. When such a belief accompanies the action, we are justified in drawing a distinction between merely expressive practices, such as pledging allegiance to the flag, and spiritually expressive rituals that are accompanied by instrumental beliefs, such as in the case of magic. It is important to note that rituals of magic may not be alone in this hybrid conceptual category. Religious rituals may also be accompanied by instrumental beliefs. Here, Frazer's explanation about the hostility of religion to magic is conceptually edifying. In magical and superstitious rituals, an attempt is made to manipulate the forces and spirits that determine the course of life. When certain magical measures fail to procure desired goals, trying new ones entails no spiritual difficulty. By contrast, religious faith or the lack of faith in God is not usually determined by having our wishes fulfilled through a ritual of prayer, blessing, or sacrifice. When it is, we say that the person is approaching religious faith as though it were a version of superstition. To switch from one religion to another or to give up on religion entirely is a spiritual transformation, not merely the adoption of new techniques.

Third, as Ayer has shown, our understanding of a given ritual and to what extent it is expressive or instrumental depends on what it involves. The practices of agriculture, which require planting in a given season, are not as amenable to the whims of magic as healing the sick might appear to be in light of modern medicine. That is because the former are rooted in historical tradition that has worked, whereas the latter is based on human concern over life and death with no clear proven medical practice and theory. We do not interpret a ritual of drawing an adopted baby through a woman's legs as instrumental magic. To suppose that it is would be to misunderstand its symbolic nature and to regard the people who perform this ritual as fools. At the most, we might say that it is a symbolic action that renders the woman into the baby's new adopting mother, albeit without misleading anyone about the fact that she has not given birth to it. We might compare it to other more familiar rituals of transformation, such as marriage ceremonies or bestowing degrees on graduates.

Fourth, Wittgenstein is sensitive both to the symbolic nature of a spiritual ritual and to the limitations of its instrumental use. "The same savage, who stabs the picture of his enemy apparently in order to kill him, really builds his hut out of wood and carves his arrows skillfully and not in effigy."[12] Performers of the ritual are quite aware that their arrows need to be skillfully carved to inflict harm on their enemy. We might compare these different practices with ceremonies at the laying of a new building's foundation or the launching of a new ship, which do not substitute for instrumental measures taken to erect buildings on solid foundations and construct ships properly, so they will not sink. We have no qualms about using both expressive and instrumental practices to satisfy our concerns. However, the issue at hand is whether a given practice of magic is instrumental or expressive.

Brian R. Clack has argued that Wittgenstein's view of magic does not necessarily run counter to an instrumentalist conception of magic such as Frazer's.[13] Indeed, Wittgenstein remarks that, since eating and drinking have their dangers, nothing is more natural than wanting to protect oneself against these dangers, using various rituals of magic to do so. As mentioned earlier, he clarifies superstition in this connection by distinguishing it from religious faith: "one springs from *fear* & is a sort of false science. The other is a trusting."[14] In my reading of Wittgenstein's insight here about superstition constituting a false science, the methodology underlying it is of generalizing from a single case. It is successful in persuading people because the attitude toward life from which superstition emerges is fear. In contrast, the attitude toward life from which religious faith emerges is putting our trust in God. Nevertheless, the description of superstition as a "false science" is more appropriate to magic, which often is accompanied by a worldview about the forces controlling life and world. Superstition may be more basic. It is to magic as children's games of hopscotch or marbles are to grown-up sports of football or basketball, which are backed by complicated rules and are conducted with referees that oversee them. Nonetheless, what he notes about the instrumental nature of superstition is also applicable to magic.

Although Wittgenstein aspires to eliminate instrumental beliefs from religious faith, this personal aspiration of his is not characteristic of religious faith in all cultures throughout the history of humanity. It seems to be an attitude of faith more prominent among religious believers in modern Western culture. In a way, it is also a response to the philosophical assault on religious faith that was expressed in Positivism, which explained religion as an early stage in human cultural development of explaining the nature of the world. From this perspective, Wittgenstein's attempt to disengage religious faith from instrumental explanations about the nature of the world typifies his own way of making room for religious faith alongside a scientific conception of life and world. This pursued goal is the launching pad for his critique of what he calls the error in Frazer's thinking, which comes down to claiming that Myth, Magic, and Religion are not of the same category as science and technology.

Wittgenstein's attempt to disengage religion from any confrontation with scientific explanations continues an earlier philosophical attempt, in his *Tractatus Logico-Philosophicus*, to limit religious claims to assertions that have no intrinsic truth value and that, as such, cannot be called false. It was also expressed later in his talk on the meaning of life, which he delivered a year before he began commenting on Frazer's discourse. In the terms he used therein, Myth, Magic, and Religion are practices used for expressing the meaning of life and what it encompasses. Science and technology are intellectual ways of explaining the causal mechanisms underlying life and world. Hence, the latter are an unsuitable substitute for the first. It is instructive to note that the very attempt to view religion and magic as merely expressive practices that provide enhancing perspectives on the meaning of life is a modern and somewhat restricted way of describing their conceptual nature.

To assert, at this point, that some religious people relate to God in a mistaken way, as believers in magic relate to the hidden forces underlying life and world, does not change the fact that, for them, religious faith has instrumental implications. My conclusion here is that there is no conceptual reason why religious practices and faith may not be more versatile than mere expressions of non-instrumental attitudes to life and the world. A philosopher who denies that religious faith has any instrumental implications is making a normative assertion. To the extent that it clarifies the meaning of religious faith to which that philosopher aspires it is an example of self-reflection and self-clarification, not clarification of a concept that is shared in the same way by others. Another way of saying this is that it presents a conception of religious faith, one that expresses the kind of religious faith to which the philosopher aspires, rather than "a grammatical remark" about the concept of religion in general.

If we now distinguish between the sort of religious faith to which Wittgenstein aspires and the way the concept is used in general, it appears to be of a mixed category, allowing for both instrumental and expressive uses. To the extent that a religious ritual of prayer to God for food, wealth, good health, redemption, happiness, the protection of dear ones, or a safe journey is of such a mixed category, it, too, serves both expressive inspirational and instrumental purposes. In this understanding, the instrumental aspect of magic and religion renders them into inspired spiritual instruments, not ordinary ones. Wittgenstein describes it thusly:

> With the magical healing of an illness, one *directs* the illness to leave the patient.
>
> After the description of any such magical treatment, one always wants to say: If the illness doesn't understand *that*, I don't know *how* one should tell it to leave.
>
> Nothing is so difficult as doing justice to the facts.[15]

In a scientific conception of life, one does not address an illness, directing it to leave. To say, as some philosophers have said, that a conception of disease based on magic has an explanatory theoretical framework, just as modern medicine has, is to miss the symbolic inspirational point of performing a ritual. Wittgenstein alludes to this as "the difficulty of doing justice to the facts." On the one hand, we have a spiritual attitude toward life and the world, holding that we can efficaciously address and manipulate diseases by enacting our wishes. On the other, we have a scientific conception of life, in which diseases are not the kind of entities that one can address or defeat simply by enacting wishes. Thus, even the concept of instrumental use has a spiritual flavor in inspired, symbolic discourse, which it lacks in a merely practical discourse. That is to say, it has a different meaning. It is as though magic has its own kind of logic and conceptual framework, not to be confused with what serves us in everyday practical matters. To appreciate this point, compare severing your connection with the doctor who is treating you, but turning to a magical healer one time, and to some other doctor another time. In the first case, we might feel as though we are converting to a new faith; in the second, as though we are pursuing a rational instrumental course of action.

It is worth noting that, while the expressive and instrumental aims of various cultural practices can be distinguished from one another, this does not entail that these aims are pursued through entirely separate and different practices. Clothes are designed both with practical and aesthetic purposes in mind. Cooking and serving food bring together the aims of rendering it tasty, nourishing, and aesthetically pleasing. Dining combines within it both the activity of eating and a cultural ceremony of doing so in refined manner. Architecture joins the practical and the aesthetic. Shaking hands upon meeting someone is a ritual that expresses friendliness while facilitating communication and social interchange. A wedding ceremony has both an expressive purpose of celebration and a legal purpose. We dress not only in a practical manner, but also in certain style. We not only bury the dead to dispose of their bodies, but also place headstones over their graves to honor and commemorate them.

My conclusion from these examples is that, while we distinguish between spiritual and instrumental aspects of human life, we also allow for their unification in certain practices. So, a prayer may be a way of both expressing existential concern and soliciting God's help. Hence, there is no reason why a ritual cannot have a dual role: as both an inspired symbolic expression of our existential concerns, attachments, fears, hopes, and sorrows, in connection with deeply meaningful events to us and as a way of affecting and influencing the course of our lives. As such, it may be used for both spiritual and instrumental purposes.

Although Wittgenstein tends to stress the expressive aspect of spiritual rituals, there is no reason to consider the use of Myth, Magic, and Religion in relation to their expressive purposes only. Just as a national flag may be used as both a symbolic expression for national pride and as a marker designating seats of emissaries from different countries, such a twofold usage also holds for certain rituals of prayer. They may be used both as symbolic expressions and as instrumental practices. Nonetheless, we ought to remember that a prayer to God for help is not exactly the same as a call for help to a lifeguard on the beach or to an emergency unit in a hospital. We do not have the same kind of expectations or letdowns in such a spiritual situation. Nor does the practice of using such a religious ritual emerge out of the same kind of cultural history and rational ways of considering evidence. Granted, in Wittgenstein's clarification, the concept of God's will is a metaphor or simile, still, to pray to God for assistance is to use a religious metaphor for more than just expressing hope. Of course, to do so out of religious conviction requires faith in both the religious practice of prayer and what the metaphor symbolizes. Thus, we may be able to accept both Wittgenstein's insight and Frazer's explanation of the ancient ritual of the priestly-king of the grove of Diana at Nemi. The former concerns its expressive spiritual meaning, the latter its instrumental meaning.

At times, the dual role of rituals is reflected in our twofold attitudes toward meaningful events in our life. Losing a wedding ring or accidentally destroying a picture of a family member who is away at war may bother us as a bad omen—this despite also knowing that the incident has no connection with what may or may not happen. (Indeed, to be bothered by the event as a bad omen is to experience it as symbolizing what we dread. As may be noticed in this connection, the concepts of omen and fate are spiritually related, both emerging from deep existential concerns.) In a similar way, we may be tempted to change the direction of our walk when a black cat crosses our path, to ward off bad luck and to not tempt fate, even without being overtly superstitious. We may only be giving vent to an attitude of apprehension over the contingencies of life. At the same time, it reveals that superstition is not merely "false science," but an expression of existential angst. What these kinds of examples show is that while it may be possible to distinguish between superstitious attitudes and superstitious beliefs, wishful gestures and rituals of magic, the observance of religious ceremonies and having faith in God, they may also run together at times.

4. Explanations of Rituals

P. M. S. Hacker has argued that we ought to distinguish two questions, which neither Frazer nor Wittgenstein did. First, how did a given ceremony come about? Second, what does it mean? The historical account answers the first question, not the second, which is hermeneutical. The second question, he claims, can be answered only "by reference to the course of the ceremony and the attitudes, beliefs, and justifying reasons of the participants."[16] He notes that, often in ceremonies, there is nothing to explain in connection with a given action. This is simply what has to be done at this point in the ceremony:

> The ceremonious act may be resonant with meaning, either qua expressive or symbolic act, or as heralding the sequel; but the remote and long since forgotten origins may well be irrelevant to its current significance.[17]

Here, we might reflect on the Western social ritual of greeting by shaking the right hand of the person we greet. The origin of this ritual of greeting is sometimes explained historically by alluding to past encounters between knights or worriers who clasped each other's right hand to avoid being stabbed.[18] Note that a ritual of greeting is not unique to Western culture. At the most, this explanation relates only to the way it is performed in the West, not to how the practice of greeting came about. If someone arriving from a different culture was unfamiliar with it and did not understand what people in the West do when they perform it, we might shed light on it by telling that person that they are performing a ritual of greeting. In doing so, we would be explaining the meaning of this ritual. However, if the concept of greeting were strange to that person, we would have a problem explaining it, resorting to such statements as "demonstrating to people we meet that we are friendly." In either case, explaining how the ritual of greeting in the West originated would not explain its meaning. If someone from an Indian or Japanese culture were puzzled about why we greet people by shaking their right hand, all that we can say is that this is the way a ritual of greeting is performed in the West.

The last remark presupposes that rituals of greeting, like language, are practices found in many human cultures. We should distinguish between understanding the meaning of a ritual of greeting and providing an explanation for it. The first has to do with understanding its expressive normative role in human interactions. This is a form of understanding manifested in the practical knowledge of how to do it properly: such as when to perform it, with whom, and in what way. The second has to do with the ability to offer an enlightening explanation of the use and value of a ritual of greeting in human interactions. Here, we might compare this ritual with the Indian ritual of greeting, which is performed by facing one another and joining one's palms together, or the Japanese of ritual of greeting, which is performed by facing one another and slightly bowing. We might then suggest that these are social rituals that express cordiality and good intentions, facilitating thereby human communication. It is worth noting that we are able to understand the social meaning of this ritual even when we do not know how to explain its meaning, not because its meaning is something mysterious, but because we are creatures that are better at understanding the meaning of rituals that we perform than we are at explaining them. Just as we are better at walking and running than in explaining how it needs to be done. In either case, to understand that a ritual of greeting has a certain social meaning is to understand that it has social use and value, expressive of social norms and attitudes of cordiality at meeting other people. These are different from those that are given expression in spiritual rituals that cater to existential concerns and attitudes of awe and wonder at the nature of life and world.

Cioffi contests the claim that historical explanations are irrelevant to our understanding of the meaning of rituals. He notes Paul Redding's insight that likens an historical hypothesis about the origin of a given ritual to giving a bereaved person the coroner's report.[19] In rebuttal, he claims that in certain puzzling circumstances, the historical explanation for certain practices equated with the coroner's report may be useful in explaining their meaning. He claims that sometimes it is not possible to answer the question about the meaning of an expressive practice without investigating its origin.

Cioffi offers a number of examples of how the question what ritual means can be answered only in connection with an historical explanation of how it came about. One is the meaning of the Passover meal, which he claims cannot be explained in a distinct way from what the original Passover meal meant to those who practiced it. A second is the meaning of the Catholic Mass, which he claims cannot be explained independent of how it developed. A third is Frazer's historical explanation of a certain detail in the ritual at Nemi, which explains why a certain branch (the golden bough) must be broken before the combat for the succession to the priesthood can take place.

It is advisable to examine Cioffi's examples of historical explanations of the meaning of these rituals in more detail. Eating Matzah instead of bread and telling the story of the exodus of the tribes of Israel out of Egypt is an integral part of the celebration of the Passover meal. The story is read aloud from the Haggadah, which was composed during the Middle Ages. But it is first told in the Bible, where the command to celebrate Passover by eating Matzah is also proclaimed. The meaning of the Passover celebration is explained therein as part of the ritual, wherein the biblical story about the exodus out of Egypt and the need to eat Matzah during this time is narrated.

The example given about the Mass and the historical explanation of how it developed is not as clear. The Mass is a very complicated ceremony, incorporating in it prayers, rites, and blessings that have all sorts of religious symbolic meanings. To explain their symbolic meaning one needs to tell the story of Christ and his call for salvation and the need to repent, as narrated in the Gospels. Against the background of this story, the symbolic meaning of the ceremony can then be explained. If this is what is meant by an historical explanation of how the Mass developed, then it is indeed an explanation of its symbolic meaning. The example of breaking the golden bough is different from the previous ones, as it relates to an unfamiliar and strange ritual about which we learn from Frazer's description of it and his explanation of its symbolic meaning. That to which Cioffi refers as the historical explanation of its meaning pertains to the need in the ritual to break off the golden bough, which Frazer explains through the ancient myths that accompanied it. Beliefs in them are supposed to explain the symbolic meaning of the actions performed in the ritual.

All these examples pertain to rituals and ceremonies accompanied by stories that are part of their symbolic meaning. When the story is missing, we may be at a loss as to what the ritual means. Typically, the stories tell of certain events in the past that the rituals incorporate into their symbolism and which, as such, explain their meaning. To the extent that these are stories that are purported to be about historical events, they purport to be historical explanations of the meaning of these rituals and ceremonies. However, to this extent, they are historical explanations that are *internal* to the expressive meaning of the practices themselves. That is to say, they express their symbolic meaning in a generic narrative. To provide an historical explanation of their origin that does not express their meaning to those who observe them is to offer an explanation that it *external* to their meaning.

Consider explaining the historical origin of the story of the exodus out of Egypt and with it the celebration of Passover, as having been invented by Jews during their exile in Babylon, as a way of providing a religious ceremony that promotes belief in divine providence over Israel and redemption. In doing so, we would be giving an empirical historical explanation for the emergence of this ceremony. In this explanation, the exodus out of Egypt is just a made-up story, not a true event. As such, it undermines the historical story told during this ceremony about the exodus out of Egypt and the need to eat Matzah on the way. Similarly, consider explaining the historical origin of the Mass and with it also the story told about Christ in the Gospels as having been invented by Jews who sought to break free from the religious jurisdiction of the Sanhedrin. Or, alternatively, as having evolved from ancient pagan rites to Dionysus or Orpheus, still prevalent in the ancient world at the time, to which the story about Christ was affixed. In doing so, we would explain the origin of the Mass in a way that undermines both the religious meaning of the story about the sacrifice of Christ and his ascent to heaven, as narrated in the Gospels and the religious meaning that the Mass has to those who observe it. Last, note that Wittgenstein's criticism of Frazer's explanation of the origins of the ritual at Nemi, in which Frazer adduces all sorts of similar rituals from which it takes off, is of a similar kind. It tells about historical influences on its creation. This is in contrast to Frazer's explanation of the myths that accompanied this ritual and the role it played in symbolizing the people's concerns about the harvest.

The distinction I am formulating between external and internal explanations is one that we sometimes express as the distinction between historical explanations and historical narratives and myths. Wittgenstein expresses it in the following remark:

> Christianity is not based on a historical truth, but presents us with a (historical) narrative & says: now believe! But not believe this report with the belief that is appropriate to a historical report,—but rather: believe, through thick & thin & you can do this only as the outcome of a life. *Here you have a message!—don't treat it as you would another historical message!* Make a *quite different* place for it in your life.—There is no *paradox* about that![20]

A characteristic feature of external historical explanations is that they do not express or explain the meaning of the rituals and ceremonies to those who observe them; that is, they do not render them meaningful to those who observe them. Sometimes they are simply irrelevant to them. Sometimes they undermine them, showing them to be based on misleading beliefs. As becomes obvious from Cioffi's examples of the Mass, Passover, and the ritual at Nemi, what he means by explanations of the historical meanings of these rituals and ceremonies and how they developed are stories that are internal to their symbolic meanings. To offer an empirical explanation of how they developed that is not internal to them would not explain the meaning of their symbols but their historical origins. It would relate to what they mean to those who observed them as the historical explanation of how our ritual of greeting originated from past encounters between hostile knights relates to the meaning for us of greeting people we meet.

Although Cioffi criticizes the philosophical attempt to cast a limit on historical explanations of the meaning of various rituals, he promotes another limiting claim on explanations of the meaning of rituals, which he ascribes to Wittgenstein. The meaning of a particular ritual can be explained, but what he calls "rituality" cannot. He notes in this connection that the sign of the cross as an expression of piety can be explained by adducing historical considerations, but the impulse of which it is a manifestation—the impulse of piety—cannot. In this insight, to have faith in God, for example, is also to have an impulse for pious behavior, which is expressed in religious rituals. He claims that the reason Wittgenstein thinks that rituals as such cannot be explained is "because he thinks them primal-Ur-phenomenal."[21] He calls this claim Wittgenstein's empirical "limiting notion."[22]

I take it that by explaining "rituality," Cioffi means explaining the very concept of a ritual, which in this insight is primal. Primal human ways of behavior arise directly from human nature. They are that to which Wittgenstein refers as "instinct action." Crying out when feeling pain or scratching where it itches are primal human impulses and ways of behavior, as are drinking when thirsty and eating when hungry. On the basis of these primal impulses, various refined, shared cultural practices are created and observed. To ask why we are inclined to cry out when feeling pain, scratch where we itch, drink when we are thirsty, and eat when we are hungry is to suppose that these are not activities expressing primal impulses, but reasoned ways of behavior. Thus, to say that rituals arise from primal impulses is to say that they do not arise from reasoning. Still, it is not clear why we have difficulty in explaining the very concept of a ritual or our impulse to perform rituals, nor why this difficulty arises because rituals are primal.

In point of fact, primal ways of behavior are often explained biologically. Darwin did so in connection with expressive behavior in general, which was supposed to reap evolutionary benefits. However, biological explanations of the functional value of expressive behavior do not explain what renders it personally meaningful to its performer. We may understand the function or economic meaning and value of farming without wanting to become farmers, as farming is not personally meaningful to us. Freud sought to overcome this difficulty by setting out to explain human symbolic behavior. In doing so, he argued that we might be deceived about its meaning for us.[23] I conclude, therefore, that what Cioffi wants to say is that rituals cannot be made personally meaningful to us, for expressing what concerns us, by means of theoretical explanations of the concept of a ritual.

Note that, in contrast to theoretical explanations, in the ordinary stream of human life, we do not explain the meaning of rituals in general or the very concept of a ritual, just as we do not explain the meaning of words in general or the concept of a word. As John Langshaw Austin noted when criticizing Wittgenstein on this point, it is senseless to ask, "What is the meaning of a word?" as the latter does in the opening to his *Blue Book*. It is sensible to ask "What is the meaning of the word 'rat?'"[24] However, Wittgenstein already knew the meaning of the word "rat." Moreover, he was not asking about the meaning of a word because he did not know the meaning of words. He was asking, because he did know the meaning of words, but found it difficult to explain what kind of a thing the meaning of a word is, and found it difficult to explain of what knowing the meaning of a word consists. He was puzzled by the metaphysical nature of the meaning of words. This was so precisely because he knew their meaning despite not being able to explain it.

To overcome this philosophical puzzlement, Wittgenstein sought to clarify the concept of a word by showing how it is related to its different practical uses. To clarify the very concept of a ritual, he sought to link it to our inclination for expressive symbolic behavior. Clarifications are, of course, not explanations that are useful to someone who does not possess the concept they explain. They are insightful remarks for those of us who are philosophically puzzled by what we already know.

In a similar way, to ask "What is the meaning of a ritual—or rituality?" is to pose a philosophical puzzlement. To respond to it by saying that explanations are limited in this case because there is something "primal" about rituals, while true, does not suffice to shed light on the nature of the problem confronted here. For just as explaining the concept of a ritual does not make it personally meaningful for expressing what concerns us, the same holds for the concepts of a word or instrument. In fact, we do not introduce our children to the use of instruments, words, or rituals by way of general explanations about these concepts. We do it by initiating them into particular uses of instruments, words, and rituals. In doing so, we make them both culturally and personally meaningful to them.

One of the basic insights emerging from Wittgenstein's discussion is that to understand the meaning of a given cultural practice is to understand its use. Another is that we do not come to understand the uses of cultural practices by means of general explanations about their meaning, as for the most part, these are not necessary, helpful, or possible. We do so by rendering particular instances of them personally and culturally meaningful to us through their use. Still another is that primal cultural practices manifest shared human forms of life that emerge from our common human nature. Cultural beings that are not inclined to express themselves in these ways are of a different cultural nature than we are. As such, we would find it difficult to explain to them what is personally and culturally meaningful to us about these practices without presupposing in the explanation our way of finding meaning in them.

To see the point of the last remark, consider once again Swift's benign Houyhnhnms, which he contrasts with the wild Yahoos. The first are incapable of understanding the meaning of arts and rituals as existential concerns and their expression are not meaningful to them. The second are incapable of understanding the meaning of instruments as they are incapable of devising and using practical means to attain their desired ends. We are different. We are creatures that have a natural ability to find meaning in both using instruments and rituals, albeit without relying on explanations of the very concept of instrument or ritual to render them meaningful to us. In my reading of Wittgenstein, these inherent impulses and abilities are part of the common (spiritual and instrumental) nature of human beings.

5. Understanding the Expressive Meaning of Spiritual Rituals

In his groundbreaking discussion of the idea of a social science, Peter Winch noted that concepts are culturally dependent for their meaning.[25] Therefore, the question arises as to which concepts we should use in striving to understand human beings in cultures different from our own, theirs, ours, or some new scientific concepts invented in so-called social theory.[26] On my reading of Wittgenstein's comments on the common spiritual nature of human beings manifested in myths, magic, and religious practices, the question does not arise. This is because their aim is not to explain a strange culture, but to note that we and human beings in strange cultures possess a common spiritual nature. As such, we are beset by the same kind of deep existential concerns and have the same kind of human inclination to express them in inspiring symbolic fashion. To note that this is the case is to acknowledge our common humanity.

Therefore, Wittgenstein's view of our ability to understand the conceptual nature of Myth, Magic, and Religion in strange cultures and to tell them apart from instrumental and technical practices transcends the discussion about meaning in two prominent philosophical traditions. He has no need for a so-called radical interpretation that aims at discovering the meaning alien linguistic practices have for their "native" users. He is not a visiting radical "interpreter" who is putting forward and testing hypotheses entertained about them, translating them thereby into his own idiolect. Nor does he have a need for a form of social hermeneutics that seeks to interpret the meaning of alien practices by interacting with the "other" who observes them, aiming thereby to arrive at a new understanding of their meaning through a mutual "fusion of horizons."

Wittgenstein seeks to bring philosophical insight to what is philosophically puzzling to us about the inclination of human beings to invent myths, employ magic, and observe religious rituals, and he does so in two ways. One is by clarifying their conceptual nature as spiritual practices that express human concerns in symbolic form and transforming them into inspiring attitudes toward life and its meaning. Another is by noting that he is able to grasp the expressive meaning of these practices without any historical explanation of their origin, as they express existential concerns and spiritual attitudes toward life that he, too, experiences. He concludes that what underlies their creation and his ability to understand their meaning is our common spiritual nature.

Wittgenstein is able to pursue this project of philosophical clarification because, although not a party to the ancient cultures in which these particular practices were created and observed, he, like all of us, is not alien to humanity. He is a party to the use of rituals and expressive language and to the conceptual distinction between them and instrumental practices based on reasoning. Indeed, one of the ways in which we are able to understand the behavior of human beings in other cultures is against the background of our common human nature and common conceptual understanding as a cultural species. Accordingly, we may note that they too have practical minds and spiritual dispositions.

By thus placing the expressive and symbolic meaning of Myth, Magic, and Religion within our immediate reach, Wittgenstein brings a broad humanistic approach toward cultural life in all its strange human manifestations.

That is not to say that our response to a given ritual captures the full meaning of the ritual to those who enact and observe it. Lacking information about the culture in which it is enacted and observed, we may be puzzled as to what exactly they seek to express through it, or why they choose a gruesome or sinister ritual to do so. However, the point of the remark that human beings have a common expressive nature is not that we are cosmopolitans who are able to adapt to every human culture and draw spiritual sustenance from it. Nor is it to claim that strange human spiritual practices never leave us baffled as to what their expressive meaning is. The point is that understanding the expressive meaning of strange human practices requires recognizing them as catering to our deep human concerns. This requirement is fulfilled when we acknowledge their expressive meaning to us. In doing so we are responding to a human nature we share with those who created and observe these practices.

That said, it is not clear from Wittgenstein's comments how much of the expressive meaning of strange rituals can be grasped without learning about the cultures from which they arise. If we were not familiar with the Japanese social ritual of greeting someone by bowing, we might still grasp it as a ritual of cordial greeting when confronted with it for the first time. This is because greeting someone cordially is a social ritual for us too, even if we perform it differently. Whether we grasp the social meaning of a strange ritual of greeting in an immediate fashion or interpret it as such depends on how far removed it is from human behavior that is familiar to us in similar social circumstances. In the case of spiritual rituals, Wittgenstein seems to assume that their expressive meaning may be grasped because it stems from a common spiritual nature of human beings, despite the fact that they may take on many different cultural expressions. However, this means that they are understood only because of their enlightening description by someone familiar with them like Frazer. Once the ritual of the Golden Bough is described as a ritual of deposing a king and the crowning of another in his place, it is possible to grasp its expressive meaning without any historical explanation about how it came to be enacted in this way.

Another difficulty with Wittgenstein's remarks is that he is wary of the attempt to bring insight into the meaning of things for us through the use of explanations, claiming that "every explanation is after all a hypothesis." However, not all explanations of meaning are hypotheses. To explain the meaning for us of a story that moves us is not to offer a conjecture or hypothesis. Sometimes it is a way of clarifying an expressive meaning we wish to articulate. Sometimes it is a way of drawing attention to a significant aspect of what is expressed. Sometimes it is a way of enriching our experience of this meaning. An example in point is Wittgenstein's own clarification of the expressive meaning of the priest-king ritual at Nemi as manifesting the majesty of death. Someone else may respond to it as a sinister ritual that evokes both our dread and fascination with murder. I tend to respond to the ritual as the enactment of a tragic drama that makes the cycle of murders an inherent feature of the aspiration for royal glory. I take it that Wittgenstein wants to express a way of understanding the meaning of this ritual that predates such overtly intellectual, interpretive clarification of how we experience it. The paradigm may be the way in which music affects us. But surely, here too, there is room for enriching interpretive clarifications of our experience, which are not in the nature of hypothesis. They are expressions of our experience of the meaning of this ritual, which do not raise hypothetical conjectures about its intended meaning by the ancients who invented it.

The concept of interpretation mentioned above offers a way of extending and enriching immediate ways of grasping the meaning of expressive symbolic practices and narratives. To interpret the meaning of the symbolism of a given practice or myth is often to describe and express our way of understanding the distinctions, values, attitudes toward life, and worldview that are manifested in it. Interpretations of expressive symbolic practices are, of course, intellectual ways of clarifying their meaning.

6. Conceptions of Life and World-Pictures

When discussing how a strange culture should be understood, Peter Winch claimed, "What we learn by studying other cultures are not merely possibilities of different ways of doing things," but also "different possibilities of making sense of human life, different ideas about the possible importance that the carrying out of certain activities may take on for a man, trying to contemplate the sense of his life as a whole."[27]

This "sense" emerges in the form of what Winch calls "a conception of life." "Unlike beasts," he writes, "men do not merely live but also have a conception of life. This is not something that is simply added to their lives." It reveals the ways in which human beings try to live and experience the meaning of their lives. He notes that it is by virtue of such a conception that "we can ask questions about what is the right way to live, what things are most important in life, whether life has any significance, and if so what."[28]

Winch's claim is illuminating, but too sparse. It does not make clear what form of expression such a conception of life takes. In my reading of Wittgenstein's comments on Frazer, in ancient cultures, it was embedded in the inspiring symbolic framework of the myths they told, the social ceremonies, magical spells, and religious rituals they created and observed. It was not a formulated worldview, an ideological doctrine, or an ethical theory. Winch's remark regarding conceptions of ethical life that arise within cultures sheds insightful light on the role that Myth, Magic, and Religion play in this undertaking. Rituals are concrete actions that express the significance of certain events in life—marriage, birth, death, war, honor, famine, abundance of food, and so forth—by enacting edifying symbols for them. Similarly, stories about the effect of such events on the lives of people attain edifying symbolic meaning for those who are brought up on them. They are not a formulated worldview, a theory of values, or a code of laws. In the same way that national flags are symbols that promote a patriotic attitude toward one's country through the ceremonies that surround them, myths promote an edifying conception of life within the linguistic space of a symbolic story. The discursive framework of a symbolic story expressed in myth is a lush breeding ground for edifying conceptions of life.

Given the important role that symbols play in acquiring a particular cultural conception of life and what it encompasses, symbolic stories serve as a very powerful tool for educating human beings into their cultural traditions. A myth provides an edifying symbolic tale for both understanding and dealing with the contingencies of life. In myths, valued cultural distinctions are expressed and enhanced by embodying them in a powerful and inspiring fashion, in formidable figures and astounding events. They thus turn into cultural symbols that inspire people with edifying points of view on life and what it encompasses, and encourage valued attitudes for engaging their own lives. It is important to mention that cultural symbols are communal products, providing a spiritual bond among those who share them. They supply what, following Winch, may be called "a shared conception of significant aspects of life," predating worldviews, ideological doctrines, ethical theories, and scientific explanations.

Reflecting in his later years on how existential attitudes that underlie conceptions of life and world are related to various propositions and beliefs asserted in their connection, Wittgenstein refers to a world-picture, or *Weltbild*, in which they are embedded. Although not itself a belief, it provides a contextual normative background for holding all sorts of beliefs. He mentions as an example Antoine Lavoisier's chemical experiment and his conclusion regarding what would happen when a certain substance was burned. The conclusion, he writes, was formed on the basis:

> of a world-picture—not of course one that he invented: he learned it as a child. I say world-picture and not hypothesis, because it is the matter-of-course foundation for his research and as such also goes unmentioned.[29]

Such a world-picture may be expressed in propositions that are above the distinction between doubting and becoming convinced. Wittgenstein clarifies their conceptual nature by noting that they are "empirical propositions" about which "no doubt can exist if making judgments is to be possible at all." Therefore, "not everything that has the form of an empirical proposition *is*."[30] It may be part of the unformulated "knowledge" embedded in our world-picture.[31] As such, a world-picture is neither true nor false. It is a normative limiting conceptual framework for entertaining beliefs that, within this framework, may be shown to be true or false:

On my understanding of Wittgenstein's use of this concept, it may manifest epistemic, existential, moral, or spiritual attitudes toward life and the world. In each of these contexts, it provides an unformulated conception of life and world that sets a limit to what we are in fact able to doubt.

To clarify Wittgenstein's use of the concept of world-picture, Anthony Kenney notes how people react to denial of what is part of their world-picture. "When one person denies what is a part of the world-picture of another, this may sometimes seem like lunacy, but sometimes a very deep difference of culture."[32]

Thus, in discussing Moore's claim to know that he has a hand or that he has spent his whole life on the face of the earth, Wittgenstein categorizes these claims as forming part of a "world-picture," rather than particular beliefs or specific items of knowledge that are confirmed or falsified:

> I did not get my picture of the world by satisfying myself of its correctness; nor do I have it because I am satisfied of its correctness. No: it is the inherited background against which I distinguish between true and false.[33]

> The propositions describing this world-picture might be part of a kind of mythology. And their role is like that of rules of a game; and the game can be learned purely practically, without learning any explicit rules.[34]

Wittgenstein also describes such a world-picture as a "form of life" that breeds an attitude of "certainty."[35] He also calls it "the substratum of all my enquiring and asserting," adding that "propositions describing it are not all equally subject to testing."[36]

Hence, it might now be said that just as scientific beliefs are entertained in the framework of an empirical world-picture, myths, magic, and religion provide a symbolic world-picture for expressing existential concerns and promoting spiritual attitudes. Beliefs emerging within these different conceptual frameworks derive from different kinds of world-pictures: empirical world-pictures and ways of reasoning in one case, and spiritual world-pictures and symbolic ways of expression in the other.

7. Spiritual Stages of Humanity

Another idea that Winch promoted was the general similarity in human cultural dispositions, and practices despite various differences between human cultures and human beings belonging to different cultures. He claimed that ethical conceptions of human life involve certain fundamental notions, which, following Wittgenstein's reflections on the limits of doubting and the attitude of certainty we have toward certain claims, he called "limiting notions." They have an ethical dimension, he explained, in the context of which, the possibilities of good and evil in human life can be experienced and exercised. He took these to rest on birth, death, and sexual relations. He noted that they "correspond closely to those that Giambattista Vico made the foundation of his idea of natural law, on which he thought the possibility of understanding human history rested." "In trying to understand the life of an alien society," he wrote, "it will be of utmost importance to be clear about the way in which these notions enter into it."[37] In my understanding of this insight, Winch's "limiting notions" emerge in the context of what Wittgenstein called "the common behavior of mankind," underlying the use of language. In this case, it is the common behavior of human beings manifested in Myth, Magic, and Religion, which are used to express existential concerns and promote spiritual attitudes toward life.

What Winch called "limiting notions" of human life are more encompassing than those he formulates. Ultimately, they include other existential concerns that are meaningful to human beings, of which, in the flow of ordinary life, we are not always aware. Avishi Margalit has claimed in this connection that rituals provide an enhancing frame for the significance of such everyday aspects of human life. They operate "like the framing of everyday objects in a museum," which "can cause us to pay renewed attention to them."[38] In doing so, they force us to focus on their significance for us and to appreciate them, something that in the everyday stream of life is lost. Margalit adds that rituals may also have an opposite effect. "Ritual, being formulaic and repetitive, is an act that dulls feelings rather than an amplifier that intensifies them." He notes, "Religions that involve revival of religious enthusiasm are generally born as a protest against elaborate, formulaic rituals that are seen by the enthusiasts as the degeneration of authentic religious feeling."[39] He connects this tendency with the Romantic urge to which Wittgenstein was also sympathetic.

Margalit's description of the framing aspect of rituals is most ample for traditional prayers and blessings. It seems less appropriate a description for the ancient rituals and celebrations that Frazer describes, many of which were conducted in ecstatic circumstances, promoting extraordinary behavior that catered to dreads and lusts, some of which incorporated human sacrifice. It is not just that the practices described by Frazer are strange to us that induces this impression of them. There is something ferocious, wild, and dreadful about them and the myths that accompanied them. They compare with present day religious ceremonies and rituals as wild beasts to domesticated farm animals.

As can now also be seen, there is indeed a connection between Vico's view of human nature and Wittgenstein's remarks on that to which I refer here as "the common spiritual nature of human beings" expressed through Myth, Magic, and Religion in ancient cultures. Vico sought to create a science of human nature rooted in an historical and cultural approach, not in paradigms of explanation drawn from the natural sciences. In the attempt to create such a science, he noted three historical stages through which human beings pass as a cultural species, making them the "three anthropological stages of humanity." Each stage, he claimed, gives rise to human beings possessed of a different spiritual nature and driven by different spiritual dispositions, manifested in what I have called here different "spiritual attitudes toward life and what it encompasses."

The driving force in the first stage, he claimed, is powerful imagination. It is poetic but weak at reasoning, leading human beings to ascribe divine properties to physical substances, as expressed in myths. The second stage is driven by heroic aspirations, ascribing to human beings majestic and divine qualities. In the third stage, the spiritual disposition is more intellectual and hence modest, benign, and reasonable, recognizing laws, conscience, reason, and duty.[40] In this view, human beings in different historical and anthropological stages have different cultural spirits. On the basis of this distinction, Vico also claimed that direct understanding of human beings in the early historical stages of cultural life is inaccessible to modern human beings and requires instead an interpretive effort.

Vico's idea that different historical stages of cultures manifest different human spiritual natures heralds two subsequent discourses with which Wittgenstein was familiar. The first is Sigmund Freud's psychoanalytic theory of human nature. In it, the attitudes, dispositions, sensibilities, conceptions of things, and ways of engaging the world expressed in myths, magic, and religion are the same as those from which dreams are cast, works of art created, jokes invented, and from which neuroses operate and the psychopathologies of everyday life are enacted. They are expressions of human psychological nature that provide ways of experiencing, perceiving, thinking, and engaging the world prior to those that underlie the lives of human beings in refined, civilized society and in rational, practical, scientific discourse. According to Freud, they derive from a psychological nature that underlies the lives of human beings in their early stages of development, forming their primary ways of thinking and conceiving of things which comprise what he calls "the unconscious." As we grow up and are initiated into refined, civilized, normative ways of behavior, this primary psychological nature is repressed, giving way to more refined and rational ways of perceiving, understanding and engaging the world.

The difference between Vico and Freud is that Vico believes that the primary poetic human psychological nature belonged only to the ancients, whereas Freud believes that it persists to this day. It lies within the souls of rational, modern human beings in the form of repressed, unconscious psychological modes of thinking and experiencing things, which are expressed in variously sublimated and transformed fashion. Both men, however, believe that there is an inherent gulf between these two different human psychological natures, a gulf that renders the primary, poetic, unconscious psychological nature inaccessible to us modern, rational, civilized human beings. We can only glimpse it from afar. Vico thus calls on us to perform a hermeneutical feat of empathy, which might enable us to understand the ancients. For the purpose of understanding the unconscious psychological nature of human beings, Freud develops a hermeneutics that is based on the principles of psychoanalytic theory and an individual's free associations.

In this particular matter, Wittgenstein thought otherwise. Thus, in his remarks on Frazer, he tries to further our appreciation of the significance of ritualistic, religious, and mythical expressions in our own lives, which he takes to embody something deep and primary in human psychological nature with which we are familiar. He emphasizes how different these primary experiences, emotions, and dispositions are from rational, reason-based ways of engaging the world and reflecting on things. They underlie the creative expressive spirit of human beings, out of which compelling images and powerful metaphors are born, not practical innovations or rational modes of thinking. He notes, however, that, although they are primary and primitive, we are nonetheless well acquainted with them. They are not features of psychological life that belonged only to the ancients. Nor are they features of an unconscious psychological life of which we are unaware. They are incorporated into our conscious lives, our primary attitudes toward life and what it encompasses, our emotions, primitive inclinations, and some of our everyday ways of reacting to things. Rituals, myths, religious symbols, and beliefs, he claims, all grow out of such primary human attitudes and inclinations. They accompany our conscious lives and are still preserved in compelling images and powerful metaphors encapsulated in the expressive language that serves us.

Elsewhere Wittgenstein notes that the ability to be amazed and to marvel at various ordinary events in life, while not enhanced by science, does not stem from being primitive. He therefore argues against Ernest Renan, who claimed that only primitive people marvel at ordinary natural events, such as birth, sickness, death, madness, catalepsy, sleep, and dreams:

> On the contrary there is absolutely no reason to marvel at such things; because they are such everyday occurrences. If primitive human beings *must* marvel at them, how much more so dogs & monkeys. Or is it being assumed that human beings suddenly awoke as it were & noticed these things which had always been there & were understandably amazed? Well, one might even assume something like this; not however that they became aware of these things for the first time, but rather that they suddenly began to marvel at them. But that too has nothing to do with their being primitive. Unless we call it primitive not to marvel at things, in which case it is precisely the people of today & Renan himself who are primitive, if he believes that scientific explanation could enhance wonderment.
>
> As though today lightning were more commonplace or less astounding than 2000 years ago . . . .[41]

Wittgenstein wants to disassociate the ability to marvel from being primitive. It is something we can still experience in our everyday lives and attitudes toward life and what it encompasses. We may share in these experiences and attitudes with the so-called primitives. They emerge out of the common spiritual nature of human beings in all cultures. Nonetheless, he also notes that they do not evince the same sort of attitude toward life that emerges out of scientific explanation:

> it is simply false to say: of course, these primitive peoples *had* to marvel at everything. But perhaps right that these people *did* marvel at everything around them.—To think they *had* to marvel at them is a primitive superstition. (Like that of thinking that they had to fear all the forces of nature & that we of course do not have to fear. On the other hand experience may show that certain primitive tribes are very strongly inclined to fear natural phenomena.—But we cannot exclude the possibility that highly civilized peoples will become liable to this very same fear again & their civilization and the knowledge of science will not protect them from this. All the same it is true that the *spirit* in which science is carried on nowadays is not compatible with fear of this kind).[42]

The second discourse that draws on Vico's ideas is Oswald Spengler's, wherein a distinction is drawn between two different human spiritual dispositions underlying two different historical stages of human beings as a cultural species, which, as I discussed earlier, he called "culture" and "civilization." The first is primary, natural, powerful, and instinctive; the second is sophisticated, rational, anemic, and contrived. It is a spiritual distinction with which Wittgenstein was on the whole in agreement. However, unlike Spengler, who relegated the primary spiritual disposition in human beings to only an early historical stage of their development, Wittgenstein thinks that despite being modern, we still possess the same underlying primary human spiritual nature as the ancients. Though different spirits may be seen to underlie the lives of ancient and modern human beings, both possess the same basic common human spiritual nature. He thinks that it is manifested in our lives in several ways, such as our use of the same inspiring mythical language to express ourselves, or our ability to make use of symbolic discourse to both express our existential concerns and promote inspiring attitudes toward life. Hence, we are not meaning-blind to the conceptual nature of Myth, Magic, and Religion, as we are still capable of tapping into the spiritual dispositions and attitudes toward life that are expressed in them. They embody our own spiritual nature, despite that we are modern human beings.

The last remark relates to what Wittgenstein perceives as the spiritual problem that afflicts modern culture. This is the problem experienced by those of us who, like Wittgenstein, have the same spiritual needs as the ancients, but find it difficult to transform our existential concerns and spiritual needs into an inspiring religious attitude toward life. In Wittgenstein's clarification of this spiritual problem, it is inherently cultural. It stems from the fact that the culture in which an inspiring spiritual attitude toward life, such as that which was expressed by telling myths, casting magical spells, and observing religious rituals is no longer at our disposal.

Although we, modern human beings, possess the same underlying spiritual nature as the ancients did, and although we are not meaning-blind to the spiritual attitudes toward life that they expressed in their myths, magical spells, and religious rituals, we differ from them in the cultural spirit that nourishes and sustains us. Therefore, we are hindered in our ability and inclination to transform our existential concerns into inspiring spiritual attitudes toward life, through such powerfully expressive cultural practices. To the extent that this predicament is experienced as a spiritual difficulty characterizing modern culture for us, it may be said to characterize its problematic spirit for us. To the extent that it is also experienced as a personal spiritual difficulty, it may also be said to characterize our own problematic spirit.

NOTES

First Study: The Spirit of the Jews

1. Ludwig Wittgenstein, *Culture and Value*, ed. Georg Henrik von Wright and Heikki Nyman; revised by Alois Pichler; trans. Peter Winch (Oxford: Blackwell Publishers, Ltd, 1998). It was originally published in 1977 under the title of *Vermischte Bemerkugan*. When quoting from it, I also indicate the year in which the remarks were written.

One: Remarks on the Spirit of Jews

1. Wittgenstein, *Culture and Value*, 1929, p. 3.
2. Ibid., 1930, p. 8.
3. Ibid., 1930, p. 14.
4. Ibid., 1931, p. 15.
5. Ibid., p. 16–17. The word in German that is translated as "mind" is *Geist*. It also means "spirit."
6. Ibid., p. 16.
7. Ibid., p. 18.
8. Ibid., p. 19.
9. Ibid., p. 23.
10. Ibid., p. 18.
11. Ibid., p. 23.
12. Ibid., 1932–1934, p. 27.
13. Ibid., 1929, p. 4.
14. Ibid., p. 3.
15. Ibid., 1939–1940, p. 40.
16. Ibid., 1931, p. 17.
17. Ibid., p. 16.
18. Ibid., 1934, p. 29.
19. For biographical information on Wittgenstein, see G. H. von Wright, "Biographical Sketch," in Norman Malcolm, ed., *Ludwig Wittgenstein, A Memoir* (Oxford: Oxford University Press, 1984). For other biographical narratives on Wittgenstein, see Brian McGuinness, *Wittgenstein: A Life, Young Ludwig 1889–1921* (London: Gerald Duckworth & Co., 1988); Ray Monk, *Ludwig Wittgenstein: The Duty of Genius* (New York: The Free Press, 1990).
20. Wittgenstein, Preface, *Tractatus Logico-Philosophicus* (New York: Humanities Press, 1961), p. 5.
21. For a somewhat different focus on these remarks, see I. Nevo, "Religious Belief and Jewish Identity in Wittgenstein's Philosophy," *Philosophy Research Archives*, XIII (1988), pp, 225–243; also D. Stern, "The Significance of Jewishness for Wittgenstein's Philosophy," *Inquiry*, 43:4 (2000), pp. 383–401.

Two: Philosophical Clarifications

1. Wittgenstein, *Last Writings on the Philosophy of Psychology*, vol. II, *The Inner and the Outer 1949–1951*, ed. G. H. Von Wright and Heikki Nyman, trans. C. G. Luckhardt (Oxford: Basil Blackwell Publishers Ltd., 1992), p. 64.
2. Wittgenstein, *Culture and Value*, 1931, p. 16. The claim that in philosophy we need "clarifications" occurs already in Wittgenstein's Notebooks 1914–1916, ed. G. H. von Wright and G. E. M. Anscombe, trans. G..E. M. Anscombe (Oxford: Basil Blackwell, 1998), p. 89.
3. Wittgenstein, *Philosophical Grammar*, part VI, ed. R. Rhees, trans. A. J. P. Kenny (Oxford: Blackwell, 1974), p. 115, #72.
4. As he is writing mostly in German, the words he uses are "*Der Jude*." For the sake of brevity, I shall mostly describe Wittgenstein's remarks as referring to "the Jew." I shall also describe his remarks as aiming to clarify the concept of Jew, as this is not a proper name but a general one that is expressed by different words in different languages. The words "Jew" and "*Jude*" derive from the Hebrew word "*Yehodi*." According to the Bible, Judah (*Yehoda*) is the name given to Jacob's fourth son by his mother Leah. It means thankful to God. The tribe of Judah that founded the kingdom of Jerusalem descends from him. It is also the name given to Judas Iscariot, who was one of the twelve apostles of Jesus, and who according to the New Testament betrayed him. The Hebrew word *Yehodi*, which means Jew, began to be used in the eighth century BCE during the Assyrian domination of the region.
5. I discuss Wittgenstein's use of philosophical clarifications further in my Third Study.
6. Wittgenstein, *Tractatus Logico-Philosophicus*, 3.2.
7. Ibid., 3.203.
8. Ibid., Preface, p. 3.
9. Ibid., 3.325.
10. Wittgenstein, Appendix: Notes on Logic, 1913, Summary, p. 96, in *Notebooks, 1914–1916*.
11. Wittgenstein, *Tractatus Logico-Philosophicus*, 4.112.
12. Ibid., 6.53.
13. Wittgenstein, Preface, *Tractatus Logico-Philosophicus*, p. 3.
14. Wittgenstein, *Philosophical Remarks*, ed. R. Rhees, trans. R. Hargreaves and R. White (Oxford: Blackwell, 1975), p. 51, #1.
15. Ibid.
16. Ibid., p. 52, #1.
17. The first manuscript that begins to express this change is Wittgenstein's *Philosophical Grammar*.
18. Wittgenstein, *Philosophical Investigations*, part I, trans. G. E. M. Anscombe (Oxford: Basil Blackwell Publishers Ltd., 1963), pp. 11–12, #23.
19. Ibid., p. 49, #122.
20. Ibid.
21. Ibid.
22. Wittgenstein, *Zettle*, ed. G. E. M. Anscombe and G. H. von Wright, trans. G. E. M. Anscombe (Oxford: Basil Blackwell, 1967), p. 123, #717.
23. Wittgenstein, *Philosophical Remarks*, p. 18, #77.
24. Wittgenstein, *Philosophical Investigations*, part I, p. 11, #23.
25. Wittgenstein, *Zettle*, p.9, #45.

26. Wittgenstein, *Philosophical Investigations*, part II, xi, p. 215.
27. Wittgenstein, *Last Writings on the Philosophy of Psychology*, vol. II, p. 4.
28. Wittgenstein, *Remarks on the Philosophy of Psychology*, vol. I, ed. G. E. M. Anscombe and G. H. von Wright, trans. G. E. M. Anscombe (Oxford: Basil Blackwell Publishers Ltd., 1980), p. 65, #326.
29. Ibid., p. 50, #243.
30. Ibid.
31. Ibid., p.68, #341.
32. Ibid., #342.
33. Wittgenstein, *Culture and Value*, 1933–1934, p. 29.
34. Wittgenstein, *Philosophical Investigations*, part I, p. 37, #79. Obviously Wittgenstein's remarks in this connection are derived from his reflections on Gottlob Frege's claims about sense and reference and Russell's claims about names and definite descriptions. For an edifying discussion of Wittgenstein's treatment in this example of proper names in relation to so called causal theories of names, see Robert J. Fogelin, *Wittgenstein* (London: Routledge & Kegan Paul, 1989), pp. 138–141.
35. Wittgenstein, *Philosophical Investigations*, part I, p. 17, #35.
36. Wittgenstein, *Remarks on the Philosophy of Psychology*, vol. I, p. 20, #94.
37. Wittgenstein, *Philosophical Investigations*, part II, vi, p.181.
38. Ibid., part I, p. 3, #2.
39. Ibid., part II, vi, p.181.
40. Saul A. Kripke discusses this experiment in connection with an experience of following a rule. See his *Wittgenstein of Rules and Private Language* (Oxford: Basil Blackwell, 1982), p. 46n29.
41. Wittgenstein, *Philosophical Investigations*, part II, xi, p.193.
42. Ibid.
43. Ibid., p. 200.
44. In his preface to Wittgenstein's *Blue Book*, Rush Rhees comments that Wittgenstein uses the locution in connection with the locution "colour-blind"; see Ludwig Wittgenstein, *Das blaue Buch; Eine philosophisch Betrachtun* (*Das braune Buch*), ed. Rush Rhees (Frankfort am Main: Suhrkamp, 1989). He suggests that its purpose is to take care of objections that his description of what he calls "our use of language" as of "operating with signs" make it look like this is some kind of mechanism. But language is not just a mechanism, as it has to do with interacting with people. The comment seems to me insightful. However, it also seems that Wittgenstein tried to enrich his former thin description of language as a use of tools and as operating with signs by emphasizing the way in which we experience the meaning of words in their use within the stream of life. This is something that a meaning-blind person does not experience. I discuss the idea of meaning-blindness further in my Third Study.
45. Wittgenstein, *Remarks on the Philosophy of Psychology*, vol. I, p. 68, #344.
46. Ibid., p. 68, #344.
47. Wittgenstein, *Last Writings on the Philosophy of Psychology*, vol. I, ed. G. H. Von Wright and Heikki Nyman, trans. C. G. Luckhardt (Oxford: Basil Blackwell Publishers Ltd., 1982–1990), p. 100 #784; also Philosophical Investigations, part II, xi, p. 214.
48. Wittgenstein, *Remarks on the Philosophy of Psychology*, vol. I, p. 50, #243.
49. Wittgenstein, *Philosophical Investigations*, part II, xi, p. 214.

50. On clarification as self-clarification, see Frank Cioffe, *Wittgenstein on Freud and Frazer* (Cambridge: Cambridge University Press, 1998).

Three: Clarifying the Concept of a Jew

1. In a somewhat similar fashion, another author of Jewish origins, Karl Marx, portrayed Jews a hundred years earlier in his *On the Jewish Question* (Cincinnati, Ohio: Hebrew Union College-Jewish Institute of Religion, 1958) as the embodiment of unrestrained human egoism.
2. Wittgenstein, *Culture and Value*, 1931, p. 14.
3. Ibid., 1948, p. 75.
4. Ibid., 1931, p. 14.
5. Ibid., 1946, p. 58.
6. Ibid.
7. Ibid.
8. Wittgenstein, *Notebooks 1914–1916*, p. 75.
9. Wittgenstein, *Tractatus Logico-Philosophicus*, p. 147, #6.421.
10. Wittgenstein, *Culture and Value*, 1929, p. 4.
11. Ibid., 1931, p. 16.
12. Ibid
13. Ibid., p. 17.
14. See David Avraham Weiner, *Genius and Talent: Schopenhauer's Influence on Wittgenstein's Early Philosophy* (Toronto: Associated University Presses, 1992), p. 21
15. Wittgenstein, *Culture and Value*, 1933–1934, p. 28.

Four: The Philosophical Background

1. Wittgenstein, *Culture and Value*, 1950, p. 98.
2. For a discussion of this theme in Wittgenstein's remarks, see Yuval Lurie, "Culture as a Human Form of Life: A Romantic Reading of Wittgenstein," *International Philosophical Quarterly*, 32:2 (June 1992).
3. In English, see Oswald Spengler, *The Decline of the West* (London: George Allen & Unwin Ltd., 1961).
4. For a different interpretation of Spengler's influence on Wittgenstein, see William J. DeAngelis, *Ludwig Wittgenstein—A Cultural Point of View: Philosophy in the Darkness of this Time* (Cornwall: Ashgate, 2007).
5. In English, see Otto Weininger, *Sex and Character: An Investigation of Fundamental Principles* (Bloomington: Indiana University Press, 2005). For further discussions of Weininger's influence on Wittgenstein, see Allan Janik, *Essays on Wittgenstein and Weininger* (Amsterdam: Rodopi, 1985); also David Stern and Bella Szabados, *Wittgenstein Reads Weininger—A Reassessment* (Cambridge: Cambridge University Press, 2004).
6. Wittgenstein, *Remarks on the Philosophy of Psychology*, vol. I, p. 167, #949; also *Zettle*, p. 81, #458. Ironically, as Wittgenstein's conceptual investigation relates to concepts, manifesting how we experience and grasp reality, it has also been dubbed a form of metaphysics: namely, "descriptive, transcendental, or conceptual metaphysics."

Five: Genius, Talent, Character, and Intellect

1. In "Wittgenstein on Jews: Some Counter-Examples," *Philosophy*, 65:253 (July 1990), pp 355–365, Gerhard D. Wassermann responds to my article "Jews as a Metaphysical Species," *Philosophy*, 64 (1989), pp. 323–347, by listing renowned Jewish creators and theoreticians to negate Wittgenstein's claim.
2. Wittgenstein, *Culture and Value*, 1931, p. 14. As in this study, for example.
3. Ben-Ami Scharfstein, *Of Birds, Beasts, and Other Artists: An Essay on the Universality of Art* (New York: New York University, 1988), pp.158–159.
4. Immanuel Kant, *Critique of the Power of Judgment* (Cambridge: Cambridge University Press, 2000), p. 186, #46.
5. See in this connection Isaiah Berlin, *Against the Current*, ed. H. Hardy (Oxford: Oxford University Press, 1981), and Berlin, *Vico and Herder: Two Studies in the History of Ideas* (London: Hogarth Press, 1975).
6. See Arthur Schopenhauer, *On the Fourfold Root of the Principle of Sufficient Reason* (Lasalle, Ill.: Open Court, 1974), p. 171. I am indebted to David Avraham Weiner's *Genius and Talent* for this reference.
7. Schopenhauer, *The World as Will and Representation*, trans. E. E. J. Payne (Oxford: Clarendon Press, 1974), vol. I, p. 377.
8. Wittgenstein, *Culture and Value*, 1932–1934, p. 27.
9. Ibid., 1939–1940, p. 40.
10. This contrasting of intellect and character has its parallel in Wittgenstein's *Philosophical Investigations* in the contrasting of opinion and attitude, which I discuss in the third study.
11. Wittgenstein, *Culture and Value*, 1948, p. 75.
12. Ibid.
13. Aristotle, *Politics*, 1327b.
14. Regarding this complex subject, see Isaiah Berlin, *Vico and Herder*, and *Against the Current*.
15. Wittgenstein, *Philosophical Grammar*, part II, p. 69.
16. Wittgenstein, *Philosophical Investigations*, part I, p. 143, #530.
17. P. A. Schilpp, ed., *The Philosophy of Rudolf Carnap* (Cambridge: Cambridge University Press, 1963), p. 26.
18. Wittgenstein, *Culture and Value*, 1946, p. 60.

Six: Stereotypes, Symbols, and Ideologies

1. Wittgenstein, *Culture and Value*, 1929, p. 3.
2. For a fuller discussion of symbolism, see my *Cultural Beings: Reading the Philosophers of Genesis* (Amsterdam: Rodopi, 2000).
3. See Allan Janik and Stephen Toulmin, *Wittgenstein's Vienna* (Chicago: Elephant Paperbacks, Ivan R. Dee, Publishers, 1996).
4. The stereotyped concept of Jews in European culture during the modern period is the counterpart of the stereotyped image of Gypsies. The latter are conceived as thieves and vagabonds who infringe on civil society and its culture from the outside. In contrast, Jews are conceived as working their way into civil society and into its cherished cultural traditions, affiliating themselves with it and changing it from within.

5. See in this connection Lurie, "Culture as a Human Form of Life."
6. George L. Mosse, *The Crisis of German Ideology* (New York: The Universal Library, 1964).
7. Yuri Slezkine, *The Jewish Century* (Princeton: Princeton University Press, 2004), p. 1.
8. The difference between Jean-Paul Sartre's phenomenological discourse on the essence of Jews and Wittgenstein's is that Wittgenstein tries to transform the stereotyped concept of Jews into a claim about the essence of metaphysical Jews, not real ones. Sartre contends that Jews can liberate themselves by stopping to think of themselves through the stereotyped concept that others use to perceive them. See Sartre, *Anti-Semite and Jew*, trans. Geroge J. Becker (New York: Shoken Books, 1965 [1946]).
9. See J. C. Nyi'ri, "Wittgenstein's Later Work in Relation to Conservatism," *Wittgenstein and His Times*, ed. Brian McGuinness (Oxford: Basil Blackwell, 1982), pp. 44–68.
10. See Janik and Toulmin, *Wittgenstein's Vienna*, p. 73.

Seven: From Prototype to Family Resemblances

1. Wittgenstein, *Culture and Value*, 1931, pp. 21–22.
2. Ibid.
3. Ibid.
4. Ibid., p. 17.
5. Wittgenstein, *Philosophical Grammar*, part II, p. 75.
6. Wittgenstein, *Philosophical Investigations*, part I, p. 32, #67.
7. Wittgenstein, *Remarks on the Philosophy of Psychology*, vol. II, p. 97, #551.
8. Wittgenstein, *Philosophical Investigations*, part I, p. 2, #1.
9. Wittgenstein, *The Brown Book, 1934–1935* (Oxford: Blackwell, 1958), II, p. 134.
10. Ibid., pp. 134–135.
11. Wittgenstein, *Last Writings on the Philosophy of Psychology*, part II, p. 30, #203.
12. Wittgenstein, *Zettle*, p. 67, #380.
13. Wittgenstein, *Philosophical Grammar*, part II, p. 60, #23.

Eight: Wittgenstein Confronts His Attitude toward Jews

1. Malcolm, *Ludwig Wittgenstein, A Memoir*, p. 30.
2. Ibid., p. 94.
3. Wittgenstein, *Zettle*, p. 80, #455.
4. M.O'C. Drury, "Conversations with Wittgenstein," in *Portraits of Wittgenstein*, vol. 3, ed. F. A. Flowers III (Bristol: Thoemmes Press, 1999), p. 208.
5. Norman Malcolm, "A Religious Man?" in *Portraits of Wittgenstein*, vol. 4, ed. F. A. Flowers III (Bristol: Thoemmes Press, 1999), p. 196.
6. Fania Pascal, "Wittgenstein: A Personal Memoir," in *Ludwig Wittgenstein: Personal Recollections*, ed. Rush Rhees (Oxford: Basil Blackwell, 1981), pp. 12–49.
7. Ibid., pp. 35.
8. Ibid., p. 36
9. Rush Rhees, "Postscript," in *Portraits of Wittgenstein*, vol 3, p. 256.
10. Ibid., p. 260.
11. Wittgenstein, *Culture and Value*, 1946, pp. 53–54.

12. Rhees, "Postscript," p. 281.
13. Apparently the fortune transferred to the Nazis was ten tons of gold.
14. Monk, *Ludwig Wittgenstein*, p. 400.
15. Wittgenstein, *Culture and Value*, 1931, p. 16.
16. Wittgenstein, *Culture and Value*, 1950, p. 95.
17. Rhees, "Postscript," p. 260.
18. Wittgenstein, *Culture and Value*, 1948, p. 85.
19. Otto Weininger, *Sex and Character*.
20. Brian F. McGuiness and George Henrick von Wright, eds., *Ludwig Wittgenstein: Cambridge Letters* (Oxford: Blackwell, 1997), p. 250. For a different interpretation of this remark, see Monk, *Ludwig Wittgenstein, The Duty of Genius*, pp. 312–313.

Nine: In Search of Less "Dangerous Places"

1. Wittgenstein, *Culture and Value*, 1939–1940, p. 42.
2. Ibid., 1949, p. 89.
3. Ibid., 1948, p. 75.
4. Ibid., 1947, p. 68.
5. Ibid.
6. Ibid.
7. Ibid., 1940, p. 43.
8. Ibid.
9. Ibid.
10. Ibid., 1931, p. 14.
11. For a fuller discussion of Wittgenstein's view on this matter, see my *Tracking the Meaning of Life: A Philosophical Journey*, part II (Columbia and London: University of Missouri Press, 2006), pp. 89–170.

Second Study: The Spirits of Culture and Civilization

One: Announcing "the Disappearance of a Culture"

1. Wittgenstein, *Culture and Value*, 1930, p. 9.
2. Ibid., p. 10.
3. Ibid.
4. When Wittgenstein was conducting aeronautical research at Manchester, he devised a plan for a door which, though not locked, would be difficult for strangers to open. The idea was that the handle would need to be lifted instead of depressed. Cf. McGuinness, *Wittgenstein*, p. 65. Accordingly, this foreword might also be characterized as a door with such a handle.

Two: A Lock Constructed from a Concealed Spiritual Distinction

1. Allan Janik and Stephen Toulmin, *Wittgenstein's Vienna*, p. 89.
2. Wittgenstein, *Philosophical Investigations*, part I, p. 49, # 122.
3. In English, see Oswald Spengler, *The Decline of the West* (New York: Knopf, 1962).
4. For a different interpretation of Spengler's influence on Wittgenstein, see. DeAngelis, *Wittgenstein*.

5. See Ludwig Wittgenstein, *Culture and Value*, p. 16. For a discussion of some ideological influences on his thinking, see G. H. von Wright, "Wittgenstein in Relation to His Times," pp. 108–126; and J. C. Nyíri, "Wittgenstein's Later Work in Relation to Conservatism," pp. 44–68, in McGuinness, ed. *Wittgenstein and His Times*.
6. Wittgenstein, *Culture and Value*, 1931, p. 16.
7. *The Encyclopedia of Philosophy*, vol. 2, ed. Paul Edwards (New York: Macmillan, 1967), p. 273.
8. Wittgenstein, *Culture and Value*, 1942, p. 49.
9. Ibid., 1946, p. 57.
10. Ibid., p. 10 (emphasis added).
11. Wittgenstein, *Philosophical Remarks*, p. 7.
12. Ibid.
13. Ibid.
14. Wittgenstein, *Culture and Value*, 1930, p. 11.
15. Wittgenstein, *Lectures & Conversations on Aesthetics, Psychology, and Religious Belief*, compiled from notes taken by Yorick Smythies, Rush Rhees, and James Taylor, ed. Cyril Barrett (Oxford: Blackwell Publishers, 1999); "Remarks on Frazer's Golden Bough," in *Ludwig Wittgenstein Philosophical Occasions 1912-1951*, ed. James Klagge and Alfred Nordman, Rush Rhees, trans. (Indianapolis and Cambridge: Hacket Publishing Company, 1993).

Three: Culture and Its Spiritual Manifestations

1. Wittgenstein, *Culture and Value*, 1949, p. 89.
2. For a discussion of the concept of acculturation and its relationship to education, see Yuval Lurie, "Education and the Riddle of Culture," in *Judaism and Education: Essays in Honor of Walter Ackerman*, ed. H. Marantz (Beer-Sheva: Ben-Gurion University Press, 1998), pp. 377–391.
3. Wittgenstein, *Culture and Value*, 1948, p. 86.
4. Wittgenstein, *Lectures and Conversations on Aesthetics, Psychology and Religious Belief*, p. 7, #22.
5. Wittgenstein, *Culture and Value*, 1938, p. 39.
6. Lars Hertzberg has pointed out that Wittgenstein misquoted Longfellow's "The Builders." The last line of the stanza reads: "For the Gods see everywhere." The full text can be found in *One Hundred and One Famous Poems*, ed. Roy Jay Cook (New York: Barnes and Noble, 1993).
7. Malcolm, *Ludwig Wittgenstein: A Memoir*, p. 70.
8. Wittgenstein's example in this connection had personal meaning for him. Before concluding after the end of the First World War that the high culture of the West no longer existed, he invested substantial efforts in choosing a dining room table for his rooms in Cambridge when he started his studies there.
9. Wittgenstein, *Lectures and Conversations on Aesthetics, Psychology and Religious Belief*, p. 8, #26.
10. Ibid., p. 6, #17.
11. Ibid., p. 7, #19.
12. Ibid., p. 7, #20.
13. Wittgenstein, *The Brown Book*, II, p. 143-144, #6.

14. For further discussion of this conceptual point, see Yuval Lurie, "Inner States," *Mind*, 88:350 (April 1979), pp. 241–257.
15. Wittgenstein, *Philosophical Grammar*, part I, p. 109, #66.
16. Wittgenstein, *The Blue Book*, p. 1.
17. Wittgenstein, *Remarks on the Philosophy of Psychology*, vol. 1, p. 62 #312.
18. Wittgenstein, *Wittgenstein's Lectures, Cambridge, 1932–1935: From the Notes of Alice Ambrose and Margaret Macdonald*, ed. Alice Ambrose and Margaret Macdonald (Totowa, N. J.: Rowman and Littlefield, 1979), part I, Philosophy, p. 5, #5.
19. Ibid., p. 38, #34.
20. Ibid.
21. Ibid.
22. Ibid., #35; see also G. E. Moore, "Wittgenstein's Lectures in 1930–33," in *Philosophical Papers* (New York: Collier Books, 1966), pp. 305–311.
23. Wittgenstein, *Wittgenstein's Lectures, Cambridge, 1932–1935*, p.39, #35.
24. Wittgenstein, *Philosophical Investigations*, part I, p. 60, #153.
25. Wittgenstein, *Remarks on the Philosophy of Psychology*, vol. I, p. 155, # 875.
26. Wittgenstein, *Culture and Value*, 1946, p. 58.
27. Ibid., 1948, pp. 80–81.
28. Wittgenstein, *Zettle*, p. 29, #165.
29. Wittgenstein, *Culture and Value*, 1948, pp. 80–81.
30. Ibid.
31. Wittgenstein, *Culture and Value*, 1930, pp.8– 9.
32. The distinction was formulated earlier by Arthur Schopenhauer. For further details, see my discussion of it in the first study.
33. Wittgenstein, *Culture and Value*, 1947, p. 68.
34. Unlike, for example, the conception of revolutionary breaks with normal science put forward by Thomas Kuhn in *The Structure of Scientific Revolutions* (Chicago, Ill.: Chicago University Press, 1962).
35. Wittgenstein, *Culture and Value*, 1931, p. 11.
36. Ibid., p. 5
37. Ibid.
38. Ibid., p. 12.

Four: Civilization and Its Spiritual Manifestations

1. Wittgenstein, *Culture and Value*, 1947, p. 73.
2. Ibid., 1930, p. 5.
3. Ibid., 1947, p. 64.
4. Ibid., 1930, p. 78.
5. Ibid., p. 9.
6. Ibid., 1946, p. 64.
7. O. K. Bouwsma, *Wittgenstein: Conversations, 1949–1951*, ed. J. L. Craft and R. E. Hustwit (Indianapolis, Ind.: Hackett Publishing Co., 1986), p. 39.
8. Wittgenstein, *Remarks on the Foundations of Mathematics [1937–44]*, part II, rev. edition, eds. G. H. von Wright, R. Rhees, and G. E. M. Anscombe, trans. G. E. M. Anscombe (Oxford: Blackwell, 1978), p. 132, #23.
9. Wittgenstein, *Culture and Value*, p. 9.
10. Wittgenstein, *Wittgenstein's Lectures, Cambridge, 1932–1935*, p. 36, #34.

11. Ibid.
12. G. H. Von Wright, "A Biographical Sketch," in Malcolm, *Ludwig Wittgenstein: A Memoir*, p. 11.
13. Wittgenstein, *Philosophical Investigations*, part I, p. 25, #50.
14. Wittgenstein, *Wittgenstein's Lectures, Cambridge, 1932–1935*, p. 37, #34.
15. Wittgenstein, *Culture and Value*, 1931, p. 15.
16. Ibid., 1931, pp. 16–17.
17. Ibid., p. 23.
18. Ibid., p. 8.
19. Ibid., p. 14.
20. Ibid., 1948, p. 75.
21. Ibid., 1949, p. 91.
22. Ibid., 1931, p. 17.
23. Ibid., 1948, p. 76.
24. Ibid., 1930, p. 5.
25. In 1935, the Nazis came out against jazz.

Five: Reflecting on Wittgenstein's Remarks on Culture and Civilization

1. Wittgenstein, *Culture and Value*, 1931, pp. 12–13.
2. Ludwig Wittgenstein, *Lectures and Conversations on Aesthetics, Psychology and Religious Belief*, ed. Cyril Barrett (Oxford: Basil Blackwell, 1966), p. 89.
3. Wittgenstein, *Lectures and Conversations on Aesthetics, Psychology and Religious Belief*, p. 10, #33.
4. Ibid., #34.
5. Wittgenstein, "Remarks on Frazer's *Golden Bough*," in *Philosophical Occasions*, eds. James C. Klagge and Alfred Nordmann (Indianapolis &Cambridge: Hacket Publishing Company, 1993), p.133. Later, in *Philosophical Investigations*, part I, p. 49, #122, Wittgenstein reformulates this remark, turning it into a philosophical call to provide "*a clear view* of our use of words," because "our grammar is lacking in this sort of perspicuity." The first remark concerns how we view and experience the spiritual meaning of things. The second concerns what is meant by a given word.
6. Wittgenstein, *Culture and Value*, 1931, p. 5.
7. Ibid., p. 12.

Third Study: The Common Spirit of Human Beings

1. James George Frazer, *The Golden Bough: A Study in Magic and Religion*, abridged edition (London, Macmillan, 1963). For the circumstances in which Wittgenstein began commenting on Frazer's book, see M. O'Conner Drury, "Conversations with Wittgenstein," in Rhees, *Ludwig Wittgenstein*. For their place in Wittgenstein's Typescripts, see P. M. S. Hacker, "Developmental Hypotheses and Perspicuous Representations: Wittgenstein on Frazer's *Golden Bough*," *Iyyun, The Jerusalem Philosophical Quarterly*, 41 (July 1992), pp. 277–299, where it is suggested that they are "incomplete" and "not intended for publication."

One: Frazer's Explanation of Myth, Magic, and Religion

1. James George Frazer, *The Golden Bough: A Study in Magic and Religion—Abridged Edition* (London: Macmillan & Co. Ltd., 1963), p. 1.
2. Ibid., p. 11.
3. Ibid., p. 13.
4. Ibid., p. 79.
5. Ibid., p. 14.
6. Ibid., p. 67.
7. Ibid.
8. Ibid.

Two: Wittgenstein's Criticism of Frazer's Conceptual Explanation

1. Wittgenstein, "Remarks on Frazer's *Golden Bough*," p. 119.
2. For a study of Wittgenstein's critique of Frazer's explanation, as based on a means-end format, see Jacques Bouveresee, "Wittgenstein's Critique of Frazer," *Ratio* (new series) 20 (4 December 2007), pp. 357–376.
3. Wittgenstein, "Remarks on Frazer's *Golden Bough*," p. 121.
4. Ibid., p. 120–121.
5. See M. O'C. Drury, *The Danger of Words* (London: Routledge, 1973), pp. x–xi.
6. Wittgenstein, "Remarks on Frazer's *Golden Bough*," p. 141.
7. Elsewhere, Wittgenstein refers to such concerns and attitudes as "the feeling we have for our life." See Rush Rhees, "Postscript," in *Portraits of Wittgenstein*, vol. 3, p. 260.
8. Wittgenstein, *Culture and Value*, p. 11.
9. Wittgenstein, "Remarks on Frazer's *Golden Bough*," p. 119.
10. Ibid., p. 120–121.
11. See J. L. Austin, *How to Do Things with Words* (Oxford: At The Clarendon Press, 1962). These are not the examples Austin uses to introduce the concept.
12. Wittgenstein, "Remarks on Frazer's *Golden Bough*," p. 121.
13. See Wittgenstein's use of the concept "further descriptions" (*Wittgenstein's Lectures, Cambridge, 1932–1935*, p.39, #35), which is discussed in my Second Study.
14. Wittgenstein, *Wittgenstein and the Vienna Circle: Conversations Recorded by Friedrich Waismann*, ed. Brian McGuinness, trans. Joachim Schulte and Brian McGuinness (Oxford: Basil Blackwell, 1979), p. 117.
15. Wittgenstein, *Philosophical Grammar*, p. 28, #129.
16. Wittgenstein, "Remarks on Frazer's *Golden Bough*," pp. 125–126.
17. What sometimes confuses Wittgenstein's discussion of the spiritual meaning of symbols in this period is that it centers on the meaning of words, in the context of which he distinguishes between concepts as "symbols" and their expression in words as linguistic "signs." In his lectures at this time, the distinction between symbols and signs is sometimes described according to the distinction he formulated in the *Tractatus Logico-Philosophicus* between propositions and propositional signs: "A symbol is a sign together with all the conditions necessary to give it significance," he claims there (Wittgenstein, *Wittgenstein's Lectures*, lecture B, viii, Lent term, 1930–1931, p. 44).

18. Leviticus 16:20–22; see also Rush Rhees, "Wittgenstein on Language and Ritual," in *Wittgenstein and His Times*, pp. 69–107. Frazer himself devotes many pages to describing rituals of "Public Scapegoats," which are aimed at the expulsion of evils, and to rituals of "Human Scapegoats," which entitle someone for a set period of time to act contrary to accepted norms.
19. The term "scapegoat" is somewhat misleading. Apparently, the ritual involved two goats. One was sacrificed to God, the other was sent into the wilderness. Rabbinical tradition opposed this ritual, claiming that it was introduced by pagans who accompanied the Exodus out of Egypt.
20. Wittgenstein, "Remarks on Frazer's *Golden Bough*," p.137–138.
21. Wittgenstein, *Philosophical Investigations*, part I, p. 89, #244.
22. Wittgenstein, "Remarks on Frazer's *Golden Bough*," p. 123.
23. In conversation, Wittgenstein described himself as "a disciple of Freud" and "a follower of Freud," despite criticizing his use of the term "unconscious mental life" and his claim that we create symbols (in dreams), the meaning of which we do not understand. In my reading of the above remark, he saw himself as following Freud in stressing the basic human inclination for inspired expressions through the invention and use of symbols. See Wittgenstein, *Lectures & Conversations on Aesthetics, Psychology, and Religious Belief*, p. 41.
24. Wittgenstein, "Remarks on Frazer's *Golden Bough*," p. 137.
25. Wittgenstein, *Culture and Value*, 1937, p. 36; cf. Goethe, Faust I.
26. Wittgenstein, *Philosophical Investigations*, part I, p.98, #284.
27. Ibid., part II, p. 178.
28. Wittgenstein, *Remarks on the Philosophy of Psychology*, vol. I, p. 38.
29. Ibid.," p. 137.
30. Ibid., p. 123.
31. Ibid., p. 125.
32. Ibid., p. 129.

Three: Wittgenstein's Criticism of Frazer's Historical Explanation

1. For some examples, see J. H. M. Beattie, *Other Cultures* (London: Routledge and Kegan Paul Ltd., 1964); "On Understanding Ritual," in *Rationality*, comp. Bryan R. Wilson (London: 1970); R.W. Firth, *Symbols Private,and Public* (Ithaca, N.Y: Cornell University Press, 1973); E. R. Leach, *Rethinking Anthropology: Monographs on Social Anthropology*, 22 (London: London School of Economics, 1961); C. Levi-Strauss, *Structural Anthropology* (London: Penguin1972); Levi-Strauss, *Myth and Meaning* (New York: Schocken Books, 1978); V. Turner, *The Forest of Symbol* (Ithaca, N.Y.: Cornell University Press, 1967); Turner, *The Ritual Process* (London Routledge & Kegan Paul, 1969); Turner,*Celebration Studies in Festivity and Ritual* (Washington D.C.: Smithsonian Institution Press, 1982).
2. Wittgenstein, "Remarks on Frazer's *Golden Bough*," p. 120–121.
3. Ibid., p. 123.
4. I am indebted to Lars Hertzberg for formulating this point.
5. Wittgenstein, "Remarks on Frazer's *Golden Bough*," p. 121.
6. Ibid.

7. Wittgenstein, *Lectures and Conversations on Aesthetics, Psychology and Religious Belief*, pp. 27–28.
8. Wittgenstein, "Remarks on Frazer's *Golden Bough*," p. 127.
9. Ibid., p.137–138.
10. Ibid., p. 151.
11. Rush Rhees, "Wittgenstein on Language and Ritual," p. 98. See also Avishai Margalit's discussion of these rituals in "Sense and Sensibility: Wittgenstein on *The Golden Bough*," *Iyyun, The Jerusalem Philosophical Quarterly*, 41 (July 1992), pp. 301–318.
12. Ibid., p. 99.
13. Wittgenstein, "Remarks on Frazer's *Golden Bough*," p. 145.
14. Cioffi, *Wittgenstein on Freud and Frazer*, pp. 86–87.
15. Bouveresse, "Wittgenstein's Critique of Frazer."
16. Wittgenstein, *Culture and Value*, 1947, pp. 69–70.
17. Wittgenstein, *Remarks on Colour*, ed. G. E. M. Anscombe, trans. Linda L. McAlister and Margret Schattle (Berkley and Los Angeles: University of California Press, 1978), p. 59, #317.
18. Wittgenstein, "Remarks on Frazer's *Golden Bough*," p. 131.
19. Ibid.

Four: Wittgenstein's Methods of Attaining Insight about Spiritual Rituals

1. Wittgenstein, *Culture and Value*, 1931, p. 16.
2. Wittgenstein, *Philosophical Grammar*, part I, p. 19, #72.
3. Ibid., p. 68, #32.
4. Wittgenstein, *Remarks on the Foundations of Mathematics*, part VII, p. 378, #16.
5. Wittgenstein, *Zettle*, p. 9, #45. Hence, it would be strange to speak of "the experience of intending to go home at the end of the lecture."
6. Ibid., p. 123, #717.
7. Wittgenstein, *Culture and Value*, 1948, p. 82.
8. Wittgenstein, "Remarks on Frazer's *Golden Bough*," p. 123.
9. Ibid.
10. In 1913, Wittgenstein wrote to Bertrand Russell from Austria: "My dear father died yesterday in the afternoon. He had the most beautiful death that I can imagine; without the slightest pains and falling asleep like a child! I did not feel sad for a single moment during all the last hours, but most joyful and I think that this death was worth a whole life." McGuinness and von Wright, *Ludwig Wittgenstein*, p. 27.
11. For a discussion of this issue, see Avishai Margalit, "Sense and Sensibility."
12. Wittgenstein, *Philosophical Investigations*, part I, p. 82, #206.
13. Wittgenstein, *Remarks on the Philosophy of Psychology,* vol. I, p. 67, #336.
14. Cioffi, *Wittgenstein on Freud and Frazer.*
15. Wittgenstein, "A Lecture on Ethics," in Klagge and Nordmann, *Philosophical Occasions*, pp. 41–43.
16. Ibid., p. 44.
17. For a fuller discussion of this lecture, see Yuval Lurie, *Tracking the Meaning of Life*, part II, pp. 175–184.
18. Wittgenstein, *Wittgenstein and the Vienna Circle*, p. 117.

19. The need to express his personal attitude toward this discourse after clarifying its conceptual meaning can serve as an example of what Wittgenstein means when he says that he approaches philosophical problems from a religious point of view. I take it that the point of religion (and ethics) is not to make us understand its concepts, but to put our faith in God. For a discussion of Wittgenstein's remark, see Norman Malcolm, *Wittgenstein, A Religious Point of View*, ed. with a Response by Peter Winch (Ithaca, N.Y.: Cornell University Press, 1994).
20. Wittgenstein, "Remarks on Frazer's *Golden Bough*," p. 123.
21. Ibid., p. 135.
22. Ibid., p. 133.
23. Ibid., p. 135.
24. Wittgenstein, *Philosophical Investigations*, part II, iv, p. 178; see also *Remarks on the Philosophy of Psychology*, vol. I, p. 54, #265.
25. Moore, "Wittgenstein's Lectures in 1930–1933, p. 107.
26. Wittgenstein, "Remarks on Frazer's *Golden Bough*," p. 131.
27. Ibid., p.133.
28. Brian R. Clack, *Wittgenstein, Frazer, and Religion* (Great Britain: Palgrave, Macmillan, 2002).
29. In English, see Oswald Spengler, *The Decline of the West.*
30. Wittgenstein's Notebooks 1914–1916, p. 84.
31. Wittgenstein, *Remarks on the Philosophy of Psychology*, p. 56, #281.
32. Wittgenstein, Philosophical Investigations, part I, p. 18, #36.
33. Gilbert Ryle, *The Concept of Mind* (London, Hutchinson and Co., 1949).
34. Wittgenstein, *Remarks of the Philosophy of Psychology*, vol. I, p. 109, #586.

Five: Philosophical Reflections on Wittgenstein's Comments

1. Wittgenstein describes the concept of inspiration in two ways, by comparing following a rule in somewhat mechanical fashion with doing so out of inspiration (*Philosophical Investigations*, part I, p. 87, #232), and by noting how we contemplate a dream with inspiration, "like an idea pregnant with possible implications" (*Culture and Value*,1948, pp. 78–79).
2. Wittgenstein, *Zettle*, p. 68, #383.
3. Wittgenstein, *Remarks on the Philosophy of Psychology*, vol. I, p. 68, #344.
4. Wittgenstein, *Philosophical Investigations*, part II, xi, p. 213.
5. Ibid., p. 214.
6. For a fuller philosophical interpretation of Swift's story, see Lurie, *Cultural Beings*, chap. 1.
7. Wittgenstein, *Remarks of the Philosophy of Psychology*, p. 44, #213.
8. Ibid., p. 39, #189.
9. See Cioffi, *Wittgenstein on Freud and Frazer*, p. 155. The commentators are A. J. Ayer, *Wittgenstein* (New York: Random House, 1985); John Cook, "Magic, Witchcraft, and Science," *Philosophical Investigations*, 6:1 (January 1983), pp. 2–26; M. O'C. Drury, *The Danger of Words*; Howard Mounce, "Understanding a Primitive Society," *Philosophy* (October 1973); Brian McGuiness, "Freud and Wittgenstein," in *Wittgenstein and His Times*; N. Rudich and M. Stassen, "Wittgenstein's Implied Anthropology," *History and Theory*, x:1 (1971), pp. 84–89.
10. A. J. Ayer, *Wittgenstein* (New York: Random House, 1985), pp. 88–89.

11. Cioffi, *Wittgenstein on Freud and Frazer*, p. 194.
12. Wittgenstein, "Remarks on Frazer's *Golden Bough*," p. 125.
13. Brian R. Clack, *Wittgenstein, Frazer, and Religion* (UK: Palgrave, Macmillan, 1999), p. 131.
14. Wittgenstein, *Culture and Value*, 1948, p. 82.
15. Wittgenstein, "Remarks on Frazer's *Golden Bough*," p. 129.
16. P. M. S. Hacker, "Developmental Hypotheses and Perspicuous Representations," p. 287.
17. Ibid.
18. The explanation is reminiscent of Rudyard Kipling's *Just So Stories*, which tell of how the camel got its hump, the elephant its trunk, and the rhinoceros its skin, all due to a generating event in their past. In this case, it still needs to be explained how, from a self-protective act on the part of distrustful worriers, a ritual of greeting emerged, which expresses friendliness and cordiality.
19. See Paul Redding, "Anthropology as Ritual: Wittgenstein's Reading of Frazer's *The Golden Bough*," *Metaphilosophy*, 18:3–4 (July 1987), pp. 253–259.
20. Wittgenstein, *Culture and Value*, p. 37.
21. Cioffi, *Wittgenstein on Freud and Frazer*, p. 188.
22. The term was coined by Peter Winch when, in another context, he referred to Wittgenstein's "limiting notions." I discuss it further in the following sections.
23. Charles Darwin did do by seeking to show that expressive bodily gestures are a natural feature of behavior on the part of all creatures, which, he argued, are useful for their survival. Freud sought to close the gap on what was missing in Darwin's functional explanation by explaining how symbolic forms of behavior emerge from basic emotional and sexual needs, which are repressed and then sublimated. Rush Rhees notes that Freud was one of the few authors Wittgenstein thought worth reading. Despite his criticisms of Freud's use of the term "unconscious" to explain human psychology, "He would speak of himself . . . as a disciple of Freud" and "a follower of Freud"; Wittgenstein, *Lectures and Conversations on Aesthetics, Psychology and Religious Belief*, p. 41. For a discussion of Freud's explanation of symbolic behavior, see my article "Psychoanalysis as a Double Dealing Rascal," in J. Rozenberg, ed., *Sense and Nonsense: Philosophical, Clinical, and Ethical Perspectives* (Jerusalem: Magnes Press of Hebrew University, 1996), pp. 163–184.
24. J. L. Austin, "The Meaning of a Word," *Philosophical Papers* (Oxford: the Clarendon Press, 1961), pp. 23–43.
25. Peter Winch, *The Idea of a Social Science and its Relation to Philosophy* (London: Routledge & Kegan Paul, 1958). One might just as well turn this insight around, suggesting that cultures are indebted to shared concepts for their existence.
26. See Donald Davidson, "On the Very Idea of a Conceptual Scheme," in *Inquiries into Truth and Interpretation* (Oxford: Oxford University Press, 1984); also Richard Rorty, "World Well Lost," in *Consequences of Pragmatism: Essays 1972–1980* (Brighton, UK: The Harvester Press, 1982).
27. Peter Winch, "Understanding a Primitive Society," in *Ethics and Action* (London: Routledge & Kegan Paul, 1972), p. 41.
28. Ibid., p. 44.
29. Wittgenstein, *On Certainty*, ed. G. E. M. Anscombe, trans. Denis Paul and G. E. M. Anscombe (New York: J. & J Harper Editions, 1969), p. 24, #167.

30. Ibid., p. 39, #308.
31. Note that such a world-picture is not an explanatory theoretical "paradigm" for the pursuit of "normal science," nor a theoretical "conception" of an ordinary concept used in the stream of life, like justice, as it is adopted and "learned as a child." It is also not a worldview, or *Weltanschauung*, which is an ontological and ideological framework for various beliefs and opinions. Nor is it a Kantian "regulative idea" that enables its possessors to make personal use of worldviews and concepts about God and natural purpose.
32. Anthony Kenny, *The Unknown God: Agnostic Essays* (London-New York: Continuum, 2004), p. 205.
33. Wittgenstein, *On Certainty*, p. 15, #94.
34. Ibid., #95.
35. Ibid., p. 46, #358.
36. Ibid., p. 23, #162.
37. Winch, "Understanding a Primitive Society," p. 43.
38. Avishai Margalit, "Sense and Sensibility."
39. Ibid., p. 311.
40. See Giambattista Vico, *The New Science of Giambattista Vico*, trans. T. G. Bergin and M. H. Fisch (Ithaca, N.Y.: Cornell University Press, 1970), pp. 316–318.
41. Wittgenstein, *Culture and Value*, 1930, p. 7.
42. Ibid., pp. 7–8.

BIBLIOGRAPHY

Austin, J. L. *How to Do Things with Words*. Oxford: At The Clarendon Press, 1962.

———. "The Meaning of a Word." In *Philosophical Papers* (Oxford: the Clarendon Press, 1961), pp. 23–43

Ayer, A. J. *Wittgenstein*. New York: Random House, 1985.

Beattie, J. H. M. *Other Cultures*. London: Routledge and Kegan Paul Ltd., 1964.

———. "On Understanding Ritual." In *Rationality*. Compiled by Bryan R. Wilson. Oxford: Blackwell, 1970.

Berlin, Isaiah. *Against the Current*. Edited by H. Hardy. Oxford: Oxford University Press, 1981.

———. *Vico and Herder: Two Studies in the History of Ideas*. London: Hogarth Press, 1975.

Bouveresee, Jacques. "Wittgenstein's Critique of Frazer," *Ratio* (new series), 20 (4 December 2007), pp. 357–376.

Bouwsma, O. K. *Wittgenstein: Conversations, 1949–1951*. Edited by J. L. Craft and R. E. Hustwit. Indianapolis, Ind.: Hackett Publishing Co., 1986.

Cioffe, Frank. *Wittgenstein on Freud and Frazer*. Cambridge: Cambridge University Press, 1998.

Clack, Brian R. *Wittgenstein, Frazer, and Religion*. UK: Palgrave, Macmillan, 2002.

Cook, John. "Magic, Witchcraft, and Science," *Philosophical Investigations*, 6:1 (January 1983), pp. 2–36.

Davidson, Donald. "On the Very Idea of a Conceptual Scheme." In *Inquiries into Truth and Interpretation*. Oxford: Oxford University Press, 1984)

DeAngelis, William J. *Ludwig Wittgenstein—A Cultural Point of View: Philosophy in the Darkness of This Time*. Cornwall: Ashgate, 2007.

Drury, M. O'C. "Conversations with Wittgenstein." In Flowers, *Portraits of Wittgenstein*.

———. *The Danger of Words*. London: Routledge, 1973.

Edwards, Paul, Ed. *The Encyclopedia of Philosophy*. Vol. 2. New York: Macmillan, 1967.

Firth, R. W. *Symbols Private ,and Public*. Ithaca, N.Y: Cornell University Press, 1973.

Flowers, F. A., Ed. *Portraits of Wittgenstein*. Volume 3. Bristol: Thoemmes Press, 1999.

Fogelin, Robert J. *Wittgenstein*. London: Routledge & Kegan Paul, 1989.

Frazer, James George. *The Golden Bough: A Study in Magic and Religion—Abridged Edition*. London: Macmillan & Co. Ltd., 1963.

Hacker, P. M. S. "Developmental Hypotheses and Perspicuous Representations: Wittgenstein on Frazer's *Golden Bough*," *Iyyun, The Jerusalem Philosophical Quarterly*, 41 (July 1992), pp. 277–299.

Janik, Allan. *Essays on Wittgenstein and Weininger*. Amsterdam: Rodopi, 1985.

———, and Stephen Toulmin. *Wittgenstein's Vienna*. Chicago: Elephant Paperbacks, Ivan R. Dee, Publishers, 1996.

Kant, Immanuel. *Critique of the Power of Judgment*. Cambridge: Cambridge University Press, 2000.

Kripke, Saul A. *Wittgenstein of Rules and Private Language*. Oxford: Basil Blackwell, 1982.

Kenny, Anthony. *The Unknown God: Agnostic Essays*. London-New York: Continuum, 2004.

Kuhn Thomas. *The Structure of Scientific Revolutions*. Chicago, Ill.: Chicago University Press, 1962.

Leach, E. R. *Rethinking Anthropology*: *Monographs on Social Anthropology*, 22. London: London School of Economics, 1961.

Levi-Strauss, C. *Structural Anthropology*. London: Penguin1972.

———. *Myth and Meaning*. New York: Schocken Books, 1978.

Longfellow, Henry Wadsworth. "The Builders." In *One Hundred and One Famous Poems*. Edited by Roy Jay Cook. New York: Barnes and Noble, 1993.

Lurie, Yuval. *Cultural Beings: Reading the Philosophers of Genesis*. Amsterdam: Rodopi, 2000.

———. "Culture as a Human Form of Life: A Romantic Reading of Wittgenstein," *International Philosophical Quarterly*, 32:2 (June 1992)

———. "Education and the Riddle of Culture." In *Judaism and Education: Essays in Honor of Walter Ackerman*. Edited by H. Marantz. Beer-Sheva: Ben-Gurion University Press, 1998, pp. 377–391.

———. "Inner States," *Mind*, 88:350 (April 1979), pp. 241–257.

———. "Jews as a Metaphysical Species," *Philosophy*, 64 (1989), pp. 323–347.

———. "Psychoanalysis as a Double Dealing Rascal." In *Sense and Nonsense: Philosophical, Clinical, and Ethical Perspectives*. Edited by J. Rozenberg. Jerusalem: Magnes Press of Hebrew University, 1996.

———. *Tracking the Meaning of Life: A Philosophical Journey*. Part2. Columbia: University of Missouri Press, 2006.

Malcolm, Norman. *Ludwig Wittgenstein, A Memoir*. Oxford: Oxford University Press, 1984.

———. "A Religious Man?: In *Portraits of Wittgenstein*. Volume 4. Edited by F. A. Flowers III. Bristol: Thoemmes Press, 1999).

———. *Wittgenstein, A Religious Point of View*. Edited with a response by Peter Winch. Ithaca, N.Y.: Cornell University Press, 1994.

Margalit, Avishai. "Sense and Sensibility: Wittgenstein on *The Golden Bough*," *Iyyun, The Jerusalem Philosophical Quarterly*, 41 (July 1992), pp. 301–318.

Marx, Karl. *On the Jewish Question*. Cincinnati, Ohio: Hebrew Union College-Jewish Institute of Religion, 1958.

McGuiness, Brian. "Freud and Wittgenstein." In McGuinness, *Wittgenstein and His Times*.

———. *Wittgenstein: A Life, Young Ludwig 1889–1921*. London: Gerald Duckworth & Co., 1988.

———, Ed., *Wittgenstein and His Times*. Oxford: Basil Blackwell, 1982.

———, and G. H. von Wright, Eds. *Ludwig Wittgenstein: Cambridge Letters*. Oxford: Blackwell, 1997.

Monk, Ray. *Ludwig Wittgenstein: The Duty of Genius*. New York: The Free Press, 1990.
Moore, G. E. "Wittgenstein's Lectures in 1930–33." In *Philosophical Papers*. New York: Collier Books, 1966.
Mosse, George L. *The Crisis of German Ideology*. New York: The Universal Library, 1964.
Nevo, I. "Religious Belief and Jewish Identity in Wittgenstein's Philosophy," *Philosophy Research Archives*, XIII (1988), pp. 225–243.
Nyi'ri, J. C. "Wittgenstein's Later Work in Relation to Conservatism." In McGuinness, *Wittgenstein and His Times*, pp. 44–68.
Pascal, Fania. "Wittgenstein: A Personal Memoir." In *Ludwig Wittgenstein: Personal Recollections*. Edited by Rush Rhees. Oxford: Basil Blackwell, 1981.
Redding, Paul. "Anthropology as Ritual: Wittgenstein's Reading of Frazer's *The Golden Bough*," *Metaphilosophy*, 18:3–4 (July 1987), pp. 253–259.
Rhees, Rush. "Wittgenstein on Language and Ritual." In McGuinness, *Wittgenstein and His Times*, pp. 69–107.
Rhees, Rush. "Postscript." In Flowers, *Portraits of Wittgenstein*.
Rhees, Rush, Ed. *Ludwig Wittgenstein: Personal Recollections*. Oxford: Basil Blackwell, 1981.
Rorty, Richard. "World Well Lost." In *Consequences of Pragmatism: Essays 1972–1980*. Brighton, UK: The Harvester Press, 1982.
Rudich, N., and M. Stassen. "Wittgenstein's Implied Anthropology," *History and Theory*, x:1 (1971), pp. 84–89.
Ryle, Gilbert. *The Concept of Mind*. London, Hutchinson and Co., 1949.
Sartre, Jean-Paul. *Anti-Semite and Jew*. Translated by Geroge J. Becker. New York: Shoken Books, 1965 [1946].
Scharfstein, Ben-Ami. *Of Birds, Beasts, and Other Artists: An Essay on the Universality of Art*. New York: New York University, 1988.
Schilpp, P. A., Ed. *The Philosophy of Rudolf Carnap*. Cambridge: Cambridge University Press, 1963.
Schopenhauer, Arthur. *On the Fourfold Root of the Principle of Sufficient Reason*. Lasalle, Ill.: Open Court, 1974.
———. *The World as Will and Representation*. Translated by E. E. J. Payne. Oxford: Clarendon Press, 1974.
Slezkine, Yuri. *The Jewish Century*. Princeton, N.J.: Princeton University Press, 2004.
Spengler, Oswald. *The Decline of the West*. New York: Knopf, 1962.
Stern, D. "The Significance of Jewishness for Wittgenstein's Philosophy," *Inquiry*, 43:4 (2000), pp. 383–401.
——, and Bella Szabados. *Wittgenstein Reads Weininger—A Reassessment*. Cambridge: Cambridge University Press, 2004.
Turner, V. *Celebration Studies in Festivity and Ritual*. Washington D.C.: Smithsonian Institution Press, 1982.
———. *The Forest of Symbol*. Ithaca, N.Y.: Cornell University Press, 1967.
———. *The Ritual Process*. London Routledge & Kegan Paul, 1969.
Vico, Giambattista. *The New Science of Giambattista Vico*. Translated by T. G. Bergin and M. H. Fisch. Ithaca, N.Y.: Cornell University Press, 1970.

Wasserman, Gerhard D. "Wittgenstein on Jews: Some Counter-Examples," *Philosophy*, 65:253 (July 1990), pp 355–365.

Weiner, David Avraham, *Genius and Talent: Schopenhauer's Influence on Wittgenstein's Early Philosophy.* Toronto: Associated University Presses, 1992.

Weininger, Otto. *Sex and Character: A Investigation of Fundamental Principles.* Bloomington: Indiana University Press, 2005.

Winch, Peter. *The Idea of a Social Science and its Relation to Philosophy.* London: Routledge & Kegan Paul, 1958.

———. "Understanding a Primitive Society." In *Ethics and Action.* London: Routledge & Kegan Paul, 1972.

Wittgenstein, Ludwig. Appendix: Notes on Logic, 1913. In *Notebooks, 1914–1916.*

———. *Das blaue Buch; Eine philosophisch Betrachtun* (*Das braune Buch*). Edited by Rush Rhees. Frankfort am Main: Suhrkamp, 1989.

———. *The Brown Book.* Oxford: Blackwell, 1998.

———. *On Certainty.* Edited by G. E. M. Anscombe and G. H. von Wright. Translated by Denis Paul and G. E. M. Anscombe. Oxford: Blackwell, 1998.

———. *Culture and Value.* Edited by G. H. von Wright and Heikki Nyman. Revised by Alois Pichler. Translated by Peter Winch. Oxford: Blackwell Publishers, Ltd, 1998.

———. *Last Writings on the Philosophy of Psychology.* Volume II. Edited by G. H. Von Wright and Heikki Nyman. Translated by C. G. Luckhardt and M. A. E. Aue. Oxford: Basil Blackwell, 1998.

———. *Last Writings on the Philosophy of Psychology.* Volume I. Edited by G. H. Von Wright and Heikki Nyman. Translated by C. G. Luckhardt. Oxford: Basil Blackwell, 1982–1990.

———. *Lectures and Conversations on Aesthetics, Psychology, and Religious Belief.* Compiled from notes taken by Yorick Smythies, Rush Rhees, and James Taylor. Edited by Cyril Barrett. Berkeley: Oxford: Basil Blackwell, 1998.

———. *Notebooks, 1914–1916.* Translated by G. E. M. Anscombe. Oxford: Basil Blackwell,1998.

———. *Philosophical Grammar.* Part I. Edited by R. Rhees. Translated by A. J. P. Kenny. Oxford: Blackwell, 1974.

———. *Philosophical Investigations.* Translated by G. E. M. Anscombe. Oxford: Basil Blackwell, 1998.

———. *Philosophical Remarks.* Edited by R. Rhees. Translated by R. Hargreaves and R. White. Oxford: Blackwell, 1975.

———. *Tractatus Logico-Philosophicus.* London, Routledge & Kegan Paul, 1969.

———. *Remarks on Colour.* Edited by G. E. M. Anscombe. Translated by Linda L. McAlister and Margret Schattle. Berkley and Los Angeles: University of California Press, 1978.

———. "Remarks on Frazer's *Golden Bough.*" In *Philosophical Occasions.* Edited by James C. Klagge and Alfred Nordmann. Indianapolis &Cambridge: Hacket Publishing Company, 1993.

———. *Remarks on the Foundations of Mathematics.* Revised edition. Edited by G. H. von Wright, R. Rhees, and G. E. M. Anscombe. Translated by G. E. M. Anscombe. UK: Athenæum Press Ltd, Gateshead, Tyne & Wear, 1998.

———. *Remarks on the Philosophy of Psychology*. Volume I. Edited by G. E. M. Anscombe and G. H. von Wright. Translated by G. E. M. Anscombe. Oxford: Basil Blackwell, 1998.

———. *Remarks on the Philosophy of Psychology*. Volume II. Edited by G. H. Von Wright and Heikki Nyman. Translated by C. G. Luckhardt and M. A. E. Aue. Oxford: Basil Blackwell, 1998.

———. *Wittgenstein's Lectures, Cambridge, 1932–1935: From the Notes of Alice Ambrose and Margaret Macdonald*. Edited by Alice Ambrose and Margaret Macdonald. Totowa, N. J.: Rowman and Littlefield, 1979.

———. *Wittgenstein and the Vienna Circle: Conversations Recorded by Friedrich Waismann*. Edited by Brian McGuinness. Translated by Joachim Schulte and Brian McGuinness. Oxford: Basil Blackwell, 1979.

———. *Zettle*. Edited by G. E. M. Anscombe and G. H. von Wright. Translated by G. E. M. Anscombe. Oxford: Basil Blackwell, 1998.

Wright, G. H. von. "Biographical Sketch." In Malcolm, *Ludwig Wittgenstein, A Memoir*.

———. "Wittgenstein in Relation to His Times." In McGuinness, *Wittgenstein and His Times*, pp. 108, 126.

ABOUT THE AUTHOR

YUVAL LURIE is Professor Emeritus at Ben Gurion Unversity in Beer Sheva, Israel, where he has taught philosophy since 1973. He received his philosophy degrees from Tel Aviv University and Cornell University. He has published articles in philosophical journals on philosophy of mind, culture, ethics, and Wittgenstein's philosophy. Among his books are *Cultural Beings: Reading the Philosophers of Genesis* (2000); *Tracking the Meaning of Life: A Philosophical Journey* (2006); and *Mavo le-kisme ha-filosofyah: etikah u-musar* (*Introduction to the Magic of Philosophy: Ethics and Morality*, 2007, Hebrew).

INDEX

VIBS

The **Value Inquiry Book Series** is co-sponsored by:

Adler School of Professional Psychology
American Indian Philosophy Association
American Maritain Association
American Society for Value Inquiry
Association for Process Philosophy of Education
Canadian Society for Philosophical Practice
Center for Bioethics, University of Turku
Center for Professional and Applied Ethics, University of North Carolina at Charlotte
Central European Pragmatist Forum
Centre for Applied Ethics, Hong Kong Baptist University
Centre for Cultural Research, Aarhus University
Centre for Professional Ethics, University of Central Lancashire
Centre for the Study of Philosophy and Religion, University College of Cape Breton
Centro de Estudos em Filosofia Americana, Brazil
College of Education and Allied Professions, Bowling Green State University
College of Liberal Arts, Rochester Institute of Technology
Concerned Philosophers for Peace
Conference of Philosophical Societies
Department of Moral and Social Philosophy, University of Helsinki
Gannon University
Gilson Society
Haitian Studies Association
Ikeda University
Institute of Philosophy of the High Council of Scientific Research, Spain
International Academy of Philosophy of the Principality of Liechtenstein
International Association of Bioethics
International Center for the Arts, Humanities, and Value Inquiry
International Society for Universal Dialogue
Natural Law Society
Philosophical Society of Finland
Philosophy Born of Struggle Association
Philosophy Seminar, University of Mainz
Pragmatism Archive at The Oklahoma State University
R.S. Hartman Institute for Formal and Applied Axiology
Research Institute, Lakeridge Health Corporation
Russian Philosophical Society
Society for Existential Analysis
Society for Iberian and Latin-American Thought
Society for the Philosophic Study of Genocide and the Holocaust
Unit for Research in Cognitive Neuroscience, Autonomous University of Barcelona
Whitehead Research Project
Yves R. Simon Institute

Titles Published

Volumes 1 - 212 see www.rodopi.nl

213. Krzysztof Piotr Skowroński, *Values and Powers: Re-reading the Philosophical Tradition of American Pragmatism*. A volume in **Central European Value Studies**

214. Matti Häyry, Tuija Takala, Peter Herissone-Kelly and Gardar Árnason, Editors, *Arguments and Analysis in Bioethics*. A volume in **Values in Bioethics**

215. Anders Nordgren, *For Our Children: The Ethics of Animal Experimentation in the Age of Genetic Engineering*. A volume in **Values in Bioethics**

216. James R. Watson, Editor, *Metacide: In the Pursuit of Excellence*. A volume in **Holocaust and Genocide Studies**

217. Andrew Fitz-Gibbon, Editor, *Positive Peace: Reflections on Peace Education, Nonviolence, and Social Change*. A volume in **Philosophy of Peace**

218. Christopher Berry Gray, *The Methodology of Maurice Hauriou: Legal, Sociological, Philosophical*. A volume in **Studies in Jurisprudence**

219. Mary K. Bloodsworth-Lugo and Carmen R. Lugo-Lugo, *Containing (Un)American Bodies: Race, Sexuality, and Post-9/11 Constructions of Citizenship*. A volume in **Philosophy of Peace**

220. Roland Faber, Brian G. Henning, Clinton Combs, Editors, *Beyond Metaphysics? Explorations in Alfred North Whitehead's Late Thought*. A volume in **Contemporary Whitehead Studies**

221. John G. McGraw, *Intimacy and Isolation (Intimacy and Aloneness: A Multi-Volume Study in Philosophical Psychology, Volume One)*, A volume in **Philosophy and Psychology**

222. Janice L. Schultz-Aldrich, Introduction and Edition, "*Truth" is a Divine Name, Hitherto Unpublished Papers of Edward A. Synan, 1918-1997*. A volume in **Gilson Studies**

223. Larry A. Hickman, Matthew Caleb Flamm, Krzysztof Piotr Skowroński and Jennifer A. Rea, Editors, *The Continuing Relevance of John Dewey: Reflections on Aesthetics, Morality, Science, and Society*. A volume in **Central European Value Studies**

224. Hugh P. McDonald, *Creative Actualization: A Meliorist Theory of Values.* A volume in **Studies in Pragmatism and Values**

225. Rob Gildert and Dennis Rothermel, Editors, *Remembrance and Reconciliation.* A volume in **Philosophy of Peace**

226. Leonidas Donskis, Editor, *Niccolò Machiavelli: History, Power, and Virtue.* A volume in **Philosophy, Literature, and Politics**

227. Sanya Osha, *Postethnophilosophy.* A volume in **Social Philosophy**

228. Rosa M. Calcaterra, Editor, *New Perspectives on Pragmatism and Analytic Philosophy.* A volume in **Studies in Pragmatism and Values**

229. Danielle Poe, Editor, *Communities of Peace: Confronting Injustice and Creating Justice.* A volume in **Philosophy of Peace**

230. Thorsten Botz-Bornstein, Editor, *The Philosophy of Viagra: Bioethical Responses to the Viagrification of the Modern World.* A volume in **Philosophy of Sex and Love**

231. Carolyn Swanson, *Reburial of Nonexistents: Reconsidering the Meinong-Russell Debate.* A volume in **Central European Value Studies**

232. Adrianne Leigh McEvoy, Editor, *Sex, Love, and Friendship: Studies of the Society for the Philosophy of Sex and Love: 1993–2003.* A volume in **Histories and Addresses of Philosophical Societies**

233. Amihud Gilead, *The Privacy of the Psychical.* A volume in **Philosophy and Psychology**

234. Paul Kriese and Randall E. Osborne, Editors, *Social Justice, Poverty and Race: Normative and Empirical Points of View.* A volume in **Studies in Jurisprudence**

235. Hakam H. Al-Shawi, *Reconstructing Subjects: A Philosophical Critique of Psychotherapy.* A volume in **Philosophy and Psychology**

236. Maurice Hauriou, *Tradition in Social Science.* Translation from French with an Introduction by Christopher Berry Gray. A volume in **Studies in Jurisprudence**

237. Camila Loew, *The Memory of Pain: Women's Testimonies of the Holocaust.*. A volume in **Holocaust and Genocide Studies**

238. Stefano Franchi and Francesco Bianchini, Editors, *The Search for a Theory of Cognition: Early Mechanisms and New Ideas.* A volume in **Cognitive Science**

239. Michael H. Mitias, *Friendship: A Central Moral Value.* A volume in **Ethical Theory and Practice**

240. John Ryder and Radim Šíp, Editors, *Identity and Social Transformation, Central European Pragmatist Forum, Volume Five.* A volume in **Central European Value Studies**

241. William Sweet and Hendrik Hart, *Responses to the Enlightenment: An Exchange on Foundations, Faith, and Community.* A volume in **Philosophy and Religion**

242. Leonidas Donskis and J.D. Mininger, Editors, *Politics Otherwise: Shakespeare as Social and Political Critique.* A volume in **Philosophy, Literature, and Politics**

243. Hugh P. McDonald, *Speculative Evaluations: Essays on a Pluralistic Universe.* A volume in **Studies in Pragmatism and Values.**

244. Dorota Koczanowicz and Wojciech Małecki, Editors, *Shusterman's Pragmatism: Between Literature and Somaesthetics.* A volume in **Central European Value Studies**

245. Harry Lesser, Editor, *Justice for Older People,* A volume in **Values in Bioethics**

246. John G. McGraw, *Personality Disorders and States of Aloneness (Intimacy and Aloneness: A Multi-Volume Study in Philosophical Psychology, Volume Two),* A volume in **Philosophy and Psychology**

247. André Mineau, *SS Thinking and the Holocaust.* A volume in **Holocaust and Genocide Studies**

248. Yuval Lurie, *Wittgenstein on the Human Spirit.* A volume in **Philosophy, Literature, and Politics**